Scottish Education in the Twentieth Century

Lindsay Paterson

Edinburgh University Press

© Lindsay Paterson, 2003

Edinburgh University Press Ltd
22 George Square, Edinburgh

Typeset in 11/13 Ehrhardt by
Mizpah Publishing Services, Chennai, India, and
printed and bound in Great Britain by
MPG Books Ltd, Bodmin

A CIP Record for this book is available from the British Library

ISBN 0 7486 1590 3 (paperback)

Contents

Acknowledgements

I am particularly grateful to R. D. Anderson, Ian Martin and David McCrone for reading a draft of the book, and for making numerous insightful and helpful comments. The final version is my own responsibility. I am also grateful to Moira Burke of the Centre for Educational Sociology at Edinburgh University for bibliographical help, and to Karen Brannen of the same Centre for help in gaining access to the data sets of the Scottish School Leavers Surveys. The librarians at the Education Faculty Library and the Main Library of Edinburgh University, and in the National Library of Scotland, have – as always – been patient and assiduous in helping to track down elusive publications and manuscripts.

CHAPTER 1

Introduction

In 1947, at the crux of the century of education with which this book deals, the Advisory Council on Education in Scotland summed up what it saw as the purpose of schooling:

> the good school is to be assessed not by any tale of examination successes, however impressive, but by the extent to which it has filled the years of youth with security, graciousness and ordered freedom.
>
> (SED 1947: 10)

The Advisory Council was not made up of outsiders. It was chaired by William Hamilton Fyfe, principal of Aberdeen University from 1936 to 1948, classical scholar, former fellow of Merton College, Oxford, former principal of Queen's University, Kingston, Ontario, and knighted in 1942; most of that 1947 report was written by James J. Robertson, rector of Aberdeen Grammar School from 1942 to 1959, and knighted in 1956. It was the sixth such Council to have been established since the Education (Scotland) Act of 1918 had made provision for one to be set up by the Scottish Education Department, the branch of the central administration which had responsibility for most Scottish education throughout the century. When Tom Johnston, Secretary of State for Scotland, spoke at the first meeting of the sixth Council in November 1942, he charged its members with the task of being 'a parliament of education', and seeking how schools could ensure that young people were 'properly equipped to discharge the duties and exercise the rights of citizenship' (Young 1986: 214).

In one respect, the Council could look back through three quarters of a century of educational progress, to 1872 when elementary schooling in Scotland was first placed on a fully statutory basis, and to the gradual growth since then of participation in it. But it could also look to the only partially fulfilled major aims of the 1918 Act, most especially to the aspiration towards a proper secondary education for all: that Act, according to the Council, 'represented the largest single advance in the history of secondary education in Scotland' (SED 1947: 2), and so was an inspiration to further reform. In this respect, as also in the incorporation of Scotland's Roman Catholic schools into the public sector, the 1918 Act seemed then, and still seems today, to be the key legislative measure in Scottish education during the entire century.

The Council mainly looked forward, however, and in three notable respects. It proposed a system of comprehensive secondary schools – 'omnibus' schools, in the currently fashionable terminology, that would take all the pupils from a neighbourhood and educate them together. Continuing its theme taken from the 1918 Act, it suggested that these could be regarded as 'the natural way for a democracy to order the post-primary schooling of a given area' (SED 1947: 36). It proposed further that the normal termination of secondary education for most pupils should be a leaving certificate that was set and marked by the school's teachers, not imposed by an external body: external examination, it argued, distorts the examined curriculum, 'depresses the status of the non-examinable', and becomes, instead of the means to educational progress, the end itself (as stated on p. 43). Consistent with this, the Council also recommended what later became known as child-centred education, but defined the child's nature as intrinsically social: 'all educational thinking must continually move between the two poles of the child in his nature and growth, and of society, as it is patterned and as we desire to modify that pattern' (see p. 15).

In all three of these respects, the Council was as prescient of the debates that would dominate the next half-century of education as it was impressed by the consistency of the progressive movement in the preceding period. Comprehensive schools were inaugurated from the mid-1960s until the mid-1970s, and became and remained popular. The resulting massive growth in external examination brought debate recurrently back to the Council's warnings. Student-centredness grew, also from the 1960s, inspired by a much broader democratisation of society, influenced indeed by social movements such as feminism that the Council only barely apprehended.

ORDERED FREEDOM

The late 1940s, as in so much of Scottish social life, were therefore a turning point in education, the moment when educational democracy became firmly established as the only way forward. That is why this Advisory Council has commanded such attention from subsequent writers, as we will see in later

chapters, even though its immediate fate was to have its most radical recommendations set aside by the Scottish Education Department.

Yet it is a peculiarly Scottish form of educational democracy, and this book
is an account of what that amounts to. The key phrase is the apparent
oxymoron, 'ordered freedom'. On the one hand, 'no democratic society can
rest content with an orderliness of individual behaviour which is not the
result of countless decisions responsibly made under conditions of real
choice'. On the other, 'order is one constituent of that secure setting within
which alone the nature of the adolescent can express itself in those spontan-
eous and purposeful activities which we call free' (SED 1947: 11). This
freedom, in other words, is to be achieved through appropriate socialisation,
and the purpose of good government is to establish the institutions which
may achieve that: in 'the community life of the school', the pupil 'confronts
a pre-existing society, a web of relationships into which his own claims and
obligations must be woven'. From that socialised individualism then comes
the 'graciousness' that would characterise a truly democratic community:
'generous in encouragement, it is temperate in reproof, and it has power to
evoke a responsive friendliness in which mistrust and hampering reserve melt
away' (SED 1947: 11).

If that seems vague and rhetorical, then – as David Northcroft (1992) has
pointed out – it is typical of the way in which the Council's report deals with
the positive aspects of freedom. We could add that it is typical more generally.
The Scots have always been ambivalent about freedom. One thing which the
story of their education system in the twentieth century seems to confirm is
that freedom is to be attained, if at all, through institutional and academic
means. The story which is told in this book is of the persisting popular preference for formally established educational institutions, and for a formally
certificated curriculum. This may also have coincided with the views of policy
makers and other elites, but it cannot be reduced to their imposing their preferences, despite what the critics of the sixth Advisory Council's idealism often
maintain. For it is a story, not only of popular preference for these things,
but also of the popular inclination to understand educational democracy as
access to them. Democracy in education, over and over again, has been interpreted as access to real education, real education has meant what happens in
mainstream schools, colleges and universities, and the main kind of learning
that happens there has been understood to be general, academic and therefore
liberal.

Indeed, despite the resistance of democratising bodies such as the Advisory
Council to what it called 'bookish' education, there has been a persisting tendency in Scotland to equate general education with academic education. In that
sense, the tradition in Scotland most closely resembles that in the USA. In the
words of Robert Maynard Hutchins, president of the University of Chicago

from 1929 to 1945, writing in 1952 about literature, through which, he believed, the 'great conversation' could take place between present and past:

> to the extent to which books can present the idea of a civilisation, the idea of Western civilisation is here presented. These books are the means of understanding our society and ourselves. They contain the great ideas that dominate us without our knowing it. There is no comparable repository of our tradition.
>
> (Carnochan 1993: 86)

Hutchins was much admired by some of the most eloquent Scottish exponents of this kind of view of the role of education in shaping a community and its boundaries – for example, Herbert Grierson, professor of English Literature at Aberdeen University (1894–1915) and Edinburgh University (1915–35), who in his rectorial address at Edinburgh University in 1936 emulated Hutchins in his protest against a conception of the university 'as intended to give a practical, technical, professional education'.

The claim that dominant Scottish interpretations of educational democracy have been for access to academic education interpreted in this way is, of course, a large generalisation, and the detailed reality – as we will see – is complex. That tradition, moreover, was brought into question in the last couple of decades of the century, under pressure from the beliefs that education ought to be mainly about preparing people for work and that academic learning could not be truly democratic. But it is the main theme which emerges. Scottish education started the twentieth century believing itself to have two important and influential institutional legacies. One was the parish school, educating the whole population of an area mainly in basic literacy, numeracy and religious precepts, and also selecting a small number of able boys for further advancement. That system had a long history, ultimately stretching back to the Reformation, and in essence had been public, national and confirmed by legislation for three centuries (Anderson 1985). The other legacy was the universities. There were two facets to the theory on which they rested. One was accessibility – the links, however tenuous, with the parish schools, so that the 'lad o pairts' could proceed from them to higher learning. The other was liberal humanism: 'to comment on the course of education at the Scottish Universities', said John Stuart Mill in his rectorial address at St Andrews in 1867, 'is to pass in review every essential department of general culture'. These have, he said – linking liberal studies to interpretations of a democratic community – 'the common end [of] strengthening, exalting, purifying, and beautifying our common nature' (Mill 1867: 11).

These two institutional legacies became the guiding ideology of democratising reformers throughout the twentieth century, although transmuted as time developed and as one phase of democratic pressure partly succeeded by creating new institutions which then became a new starting point for further reform. The parish school and the democratic, liberal university became, for Scottish education, 'defining institutions', in the term coined by Hilary Steedman to describe the quite different influence of the great English endowed schools during that country's transition to universal secondary education in the first half of the twentieth century (Steedman 1987). These two Scottish institutional legacies became the repository of ideologies around which democratic pressures were exerted and conservative resistance was mounted. At times, as will be discussed later, the conflicts became intense, and many of them are still with us today, exactly as the Advisory Council foretold. But unless we understand the nature of the legacy – both public and selective, both for a community and also academic – then we will be in danger of misunderstanding what people in Scotland have meant by educational democracy, and misinterpreting some of the ambiguous results which these struggles over education have produced. Giving access to common types of educational institution, but continuing to define real education in general, academic terms, has been Scotland's attempt to answer the conundrum of all mass systems of education: how to reconcile democracy with the necessity of selection, both selection of culture in the maintenance of excellence, and selection of people, allocating individuals to differentiated occupations while also preparing them for life as equal citizens in the common culture of the community.

EDUCATIONAL MYTHS AND EDUCATIONAL CHANGE

These reinterpreted legacies have come in for much criticism in Scottish educational debates over the past thirty years. The selective, partial character of the rudimentary educational democracy of late-nineteenth-century Scotland has been frequently pointed out – notably in the definitive works by R. D. Anderson (for example 1983, 1985, 1995) – and the resulting ambiguities of twentieth-century education have been traced to the various interpretations of the theme of liberal opportunity which these main traditions encouraged: the most important writers in that respect have been Andrew McPherson (for example 1973, 1983, 1992a, and – with Raab – 1988), and David McCrone (2001, and – with Bechhofer and Kendrick – 1982). The tensions and ambiguities form large parts of the material that is discussed in later chapters. These writers have referred to the belief in the democratic tradition as a 'myth', using that in an anthropological sense rather than straightforwardly as an accusation of falsehood. In the words of McPherson and Raab (1988: 407), 'myth is simultaneously expressive and explanatory ... It asserts identity, celebrates values, and explains the world through them.'

Thus, as McPherson argued elsewhere, the members of the sixth Advisory Council were inclined to believe in the democratic myth because many of them had experienced it at its best – growing up in small burghs where there really was something like equality of access to the same primary and secondary schools, even in the 1930s or earlier (McPherson 1983). He memorably labelled this the 'Kirriemuir career', after the town in Angus from where came probably the most famous such product of Scottish education in the late-nineteenth century, J. M. Barrie.

However, whereas McPherson and McCrone used the term 'myth' in this strictly neutral sense, some of their successors have concentrated on the falsity more than the social scientific description: in that sense, the volume to which McPherson contributed in 1983, edited by Walter Humes and Hamish Paterson, has been more influential than McPherson's own essay (Humes and Paterson 1983). An equally influential and ascerbic account was published at much the same time by Smout (1986: 209–30), similar sentiments were found in numerous works of fiction (Malzahn 1987: 237–8), and Humes influentially attributed the false self-confidence of the system to a secretive and unaccountable 'leadership class', a theme which resonated with the Scottish opposition to the Conservative government and in the emerging campaign for a Scottish parliament (Humes 1986).

For our purposes here, McPherson's warning about this tendency is valid: 'the demythologiser is as likely to de-historicise ... as is the prisoner of myths who interprets present institutions as the unchanged expression of a timeless ideal' (McPherson 1983: 217).

The political potential of myth has been best described by Raymond Williams, writing more generally:

'Tradition' has been commonly understood as a relatively inert, historicised segment of a social structure: tradition as the surviving past. [But it is, rather,] an intentionally selective version of a shaping past and a pre-shaped present, which is then powerfully operative in the process of social and cultural definition and identification.

(Williams 1977: 115)

Alasdair MacIntyre has summed up a similar argument very neatly: 'traditions, when vital, embody continuities of conflict' (MacIntyre 1981: 222).

Looking back over the century, the striking feature about the myth is its mobilising capacity – precisely the capacity of human beings to select parts of it into programmes for shaping the present and the future. It has repeatedly been used by reformers to gain legitimacy for change, and the most recent episodes in that stem from the period of criticism of the myth that started from the early 1980s. Myth is a source of effective political ideology, especially when – as repeatedly in the twentieth century – its interpretation is in the hands of radical political movements purporting to express the interests of marginalised social groups, such as the working class in the extension and democratisation of secondary education between the 1920s and the 1960s, girls and women from about then until the present day, and minority ethnic groups since the 1980s. The history of the century is definitely not about a smooth transition to educational democracy presided over by a benevolent elite that always knew where it was going. It is indeed about struggle and conflict, partly forced by wider social changes – such as the emancipation of women – but partly also achieved through the deliberate democratising actions of political outsiders. Some of these outsiders, however, became insiders – such as the Labour movement people, of whom Tom Johnston, setting up the sixth Advisory Council, was a noted leader – and some of the previous insiders, such as James J. Robertson, were sufficiently critical of the heritage to open their minds to the radicalising thought.

These changing and conflicting interpretations of myth are also why understanding where we are today in Scottish education requires that we understand how we got here. If we want to explain why Scots have resisted a fully developed vocational track in their educational system, or why public examinations have grown to dominate the last four years of secondary school-ing, or why there has been consistent popular preference for liberal, academic studies in higher education, we have to look at the history of these ideas. If we do that, we might see that these preferences are the consistent outcome of pressure for educational democracy, and not only the confusing mess of selection, control and liberal individualism that critics have alleged.

This book, therefore, is an attempt to understand how education has changed in the past century, how the guiding ideas for change gained support and were effective, and how – in that process – certain other ideas, both less and more radical, were discarded. The book is organised broadly into two parts, dealing with two periods, and, within that, into chapters dealing with the different sectors of education. There is, in truth, no neat and accurate div-ision of the century into periods like this, and any particular classification would suit some sectors more than others, but there is some reality to the broad social ethos of the two periods which are used here.

The first is from the beginning to the outbreak of World War II. The beginning itself depends on the educational sector in question: for elementary education, the key date, as we have noted already, is 1872, for secondary it is from the mid-1880s, for universities it is the important reform Act of 1889, and for technical and adult education it is probably in 1901, when there was the first serious attempt by the Scottish Education Department to establish a system of continuation classes and to build up a system of higher technical education. In effect, then, the first period lasts from the 1880s to the 1930s. During this period, the ideology relating to schools was dominated by the consolidation of primary education, and by the bitter disputes about access to secondary schools. There was a growing tension between adult education conceived of as a means of economic regeneration and adult education as a means to liberating the working class, and by the end of the period radical adult education was no longer widely felt to be an important route to working-class emancipation. In university education, there was an emerging ambiguity about the very nature of the Scottish universities, both of the country and also partly outside it, as they moved into an increasingly British realm following the setting up in 1919 of the University Grants Committee that funded universities throughout Britain. All of the resulting political conflicts in this era referred back to the democratic impulse behind the 1872 Act, or behind what was perceived as the main university tradition, and all used the success of this pressure in the 1918 Act to push for further democracy.

The second period deals with the remaining half century or so – from the 1940s until the 1990s. It started with the democratising movement that emerged from World War II, Scotland's educational response to the much wider movement across Europe in the post-war period, just as the 1918 Act had emerged from an earlier promise to build a land fit for heroes. Some of the main themes have already been outlined in the sketch of the ideas of the sixth Advisory Council above, but – precisely because its most radical recommendations were not implemented immediately – these themes remained to dominate debate for many further decades. The story from then until the aftermath of the 1960s was the slow growth of a more child-centred style of schooling, the strengthening opposition to selection between different types of secondary school, the re-emergence of a liberatory interpretation of adult education, and the bringing into question of the national role of universities as the first phase of expansion started, but as their British character seemed all the more secure. The final couple of decades of the century may be interpreted as the following through of the consequences of the reforms introduced in the 1960s. In the primary sector, there was the emergence of a compromise between the most radical forms of child-centredness and the traditional role of the teacher – the Scottish interpretation of individualism that sought to reconcile it with respect for academic study, and for the influential role of institutions and teachers in deliberately shaping children's development. In secondary education, the ending of selection between schools in the public sector raised open-ended questions about what to do with the new, more diverse clientele, in the form of curriculum, examinations, and pastoral care. For post-school education, the legacy has been the massive expansion of higher education as what is interpreted as the next stage in democratic expansion, the repatriation of universities into the Scottish political realm, and the pushing to the margins of any coherent, developed programme of vocational or non-academic adult education.

The educational sectors with which this account deals are not much more clearly defined than the periods, especially in Scotland. It was not until the 1920s that a distinction between elementary and secondary education was finally accepted in Scotland. One of the reasons why the most radical kinds of adult education never gained more than a precarious position is that popular views mostly did not distinguish among the liberal humanism of university education, the general part of the preparation for specific professions, and the kinds of liberal studies to which adults might aspire if they had lost out on education as children. That is part of the consequence of the sheer power of the paradigms which the century inherited – the ideological power of the myth of the democratic parish school and the democratic university. Under pressure from that, all institutional types and all differentiated programmes have been gradually subsumed into a common form. The implications of this are assessed in the concluding chapter.

To start with, however, in Chapter 2, some ideas are discussed that might help us to explain the history. The Scottish experience as outlined in this book may, like every national system, be peculiar, but it shares many features in common with the growth of education systems throughout the developed world. That chapter examines what writers on that common experience have had to say, and how their interpretations may apply to Scotland. The book does not, however, attempt any detailed comparison between Scotland and other countries, whether inside or outside the UK: the comparison is at the level of explanatory theories. A comparative history of Scottish education in the twentieth century would be illuminating, but requires first that we establish how that system itself developed.

The book, then, is an attempt at explanation. It is not a narrative history, although it does try to deal with all the significant events and developments. It also depends heavily on the interpretations of many other writers, especially on the flourishing scholarship about Scottish education of the last thirty years. Education is perhaps rather odd in that respect, insofar as its practitioners tend to be voluble and assiduous, and so it is surrounded with articulate and well-researched points of view. Any writer trying to contribute to our understanding of how Scottish education has developed cannot help but be aware of how many people have done so before. Any Scottish academic inevitably does so from a position inside the system. I hope that what this may lose in detachment is made up for by a confirmation of the Advisory Council's sense that the tradition with which we are concerned here is a matter of both individual and social significance.

CHAPTER 2

Expansion and Democracy

For the century as a whole, three changes stand out above all others. The main purpose of this chapter is to outline some ideas that may explain these. The details of the changes are for later chapters, but it will help here to set the context with some brief summaries of what the changes amounted to.

The first is expansion. At the beginning of the century, only elementary schooling had reached anything approaching universal coverage: according to the 1901 census of population, the proportion of children aged between six and twelve who were attending school was over ninety-five per cent, although the authorities still had difficulty in persuading Scottish parents that children as young as five should attend school, the proportion at that age being only sixty-three per cent (Anderson 1995: 234). The age-five problem seems to have been solved by the 1920s. Indeed, there was then a very slow growth in nursery provision from a base of almost nothing. In 1934, one survey found just nineteen nurseries catering for no more than about 650 children in the whole country, less than one per cent even of four-year-olds (Muir 1934), and by 1941 there were still only fifty-five nursery schools or primaries with nursery departments (Lloyd 1979: 321). In 1970, the numbers had crept up to 185 nursery schools or departments, catering for 10,647 children, which would have meant that at most about one in ten of four-year-olds were enrolled (SED 1971b: 57). But then the real expansion started: in 1986, forty-one per cent of children aged four were in a public-sector nursery, in 1994 the figure was fifty-six per cent, and in 2001 it was ninety-seven per cent (SOEID 1995a: 4; Scottish Executive 2001a).

Nearly all the other sectors were transformed in size as the century progressed. To allow for varying definitions of the age range of the secondary stage, a commonly used measure is to relate the number of pupils in secondary schools to the total population. By this index, secondary schooling grew more than eightfold. In 1912, the number of pupils in secondary education for every thousand people in the total population was eight; in 1951 – aided by the raising of the school-leaving age to fifteen in 1947 – the ratio was forty-six; in 1995, by which time the leaving age was sixteen, it was sixty-seven (derived from Anderson 1983a: 246; SED 1952a: 92; SOEID 1997a: 2). One aspect of this secondary expansion was the growth in public examinations. The Leaving Certificate was inaugurated in 1888 with 972 candidates; by 1951, there were 10,286; in 1991, there was a total of 136,159 candidates for the various levels of public examination, which by then included not only the Higher Grade that dated from the beginning, but also the Ordinary Grade that was being replaced by Standard Grade (Philip 1992: 19, 110, 220).

Expansion in the universities happened later, but has been very striking since the 1980s. In 1901, the ratio of full-time students at Scottish universities to total population was 1.4 per thousand (derived from Anderson 1983a: 357). In 1951, it was 2.9 (derived from UGC 1952: 10). In 1991, it was 10.8, higher than the secondary ratio in 1912 (derived from UFC 1992: 20). Part of this expansion was accounted for by growing female participation, from fifteen per cent of university students in 1901, through twenty-six per cent in 1951, to forty-four per cent in 1991. The number of people training to be teachers grew steadily, quotas being set by the Scottish Education Department to reflect the current needs of schools: in 1912, there were 2,570, in 1951 there were 3,777 and in 1991 there were 4,225, although this apparent rise masks even higher levels in the 1970s – for example, 13,826 in 1970 (SED 1913: 30; SED 1952a: 112; SED 1972c: 148; SOED 1991: 6).

Alongside the expansion in universities and training colleges was the steady growth of the technological colleges that had been set up by the Scottish Education Department after 1901, the so-called central institutions. The number of their students – full-time and part-time – per thousand population was 2.4 in 1902 (derived from Cowper 1970: 185). In 1951, it was 6.2 (derived from SED 1952a: 98). In 1991, a couple of years before most of these institutions became universities in their own right, the ratio was 6.9, but by then they had been joined by another 6.6 per thousand higher education students in a sector that had not even existed in 1951: the further education colleges (derived from SOED 1991: 6). The main work of these new colleges, however, was to provide mostly part-time vocational education, the successor of the continuation classes that were first formally organised in 1901. In that year, 78,171 students were enrolled in such classes, and this rose to 144,815 in 1912 (SED 1913: 21). In 1951, there were 227,878 students in continuation classes (SED 1952a: 47). In 1991, the number in non-advanced courses in the further education colleges was not much more than this, at 228,956, reflecting the growth of advanced – that is, higher education – courses, and the almost complete conversion of the central institutions into higher education institutions (SOED 1993: 3).

Informal adult education is more difficult to measure – and, indeed, in one sense is unquantifiable, because the most informal kinds of education are never counted by government statisticians. Nevertheless, here, too, there seems to have been growth. The Advisory Council reported that the number of students attending adult education classes funded by local Education Authorities had risen from just over 1,500 in 1927 to around ten times that amount in 1949 (SED 1952b: 61); this would have included most classes run by the Authorities themselves, the Workers' Educational Association, and the university extra-mural departments. To the 1927 figure could be added just under 5,000 students in the Scottish classes provided by the National Council of Labour Colleges, but by 1949 that had dropped to no more than about 1,700 (Roberts 1970, Appendix: ii). The post-war expansion was then very striking. Horobin found around 205,000 enrolments in adult education classes in 1971 (Horobin 1980: 6). The sensitivity of this non-statutory sector to public expenditure cuts was then shown by the fall to just under 140,000 in 1981 (Horobin 1983: 8), but, by 1996, official statistics showed over 250,000 adults taking part in community education groups (SOEID 1998a: 3).

Most of this expansion was financed by public agencies, the three most important of which after World War I were the Scottish Education Department, the locally elected education authorities and the University Grants Committee or its successors. Allowing for any double counting represented by transfers among these bodies, their total spending on education in current prices grew from about £13m in 1925 to £38m in 1950, £307m in 1970 and £4bn in 1994 (SED 1928: 31, 45; UGC 1936: 58; SED 1951: 59, 80; UGC 1952: 35; SED 1972c: 189; Scottish Office 1996: 19). Compared to 1925, and indexed to 2001 prices, this represents real growth by a factor of 1.5 in 1950, 6.0 in 1970 and 9.9 in 1994.

The second major change during the century was that the institutions of education became less differentiated. Again, primary was already well on the way to that as a result of the effects of the 1872 Act – which had absorbed most of the schools run by Protestant denominations into the public sector – but there, as in secondary schooling, there were still in 1901 the distinction between the public schools, of which there were 2,788, and the schools run by various religious denominations: 189 Catholic schools, sixty-seven Episcopalian, twenty-four Church of Scotland, four Free Church, and sixty-nine other non-public schools (Anderson 1995: 309). The 1918 Act essentially brought almost all of these into the public sector: as we will see in Chapter 4, the fact that Catholic schools would not be able to remain voluntary schools, but would become fully public, was a point of controversy in the debates leading to that Act. From then until the end of the century, there was essentially only one kind of public-sector primary school in Scotland, catering for around nineteen out of every twenty pupils. In 1994, there were 355 Catholic primaries out of a total of 2,336 public primaries (SOEID 1995b: 2). At no point in the century were there more than a very few single-sex primary schools.

The secondary sector was in its infancy in 1900, consisting of three broad segments: the long-established burgh schools and the endowed schools, of which together there were fifty-six, and 348 Advanced Departments in some eleven per cent of the elementary schools (Anderson 1983a: 222). Between then and the 1920s, the Scottish Education Department added to the complexity by encouraging the creation of a couple of hundred Higher Grade schools. In the 1920s, these were absorbed into a common secondary sector alongside the burgh schools and the endowed schools, and some attempt was made to organise what were by then called Advanced Divisions into a coherent programme of education from twelve to fourteen. From this had emerged by 1936 a structure of secondary schooling that had two main parts – senior secondary courses providing five years of academic education, and junior secondary courses that would provide three years after the leaving age had been raised to fifteen, as it was intended to do in 1939 but which was postponed because of the war. Then, from 1965 until the mid-1970s, that distinction, too, was removed, and since then there has been just one kind of public-sector secondary school, modified in the case of the schools designated as Roman Catholic by the continuing but limited influence of the church. In 1994, there were sixty-five Catholic secondaries out of the total of 405 public secondaries (SOEID 1995b: 2). The small independent sector – successor to most of the endowed schools – educated only around five per cent of secondary pupils. At the end of the century, in the secondary sector there was only one public-sector school that was single-sex (a Catholic girls school in Glasgow), and only around half a dozen independent schools that were single-sex.

Higher education was sharply differentiated for most of the century, the main division being between the four long-established universities in St Andrews, Glasgow, Aberdeen and Edinburgh and the colleges which were built up by the Scottish Education Department. These latter were in two main groups. The first were the central institutions, established mainly in the cities as central sources of technological advice for the various regions: by 1908, there were sixteen of these, and a further three were added between 1922 and 1950 (Cowper 1970: 3). Following various mergers, with each other or with neighbouring universities, the upgrading of two institutions that had been founded as local authority further education colleges, and the transfer of one of the central institutions into that local authority sector, there remained twelve in 1991. The second group consisted of the institutions for training teachers. At the beginning of the century, these continued to be divided on religious grounds. Both the Church of Scotland and the Free Church ran colleges in each of Glasgow, Edinburgh and Aberdeen. The Roman Catholic church and the Episcopal Church each had one college (Scotland 1969: 110).

The Protestant institutions were then taken into a common state sector in the years following new regulations governing teacher training in 1905. The Catholic Church continued to maintain its own training facilities, consisting, from the 1920s until the 1980s, of one college in Glasgow and one in Edinburgh. New colleges were added in the 1960s, to cater for the rapidly expanding schools, and some of these were closed again in the 1980s. By 1991, there remained five colleges of education, one of them Catholic.

After 1992, most of the central institutions and colleges of education either merged with a neighbouring university or themselves became universities, and in any case all were subjected to the same set of policies and funding rules. So, for the first time since the nineteenth century, there was a single, relatively undifferentiated structure of higher education institutions, and for a while the term 'tertiary education' was commonly used, being replaced at the end of the century by 'lifelong learning'. The only higher education institution to remain outside this structure was the college of agriculture, itself formed by the merger in 1992 of the three colleges of agriculture that had lasted throughout the century. The main differentiating feature remaining in higher education concerned the further education colleges that had been developed since the 1950s; by the end of the century they were providing nearly a third of higher education places alongside the non-advanced further education that formed four fifths of their activity (Scottish Executive 2001: table 2). The history of gradual convergence of the universities and the former colleges and central institutions then encouraged suggestions that these newer colleges could also join a common post-school system.

Education in Scotland, therefore, at the end of the century was much simpler in its institutional types than it had been a century before. But it had also come to be far more open to ideas of responding to individual student needs – the third change. The key symbolic moment for schooling was the promulgation in 1965 by the Scottish Education Department of a set of recommendations proposing that education ought to become much more child-centred, noting 'the growing acceptance by teachers of the principles under-lying an education based on the needs and interests of the child' (Darling 1994; SED 1965a: vii). In fact, a relaxation in this direction had been evident from much earlier in the century, as we will see, and the apparent revolution inaugur-ated in 1965 was never as far reaching as was claimed by its most enthusiastic advocates, or by its most sceptical critics. But the whole atmosphere of schools undoubtedly became more relaxed from the mid-century onwards. This grow-ing individualism then received rather paradoxical help from the policies of the Conservative government after 1979, whose brand of individual choice may have been modelled on ideas about consumers in markets, but which seemed to be received in Scotland as a further extension of the student-centred develop-ments already under way. Concepts of parental rights, of students' rights in higher education, and even of children's rights encouraged the education system to be more responsive, and helped other social changes to have their effects: thus the emphasis on rights helped establish a principle in the 1980s that the curriculum should not be differentiated between boys and girls.

These are the three dominant changes that are traced in later chapters – expansion, gradual un-differentiation of institutional types and gradual differentiation of attention to individual students. These are not peculiar to Scotland, however, and some version of them can be found in most developed countries. Therefore, before we look in more detail at the Scottish experience, the main purpose of this chapter is to suggest some explanations of these changes.

EXPANSION

In expanding its education system massively, Scotland shared in a social movement that crossed the developed world, and, in some respects, the whole world. The expansion of elementary education is one of the most important global phenomena of the last century, especially of the first half of it. Benavot and Riddle (1988: 200) calculate that by the middle of the century, nearly one half of the world's children aged 5–14 were attending some kind of school. For the more developed countries, the rate was around two thirds, and northern Europe had a rate of about three quarters (Benavot and Riddle 1998: 202). Scotland's rate in 1951 was well ahead of this: around ninety-three per cent of children aged five to fourteen were then in school (SED 1951: 86). Thus Scotland had a primary enrolment rate that was almost identical to the ninety per cent found for the world's richest countries in 1950 by Meyer et al. (1977: 244).

The period of expansion after 1950 has been described as an 'educational revolution' (Meyer et al. 1977: 244). By 1970, some forty-six per cent of the relevant age group of the richest countries were in secondary school. For Scotland, with a minimum leaving age of fifteen, the proportion was higher than this, at fifty-seven per cent (SED 1971b: 50). As with the primary-school enrolments, there was a great deal of convergence in enrolment rates in secondary schooling in the second half of the twentieth century.

Higher education, too, has expanded massively, helped in most countries by the admission of women for the first time in the late-nineteenth century. Outside the USA – as in Scotland – the most spectacular changes were in the second half of the century. In the first three decades, the size of university enrolments doubled in Britain as a whole, trebled in Germany and Russia, and rose fivefold in the USA (Jarausch 1983: 13). In roughly the same period, enrolment in non-university technical higher education trebled in Britain, rose by around three quarters in Germany, multiplied twenty-six times in

Russia, and multiplied around 7.5 times in the USA (Jarausch 1983: 15). The growth in Scotland in the first three decades, starting from a relatively high base, was more modest: approximately a doubling (Anderson 1985: 467). Nevertheless, in all countries apart from the USA this still left only between about two and five per cent of each age cohort entering higher education; in the USA, it was eleven per cent (Jarausch 1983: 16). Scotland, with only around 2,300 students entering university for the first time each year in the 1930s, and with annual age cohorts of around 95,000 at this time, cannot have had a rate of entry of more than about three per cent (UGC 1936: 54). By the end of the 1950s, rates of entry to all kinds of higher education (university and non-university, part-time and full-time) had risen to no more than around one in eight: in 1958, they were thirteen per cent in Britain, nine per cent in France, seven per cent in West Germany, seven per cent in the Netherlands, and thirteen per cent in Sweden; in the USA, it was thirty-five per cent (Committee on Higher Education 1963b: 42). In Scotland, the rate was twelve per cent (Committee on Higher Education 1963b: 26). But then the explosion came, and by 1995 in most developed countries well over one quarter of the age group entered: the rate of entry was forty-three per cent in the UK, thirty-three per cent in France, twenty-seven per cent in the former West Germany, thirty-four per cent in the Netherlands, and about twenty-five per cent in Sweden; in the USA, it had reached fifty-two per cent (OECD 1997: 164; DfEE 1998: 105). In Scotland, the rate for full-time courses was forty-five per cent, and, since around one third of all students in higher education were studying part-time, the rate would almost certainly have been well over one half if they had been included (Scottish Executive 1999: tables 1 and 12).

Academic writing on this expansion has advanced three main explanations. The first is that it was a product of industrialisation, urbanisation and – above all – modernisation, the transformation of traditional societies into the industrial, capitalist economies that had spread over most of Europe by the early twentieth century. Education became necessary to provide an educated workforce, and to allocate people efficiently to social roles. The original exponent of interpretations of this sort was Max Weber, and approaches which follow him have remained popular ever since (for example, Marshall 1950; Blaug 1968). There are likely to be elements of truth in this for most systems, if only because it became popular with politicians: thus, in Scotland, as in most European countries, the reason given by the government for attempting to build up a system of higher technical education was as a means to modernising the economy. But empirical studies of the development of mass schooling between the late-nineteenth and the late-twentieth centuries tend to find at best weak support for this plausible speculation (Meyer et al. 1992). Scotland is actually a rather good case in point, as Anderson (1985) points out: it had, in effect, a mass, public and – in aspiration – compulsory system of elementary schooling well before its industrial revolution, because of the origins of its parish school system in the presbyterian church in the eighteenth century. Green, more generally, points out that the development of mass literacy 'was less an effect of industrialisation than a prior facilitating agent' (Green 1990: 41).

The second plausible theory is that mass education was mainly about a new kind of socialisation – a new way of inducting young people into society, and to provide a new ideology for legitimising social inequalities by placing them on the basis of educational merit rather than on the straightforward inheritance of wealth. If Weber was the founder of the first school of thought, the originator of this one is Emile Durkheim, who suggested in 1911 that:

> if [a] society has reached a degree of development such that ... there is more division of labour, [education] will arouse among children, on the underlying basic set of common ideas and sentiments, a richer diversity of occupational aptitudes.

> (Durkheim 1956 [1911]: 71)

This view then came to dominate the sociological thinking about education in the second half of the twentieth century. It was argued, for example, that the increase in the proportion of people gaining public certification for their attainment in school and university represented a new form of 'status attainment', a society based on credentials certainly, but not really on any more accurate measure of human potential (Collins 1979). The main attention of educational sociologists then turned to the means by which education reproduces social inequalities – why the winners in the credentialling race tend to be those who are born with the advantage of having well-educated or affluent parents (for example, Bowles and Gintis 1976; Willis 1977). The education of parents gives them 'cultural capital' (the term used by one of the most influential thinkers in this tradition, Pierre Bourdieu (1997 [1986])), which can then be 'inherited' and 'invested' by their children somewhat like the financial capital that would have been the main basis of inheritance in previous eras, but in ways that are much less obviously a reproduction of advantage because they appear simply as the capacity to do well inside the education system; empirical confirmation of this is provided by, for example, Savage (2000: 91). Particular attention has been paid by writers of this persuasion to questions of language, or 'linguistic codes' as described by Basil Bernstein (1971). Middle-class children, it has been claimed, have access through the culture of their homes to an extended linguistic code that allows them to engage more readily than working-class children in the characteristic discussions that take place in classrooms.

UNIVERSALISTIC INDIVIDUALISM

Productive though such theories about modernisation, cultural capital and meritocracy are, they are ultimately not adequate, which brings us to the third theory. This is a combination of views about the relationship between education and the state and views about the cultural content of education. One of the most sustained critiques of Durkheimian views was by Ringer (1979), who argued that there was no neat correspondence between educational expansion and the needs of society or the economy in the period from the late-nineteenth century until the middle of the twentieth century. That is, he says, because education has cultural content, not just a social function, and it encourages its students to think even while also undertaking the most competitive of examinations: 'at least until 1930, European secondary schools and universities mediated not only between the social positions of fathers and sons but also between past and present' (see p. 18), and the survival of ideas from the past into this era underlay many critiques of capitalism and industrialism, including a certain resistance by middle-class professionals to attempts to control their work in the name of economy or efficiency.

The content of education is also all the more relevant the closer it comes to being universal. Boli et al. (1985: 157) argue that mass education provides knowledge and understanding to its students that go far beyond the structural requirements of a capitalist labour market. In particular, especially since about the 1960s, 'it focuses too much on the individual as chooser and actor to be conceived as a simple instrument of passivity and labour control in a differentiated society' (see p. 157). They conclude by emphasising the cultural or ideological role of schooling: 'mass education accompanies not differentiation per se but universalistic individualism' (see p. 156) – by which is meant an individualism that, because it aspires to be universal, is inevitably also social, inevitably concerned with establishing the conditions under which all persons can be truly individuals.

There are three aspects to this. One is to emphasise the role of the state in expanding education. Educational growth is itself a way in which the modern state has sought to acquire democratic legitimacy (Green 1990: 77). But that can only be true if the aspiration to better education is a popular movement, not something imposed. The state can certainly be an effective agent of change. It can expand the supply of schooling, ensure that the labour market rewards proper training and encourage students and their parents by outlawing child labour or providing bursaries and other kinds of subsidy (Fuller and Rubinson 1992: 25). In the twentieth century, an important task which the state performed was to reorganise education into a sequence of end-on stages, of primary, secondary and then tertiary, which then is a better basis for common standards of selection during and between

levels of education: Archer (1979: 176–8) argues that, without such a structure, expansion could not happen smoothly.

Nevertheless, these are all mechanisms, not what education is about.
The second aspect of the development of universalistic individualism does get
closer to purpose, because it lays emphasis on the link between educational
growth and nation-building or nationalism (Boli et al. 1985: 161). Mass
schooling is not usually a centralised imposition, although it is centrally sanctioned, as in the insistence that children learn a standard language. This was
well documented for France by Eugen Weber (1977), but an equally telling
instance would be from Scotland, where, until at least the 1970s, Gaelic was at
best tolerated in the education system as a means to the better acquisition of
English. But even this kind of linguistic assimilation is not straightforwardly
an imposition, insofar as parents continued to believe that children ought to
learn English if they were to have any chance of getting on.

So the best way to understand the nationalism which this role for education
underpins is as a branch of liberalism (Tamir 1993). That is the third and most
important aspect of universalistic individualism. Mass education has been the
link between politics and the individual in the very construction and definition
of what Ramirez and Boli (1987: 10) call 'the European model of a national
society', a model that is being exported all over the globe. The model includes:

> the legitimating myths of (1) the individual, (2) the nation as a society
> made up of individuals, (3) progress, (4) childhood socialisation as the
> key to adult character, and (5) the state as guardian of the nation and
> guarantor of progress.
>
> (Ramirez and Boli 1987: 10)

From these principles come the standard panoply of liberal beliefs,
modernised for a century in which social reform and public provision of basic
services came to be accepted as the only way of entrenching and universalising
the freedom that liberalism asserts. In a society whose dominant ideology is
this form of universalistic individualism, pursuing personal advancement is
simply not believed to be contradictory to supporting public provision: 'most
actors who pursue education for themselves do so with the understanding that
it is a legitimate collective good, a credible way of surpassing one's fellows'
(Meyer 1992: 226).

This point then links the explanation of expansion to explanations of the
other two main changes in Scottish education in the twentieth century – the slow
standardisation of institutions, and the slow individualisation of instruction. The
standardisation was the only way in which individualism could be made universal: the whole story of Scottish attitudes to education in the twentieth century
can be interpreted as a refusal to accept official assurances that parallel kinds of

institution with different educational purposes could ever be of equal status. That is why the apparent ideological rupture represented by the coming to power of parties of the New Right did so little to disrupt the trends of expansion, and – as we will see in detail in Chapters 7 and 8 – in Scotland no more than modified at the edges the slow growth of individualism.

Some of the central dilemmas of education at the end of the century are consequences of the growth of individual assertion, itself encouraged by education – the apparently insatiable demand for ever more education, the insistence on the extension of that to any groups who still remain outside its main provisions, the challenge to the authority of the teacher and the questioning of the very cultural tradition to which the earlier reformers intended that democratisation should give access – what Beck (1992: 128) calls 'disenchantment'. The same individualisation also accounts for the alienation from education of the now small minority who drop out at early stages that would have been the common end-point for the majority half a century ago. In a process that was pointed out as long ago as the 1950s and 1960s by such writers as Michael Young (1958) and Raymond Williams (1963), meritocracy has individualised failure, in the sense that, if social selection is apparently based on 'merit', then failure is due to individual incompetence or laziness rather than to structural obstacles. Not to succeed is therefore potentially to be denied full citizenship.

POLITICAL CULTURE

This is not a book primarily about the politics of Scottish education (for which, see Humes (1986), Hutchison (1993), McPherson and Raab (1988) and Paterson (2000a)), but politics are unavoidable precisely because the state is involved, and because it in turn is subject to the democratic pressures outlined by the writers we have just been examining. The major twentieth-century changes in education were driven by political campaigning based on a developing ideology of universalistic individualism, not by the needs of the economy, and not by the wishes of state functionaries, although these shaped how popular preferences were enacted, and during periods of consolidation did become very influential. The democratic state is an agent, and it is no accident then that state power and individual autonomy, far from being antinomies, have grown together: 'the national state and the individual are strongly institutionalised entities within world culture, linked to one another through the institution of citizenship. The latter, in turn, presupposes an institutionalised and expanded state educational system' (Ramirez and Boli 1987: 14).

Therefore, if we want to explain the growth of mass education, the penetration of the ideology of universalistic individualism and the particular forms the resulting institutions take in any particular country, then we have to pay attention to reforming politics, for it is out of that milieu that ideas for transformation have come. Considering the century broadly, it was radical political movements that legitimised change, and that focused more diffuse pressure into authoritative reform. In Scotland in the twentieth century, that meant the Liberal Party for the first couple of decades, but thereafter mainly the Labour movement, acquiring an ideology of the socialised individual from the decaying Liberals, and marrying that with presbyterian and Catholic social rectitude. They also modified it all once in power with a respect for the actual democratic potential of inherited national institutions such as the parish school and the democratic university. In Scotland, reforming politics was always mediated through the powerful alliance between civil servants in the Scottish Education Department and the semi-autonomous professionals who actually ran the daily aspects of the education system: the absence of an indigenous parliament until the very end of the century gave these networks particular power in moulding radical ideas in practice.

In these respects, Scottish Labour movement people and their professional allies were in the mainstream of reforming European thought. Nowhere in Europe at any time during the century was there ever any serious prospect of the educational legacies of previous expansion being abandoned. Nowhere was there more than minority support for what later came to be called the deschooling movement – the idea, proposed by Ivan Illich in his book of 1973, that educational institutions were the problem, and that true educational freedom required that children be liberated from them. And nowhere was there any widespread support for the idea that the inherited academic curriculum was corrupting, a claim that, since the 1970s, has formed part of the more general critique of education as an alleged agent in social reproduction (for which debates, see Carnochan 1993; Feinberg 1998).

Three examples will illustrate how absolutely normal Scotland was in these respects. The first is the educational ideas of the Italian Marxist intellectual Antonio Gramsci, writing mainly from prison cells under the Fascist regime of the 1920s. One reading of some of Gramsci's writings became popular among radical critics of institutional education in the 1970s and more recently, and the term which attracts them to his work is 'hegemony'. This is a complex idea, but the essence of it is that it involves rule by means other than physical coercion. As Harold Entwistle puts it in his book on Gramsci:

> hegemonic direction is by moral and intellectual persuasion rather than
> control by the police, the military, or the coercive power of the law ...
> Control ... operates persuasively rather than coercively through
> cultural institutions – churches, labour unions and other workers'
> associations, schools and the press.
>
> (Entwistle 1979: 12)

Thus, according to Gramsci, 'every relationship of "hegemony" is necessarily a pedagogical relationship' (quoted by Entwistle 1979: 12).

However, Gramsci was very clear that he saw the hegemony of education as being the consequence of the structure of the school system, rather than of the content of the curriculum or of the practice of teachers. In Gramsci's words: 'the traditional school system was oligarchic because it was intended for the new generation of the ruling class, designed to rule in its turn: but it was not oligarchic in its mode of teaching' (quoted by Entwistle 1979: 92–3).

The social character of a particular kind of school was not created by the teaching that went on there, but by the selection of the kind of pupils who entered it. The goal of radicals, therefore, should be to create a common type of school that would serve all children equally. Even that, however, would have to be introduced gradually, and in the meantime the fairest way to modify the existing divided systems of schooling was to make sure that selection into the highest-status academic schools would be as meritocratic as possible (Entwistle 1979: 98). Gramsci, in common with most European socialists, was a strong admirer of mainstream humanistic culture, and saw it as a necessary corrective to the uninformed 'common sense' of ordinary people. Creating a new culture, he argued, meant mainly 'the diffusion in a critical form of truths already partly discovered, their "socialisation", as it were' (quoted by Entwistle 1979: 122).

Gramsci's ideas on politics and culture became highly influential on left-wing thought in the late-twentieth century, including in Scotland, but his educational thinking has been less clearly remembered. Yet, on this, he was in the mainstream of European socialist thinking. A second illustration of this is the history of actual social democratic reform of education in Scandinavia between the 1920s and the 1960s. The trajectory of Swedish education in the twentieth century until about the 1970s is, in fact, remarkably similar to Scotland's (Boucher 1982; Paulston 1968). Before 1918, the main exponents of what was called 'educational unity' were liberals, influenced by progressive clergymen from the Lutheran church and by radical teachers. They persuaded the Social Democrats to include the aim of the unity school – what would be later called the comprehensive school – in their programme, and the minister of education in the first, minority Social Democratic government in 1918, Värner Rydén, set up a schools commission in 1922, analogous to Scotland's Advisory Council. Like that Council, as we will see in Chapters 4 and 8, the commission recommended a common *folkskola* providing six years of common education from ages seven to thirteen followed by four years of secondary education based on selection into different kinds of school (Paulston 1968: 45). The proposals were, however, rejected in 1924 by the new Conservative minister. The Social Democrats did gain an overall majority in 1932 (which they retained until 1977), but their first concern then was dealing with the effects of recession, and so their educational policies concentrated on the welfare aspects of schooling rather than its structure – free meals and medical inspection, providing clothing allowances and bathing facilities, and encouraging outdoor sport (Paulston 1968: 67).

The crucial reforming government was that led by Tage Erlander after 1946. As education minister he had established in 1946 a new schools commission, this time much more political, and including all the political parties; indeed, he chaired it until he became prime minister. Its 1948 report was the turning point. It recommended a nine-year period of compulsory schooling in a common unity school, from age seven to sixteen. For those who left then there would be part-time continuation classes. The commission also recommended that schools pay much greater attention to the pastoral needs of students, and proposed a properly established system of child guidance.

All this closely resembled the proposals of the 1947 Scottish Advisory Council. The ensuing reforms also followed a similar trajectory to those in Scotland between 1950 and the mid-1960s, even though the Scottish Council's report had not been officially accepted. The price which Erlander and his colleagues paid for proceeding by consensus was conceding that there would be a decade of officially sponsored experimentation. These experiments led to the eventual adoption of the unity school as the only form of schooling from 1962. The reform programme was fully implemented by 1969 (Boucher 1982: 31). The Scottish experimentation was not so officially encouraged, but the dates of reform were very close.

Sweden, therefore, can be taken as an example of what a powerful Labour movement actually did in power. By and large, the dominant concern was with structural reform. Despite the period in the 1930s when a more direct attack on social inequalities dominated thinking in the party, the main educational tradition was to make the school system structurally less differentiated in order to provide equal opportunities for working-class children. Swedish social democrats were not alone in Scandinavia in defining democratising reforms in this institutional way. The Norwegian Labour government, for example, introduced in 1936 a structure of schooling which consisted of seven years of common education (ages seven to fourteen), and then selection into one of two main tracks (Rust 1989). The Labour government of 1945 set up a commission which recommended in 1952 that there should be a comprehensive school system up to age sixteen by the mid-1960s. As in Sweden, this led in the 1950s to officially encouraged experiments, and a system of common schooling was legislated for in 1969.

If the most politically successful Labour movements in Europe were taking this approach to structural reform, and if, from a completely different tradition, Marxists such as Gramsci also saw the problems of education in broadly the same way, it is hardly surprising that Scottish radicals were inclined to the view that democratisation meant above all institutional reform. There was also, however, another reason closer to home – the rest of the British Labour movement, and this provides our third illustration of the ways in which Scottish reformers were in the European mainstream.

In his extensive study of the educational politics of the British Labour Party in the first half of the twentieth century, Barker notes three sources of ideas: socialist thought, liberalism and the kind of social criticism found in the writing of Carlyle, Ruskin and Arnold (Barker 1971: 5–7). The last of these links directly to the notion that the purpose of democratising education is to give everyone access to mainstream culture, and that the problem in unreformed capitalism is that the middle and upper classes monopolise it. Labour inherited this tradition in which the spread of public education would increase 'the level of intelligent citizenship and of articulate and democratic political self-assertion' (see p. 138). Thus the Labour leader Ramsay MacDonald, whose formative influences were in the Scottish section of the Independent Labour Party, wrote in 1900 that 'democracy can be made efficient only by the education of the individual citizen in civic virtues' (see p. 138).

These ideas can all be found in the writing and activism of R. H. Tawney, the main intellectual influence on Labour Party thinking on education, whose report for the party in 1922 entitled *Secondary Education for All* shaped its programme until the 1950s. He believed that ultimately the only way to secure educational democracy would be by a system of comprehensive secondary schools, but – like Gramsci and the Swedish reformers – he was willing to accept that, in the meantime, a more efficiently operated selective system would be a step in the right direction (Tawney 1964: 77). As well as his pervasive influence on Labour Party thinking for three decades, Tawney influenced thinking about educational policy in two particular ways. One was by his membership of the English Board of Education's consultative committee from 1912 until 1931. His most lasting contribution in that role was the report on education and the adolescent in 1926, named after its chair, Sir Henry Hadow, vice-chancellor of Sheffield University. The report in effect gave support to the policy which Tawney had given to the Labour Party, and its main recommendations have usually been attributed to him (Barker 1971: 57; Simon 1974: 232). It recommended some form of planned post-primary provision for all, and the raising of the leaving age to fifteen (Simon 1974: 128).

Tawney's other influential policy role was through his helping to establish the Workers' Educational Association. He was a member of the official committee that produced the 1919 report of the Ministry of Reconstruction, a radical document which recommended that a properly constituted adult education service was as necessary to securing mass democracy as a system of elementary and secondary schools (Barker 1972: 125). Tawney remained associated with the WEA for the rest of his life. In this respect, he resembled

Gramsci, who had proposed that developing a working-class consciousness would require the political education of intellectuals who were organic to the working class, in the sense of providing leadership against the traditional intellectuals (Entwistle 1979: 113).

For Tawney as for Gramsci, and as for nearly all the significant educational thinkers in the British Labour Party at this time, the point was to democratise culture, not to reject it. As Barker (1972: 43) notes of *Secondary Education for All*, these radicals saw the education system as the means by which a competitive society could be replaced by one that was 'properly attuned to intellectual and spiritual values'. A 'humane education', Tawney wrote in 1914, is not in itself reproachable; what had to change was its being confined to 'persons entering a certain restricted group of professions' (Tawney 1964: 75).

These currents of radical thought were highly influential on the Scottish Labour movement. If anything, indeed, the focus on institutional reform, and the acceptance of existing culture, were even stronger there, as we will see in later chapters. The WEA always struggled to gain a secure place in Scotland, and its Marxist rival in the Labour movement, the National Council of Labour Colleges, was energetic but persistently on the margins, and vanished in the 1960s. The most radical MPs in this respect in the 1930s, such as Tom Johnston and James Maxton, believed that all children should have access to secondary education of a fairly traditional sort (Stocks 2002: 31). They, like Gramsci, did not even favour an ending of selection immediately, preferring to argue that it should operate fairly and that adequate bursaries should be available to enable working-class children to realise their potential. The main point of the European comparisons that have been sketched here is that, if Scottish reformist thinking was out of line, it was only in the intensity of its respect for the existing cultural order, having inherited a firm belief that it could be made accessible. As Barker concludes, it was thoroughly normal for radicals, including socialist radicals, to seek 'to distribute the benefits of that order, not to change it' (Barker 1972: 159).

INSTITUTIONS

Thus the dominant reforming tradition in twentieth-century European education has been directed at changing the structure of institutions and the patterns of access to them. That is the main reason why national traditions in education remain fundamentally important. By committing themselves to extant culture and to democratising existing institutions as a means of widening access to it, reformers also implicitly accepted the cultural values that were embodied in the existing practices of the traditional institutions.

Steedman's concept of 'defining institutions' is particularly potent here. She argued that the expansion of secondary education in England was modelled on the so-called 'public' schools there (Steedman 1987). Unlike France and Germany, England at this period had no 'defining authority' – no state agency powerful or legitimate enough to set up new endowed grammar schools in the image it wanted. The old 'public' schools therefore provided the definitions of what would constitute a proper secondary education in the new grammar schools. The key elements of that definition were aspiring to give their pupils access to Oxford and Cambridge scholarships, instituting an appropriately high school leaving age (at around eighteen), giving high status to a classical curriculum, organising the school along the lines of the 'public' schools (grouping pupils into houses, for example) and 'strengthening of boundary definition between school and the outside world', for example through school uniforms, organised team games and religious assemblies. The inheritance which the grammar schools gained from the 'public' schools then, in turn, shaped the character of English selective secondary education until the 1960s, and further became the model on which English comprehensive schools were based after 1965.

One of the mechanisms by which that wider diffusion happened was through the outlook of the expanding professional class which went on to staff the new welfare state in the middle of the century. This, then, created a whole society modelled on the professional ideal. As Perkin (1989: 8) argues, 'only the landed few could be leisured gentlemen, only those who acquired capital [could be] entrepreneurs', but 'the professional ideal could in principle be extended to everyone', precisely through the expanded education system. Perkin finds, pervading professional culture generally, the same kinds of values as Steedman noted in the secondary schools.

Although Steedman distinguishes between English defining institutions and French or German authoritative ministries, in fact the same kind of idea is relevant much more widely, precisely because so much of educational democratisation sought to open access to institutions that continued to be defined in fairly traditional terms. Insofar as the main twentieth-century reforms unified and systematised previously more fragmented patterns of schooling, in each country the power of the nationally dominant image of a proper educational institution was all the greater. Administrative unification always entails, in the words of Archer (1979: 174), 'the standardisation of inputs, processes and outputs', and so the key question becomes the model on which this standardisation takes place. However, to say that institutions shape meanings is not to imply a necessary stasis, because institutions may embody the capacity for change, expansion or democratisation, depending precisely on their lineage and the ideologies or myths with which they are imbued. As Kogan says of 'institutional values': 'it is too easy to assume that they are inherently defensive of professional or bureaucratic interests. If construed objectively they can be seen to relate to such basic values as equity or freedom or a sense of community' (Kogan 1975: 65).

So, in understanding the model to which Scottish education has aspired in the twentieth century, it would be informative to look to its defining institutions, the parish school, the putatively democratic university and the general education programmes that were supposed, paradigmatically, to take place within them. Through this extension of a particular view of the democratic significance of the inherited structures to which a democratised system sought to aspire, the Scottish professional society of the second half of the twentieth century would have acquired quite different values from those which Perkin found in England. We might then better understand why Scotland at the end of the century had a particular structure of attitudes to educational democracy, both at a popular level and among governing groups – a view in which academic education is believed to be a democratic heritage rather than, as in England, one that is derived from the most privileged institutions imaginable.

SCOTLAND

There are five points from this discussion that might provide a guide to interpreting the story of Scottish education that follows in later chapters.

We have summarised the evidence on expansion, systematisation and unification at the beginning of this chapter. The first point of interpretation of these is to pick up on the idea of the defining institution. Scotland had a system of public education long before the twentieth century, provided by the Church and legislated for by the national parliament until the late-seventeenth century and later by the parliament in London. It also had a system of universities that were engaged in professional preparation long before the period to which Jarausch (1983) ascribes this process elsewhere. The legacy was therefore already imbued with national and ostensibly democratic potential. As Anderson (1983b: 519) puts it, before 1872, 'the parish schools already existed as the basis of a "public" system and as a model for future development' – a model, we could now say, of exactly the defining kind which Steedman suggests, but, in the hands of twentieth-century reformers, of quite different ideological significance from the grammar-school tradition which she explains. Even if we confine our attention to the small number of secondary schools that existed before the late-nineteenth century, we still reach conclusions about the potential legacy that indicate a rather different significance to the quite different legacy in England: the endowed schools in Scotland 'were public institutions whose legal endowment guaranteed permanence' (Anderson 1983b: 534). The attitude to the universities was that they were similarly public.

Second, we must be careful how we define that word 'public'. As in England, the state was indeed not as centrally involved as it was in, say, France after 1789, but that does not mean that the Scots gave to the twentieth century a meaning for 'public' that could be equated with, say, 'voluntary'. In the absence of the formal trappings of a separate state after the Union with England in 1707 – a Union that was probably never more popular in Scotland than at the dawn of the twentieth century – Scots had to evolve a rather specific sense of 'public', rooted in civil society rather than the state. Anderson argues that, in terms of principles such as systematisation and unification, Scottish policy was closer to the thoroughly dirigiste French state than to England, although the directing was civic, not statist.

Third, if one of the central aspirations of European twentieth-century reformers has been to reduce what Ringer (1987: 7) calls 'segmentation', or division into 'parallel segments or "tracks"', then the democratic pressure in Scotland has been as thorough as in other countries, including those such as Sweden that are usually regarded as having taken the process furthest. The policy response has generally been rather laggard, at no time more so than in the period after 1980 when the eventually successful outcome of half a century of pressure for a common secondary school happened to coincide with the election in the UK of a government that was inveterately hostile to that idea. That this government never commanded more than minority support in Scotland, and steadily lost what it had throughout the period from 1979 to 1997, was itself partly because of this conflict of educational ideas. The same can then be said of the referendum vote for a Scottish parliament in 1997, a large part of the motive for which was a belief that the education system needed to be safeguarded and, probably, that the reforms that had been achieved in the 1960s and after needed to be taken further, with Sweden and other Scandinavian countries as possible models (Paterson 2000a: 29–46).

Fourth, as in England and everywhere else, the cultural and curricular implications of the Scottish defining institutions were nationally specific. To many critics of Scottish education in the last two or three decades of the twentieth century, the extension of academic education to everyone was a parody of democracy, a stifling of working-class Scots culture, or of Gaelic culture, an elevation of book-learning over dialogic discovery, a denial of children's creativity. So far as actual democratic aspirations are concerned – as distinct from the educational utopias which radicals have been painting for centuries – these accusations miss the point. The extension of access to academic, English-language, largely written culture through education was not imposed; it was what people seemed to want, as expressed through their actions (in choosing types of school), their characteristic social movements and their votes. Neave put the Scottish specificity clearly:

> In most Western countries the distinction between 'academic' and
> non academic courses is regarded as one of the major historic
> obstacles to a democratic system of education. In Scotland, the

reverse is true. The concept of a curriculum dominated by a highly
academic content has been justified in the name of creating a
'common course' for all.

(Neave 1976: 131)

So the fifth and last point in conclusion here is that the institutional legacy
through which Scottish democratic reform has taken place leaves a very
specifically Scottish ideology of education, even though the process of
democratisation and of inheriting institutions may be much the same everywhere. The changing character of that twentieth-century Scottish ideology is
something which is explored throughout the book, but the key components
can be identified at the outset as a particular tension between the individual
and the collective. McPherson (1973: 167) called these the 'organising principles of action' in Scottish reform. The aspiration in the successive waves of
reform has been to use education as the means of refining what the Scottish
philosophers called 'common sense', in a process very similar to Gramsci's
notion of developing 'good sense'. This principle links the individual to the
collective through education: it is collective because it is common, and it is
individual because it relates to an educated understanding. Thus the shift
from individualism to collectivism that was underway at the beginning of the
century was a shift within this democratic tradition, and the more recent
extension of individualism has probably been interpreted as similarly
enclosed within a Scottish interpretative framework. That is why the individualising reforms of the Thatcher government – such as giving parents more
choice over where to send their children – could be interpreted in Scotland
as being consistent with the collective principles that underpinned, say, the
introduction of comprehensive secondary schooling. The same was true in
Scandinavia: as the Swedish prime minister, Tage Erlander, himself said in
1954: 'it is a mistake to believe that people's freedom is diminished because
they decide to carry out collectively what they are incapable of doing
individually' (Tilton 1990: 268–9).

Thus the whole purpose of collective reforms in places such as Scotland
and Sweden has been interpreted popularly as being to free the individual
from structural constraints, and so policies that seem further to advance that
freedom are accepted as consistent with the original reforms.

If this structure – of a predominantly academic education through
predominantly formal institutions at school or university level – does not seem
very democratic to critics, now or in the past, then that may partly be because
they are looking at it through the wrong lens, as Neave warns. For the future, a
new generation of reformers may want further to change the Scottish common
sense so that worthwhile education is no longer seen as mainly academic or
institutional. Less deliberately, the belief in the democratic potential of

academic education may also have been eroded by the absence of questions of philosophy and educational purpose from officially sponsored discussions of educational policy in the 1990s, as we will see in Chapters 8 and 9. However, for interpreting the experience of most of the twentieth century, the potency of that idea seems undeniable – including its potency in the two or three decades since writers such as Andrew McPherson and R. D. Anderson first developed their searching critique of its accuracy as a description of the past.

PART I

Competition and Opportunity, 1880s–1930s

From Individualism to Collectivism

The Education (Scotland) Act of 1872 was profoundly significant, but left as many issues unresolved as it settled. In some respects, indeed, the entire period from then until 1918, at least, can be understood as an attempt to address some of the disappointments of the campaigners whose activities led to the passing of the Act. Chapter 3 explains why it was important, assesses its impact on elementary education and then follows through the consequences to the 1930s. One of these consequences by the beginning of the new century was the growing sense that compulsory elementary schooling was likely to lead to a much more widespread provision of secondary schooling than hitherto; indeed, the very definition of an elementary stage for the first time in Scotland then raised questions about what should happen to those children aged over twelve who traditionally had stayed on in the parish school. Chapter 4 therefore deals with the complex changes through which post-elementary education went from the 1890s until the 1930s. The key moment was the 1918 Act, the main purpose of which was to bring some system to the complexity. The universities were affected by the 1872 Act only insofar as there remained a residual interest in the route into them directly from the parish schools. However, the reform of secondary schooling did directly affect the universities, and debates about access, in terms of social class and gender, became normal. The universities also started the slow process of gradually becoming more British in their outlook, although – despite their critics then and later – there was never any real chance that they could sever their links with the rest of Scottish education, even if only because they continued to provide the academic education for large numbers of schoolteachers. This is dealt with in Chapter 5. The universities were also being supplemented from 1901 by the new central institutions, colleges which the Scottish Education Department intended to provide a higher technical education that would be on a par with the universities' provision in the arts or in pure science.

Beyond them there grew up a plethora of mainly vocational continuation classes and various kinds of workers' education that ranged from the academic to the directly political. The significance of all these vocational and informal educational activities is traced and assessed in Chapter 6.

If there is a common set of themes for this first period, it can be encapsulated in an oft-quoted passage by Duncan MacGillivray, the highly influential president of the main teachers' union, the Educational Institute of Scotland, writing during the first wave of post-war optimism: 'The wheel has come around almost full circle from individualism to collectivism, from competition to co-operation, and from the doctrine of laissez-faire to that of State control' (MacGillivray 1919: 1).

So it is with the working-out in practice of these tensions that this first part is mainly concerned.

CHAPTER 3

Elementary Education

The 1872 Act was the outcome of the protracted mid-nineteenth-century debate about setting up a national system of schooling, which itself had been provoked by the crisis in education caused by the growth of industry and by the split in the established church at the Disruption of 1843. It seemed no longer then plausible to claim that the parish schools were adequately meeting the needs of the nation: too many children in the industrial districts were ill-served by any sector, established or not, and rivalry among the denominations dissipated effort in ways that were not always productive. The subscription schools that had grown up in response to the dislocation of industrialism and its accompanying shifts of population were doing no more than filling in gaps. Out of these concerns came in 1864 the Commission of Inquiry chaired by the Duke of Argyll, the reports of which in the second half of the 1860s led to the framing of the eventual legislation (Anderson 1983a, 1995; Lenman and Stocks 1972; Myers 1972; Withrington 1972, 1983).

The Act had seven main provisions (Anderson 1995: 313). Every parish and burgh was to have an elected school board. Initially there were about 980 of these, and this declined slowly through mergers to 947 in 1918, when the boards were replaced by thirty-eight elected education authorities (Scotland 1969: 13). The boards would immediately become responsible for all the parochial and burgh schools, and could accept the transfer, without compensation, of any denominational school or subscription school; the schools under the administration of the boards were called public schools. The boards would receive grants from the Scotch Education Department, which was constituted for the first time, technically as a committee of the Privy Council; 'Scotch' did not become 'Scottish' until 1918. Religion would continue to be taught in accordance with local custom, although parents would be entitled to withdraw their children from that if they objected; this practice became known as providing religious instruction according to 'use and wont', although these words did not actually appear in the legislation. Children had to attend school between the ages of five and thirteen, but could be exempted if they could show they had sufficient competence in reading, writing and arithmetic. Teachers in charge of schools had to hold a certificate of competency granted by the SED. Additionally, former burgh schools which had been providing significant amounts of post-elementary education were relabelled 'higher class' schools, although no grants or aid from the local rates were available to promote their development.

So it was far-reaching. Nevertheless, the immediate aftermath was controversial. The severest critics claimed that 1872 marked the defeat of an opportunity to revive the Scottish tradition of universal parish schooling (Myers 1972: 73; Lenman and Stocks 1972). One of the main objections was that the supervision of the system was placed in the hands of a body based in London – the Privy Council; the SED did not move to Edinburgh until the 1930s. Lyon Playfair MP, an exponent of the Scottish tradition, claimed in parliament in 1872 that the proposer of the Bill, the Lord Advocate George Young, and his counterpart responsible for the 1870 Education Act in England and Wales, W. E. Forster, did not have 'that inner faith in the advantages of a Scotch system that induces me to put unreservedly into their hands the unknown future'; later he extended this view into opposing the transfer of responsibility for Scottish education to the new Secretary for Scotland after 1885 (Myers 1972: 87). James Donaldson, rector of Edinburgh High School, believed that the Bill was a thoroughly anglicising measure (Anderson 1995: 70).

There is no denying the disputes, but the main subsequent effect of them over the ensuing half-century was the gradual incorporation into the practice of elementary education of many of the principles which the proponents of the national tradition advocated (Withrington 1972). The Act did, after all, provide for a truly national system, even if the department overseeing it was based in London; in any case, the schools inspectorate, founded in 1840, continued to be based in Scotland and to have a close involvement in the development of policy, especially in the drawing up of the Codes which governed what actually was taught (Bone 1968: 76). The first six years of the operation of the Act were, moreover, overseen by a temporary Board of Education based in Edinburgh, and the SED came under the auspices of the new Secretary for Scotland after 1885. The placing of the schools under the control of locally elected boards also avoided any domination of their governance by landlords, one of the fears of radical campaigners such as Duncan McLaren, Liberal MP for Edinburgh (Withrington 1972: 121). As the historian of the boards in Fife between 1873 and 1919 put it, 'the opportunities provided by the Act of 1872 for a wider range of participation in the administration of local schools were to an impressive extent taken up' (Bain 1998: 116; see also Anderson 1995: 166–70). Thus, out of 2,536 elections to places on the boards in Fife over that period, twenty-eight per cent were won by people who worked in various skilled working-class trades or as shopkeepers or small merchants, fourteen per cent by middle-class professionals, and the remainder by commercial and industrial owners and various farming occupations (Bain 1998: 93). In most areas, religious interests were strongly represented at first, partly because the electoral rules allowed voters to give all their multiple votes to single candidates, with the result that well-organised factions could secure places (Anderson 1995: 168–73). However, by the first decade of the new century conservative evangelicalism had given way to a form of Christian welfarism, under the influence of a vocal minority of members representing the Labour movement (Brown 1997: 143–4). Some of this moderate radicalism also came from the small number of female members. Because the franchise for the boards had been open to middle-class women from the start, their participation grew slowly even though at a very low level: for example, only thirty-eight women were elected in Fife in the whole period. The most famous female board member nationally was Flora Stevenson, who was elected to the Edinburgh board in 1873 and became its chair in 1900 (Anderson 1995: 171; Corr 1990b).

Another of the aims of the campaigners had also been realised, in that the Act had resulted in schooling being made compulsory, although with the possibility of exemption. Moreover, there was an important principle recognised in the phrasing of the purpose of the Act. Henry Craik, then an official with the Board of Education in London, and from 1885 until 1904 the head of the SED, was not the only person to claim significance for the fact that the Act was declared to be 'for the whole people of Scotland'. It was not an elementary education act, unlike the 1870 measure south of the border (Craik 1884: 143).

EDUCATION AND SOCIAL REFORM

Given the controversy, however, it is perhaps then not surprising that 'to most Scots 1872 was both a fulfilment and a challenge to further struggles' (Lenman and Stocks 1972: 104).

The first, and most visible, activity of the boards was new building. The inadequacy of existing premises was one reason why the presbyterian denominations gave up their schools quickly, and by the beginning of the new century only twenty-four schools remained in the hands of the Church of Scotland, and four with the Free Church, while 2,788 were run by the school boards (Anderson 1995: 309). Anderson (1995: 223) notes that the larger boards had constructed new schools for most of their children by 1882, a remarkable instance of public intervention to promote a public, national end. The resulting two- or three-storey, stone-built edifices became symbolically associated with Scottish education throughout the twentieth century.

A particularly onerous task was faced by the Roman Catholic church, which had kept its schools out of the new system because it did not trust the boards to respect their religious character. The Catholic population was growing rapidly, from a total of 333,000 in 1878 to 513,000 in 1911, by then making up eleven per cent of Scotland's population (Fitzpatrick 1986: 13). However, it remained very poor, since most of it consisted of immigrants from Ireland seeking unskilled work in the industrial areas of west-central Scotland. Between the 1870s and 1918, the church constructed its own system, in receipt of government grants but owned and managed by the ecclesiastical authorities. The number of such schools rose from sixty-five in 1872 to 138 in 1882, an effort that was as impressive as that of the boards. There were 188 in 1900 and 224 in 1918. The number of pupils in attendance rose from 12,000 in 1872, through 33,000 in 1882, to 58,000 in 1902 and 94,000 in 1918 (Treble 1978: 113). The inspectorate were full of praise, commenting in 1876 on Lanarkshire that:

> comparing the condition of the education of children before the [1872] Act with the present, no greater improvement has been made by any class than by the Roman Catholics. This is largely due to the zeal of the clergy.
>
> (Treble 1978: 114)

The second change which the Scotch Education Department sought to bring about over the next half century was an improvement in the quality of teaching. The aim was to reach a position where all teachers were certificated, achieved either by going through a course in a training college, or by serving a five-year apprenticeship as a pupil teacher. By the beginning of the twentieth century, the SED's aim was to phase out the latter route (which had been modified in various ways) so that all teachers would have been formally trained. The process of educating the teachers is discussed more fully in Chapter 5 below, but the improvements in supply can be readily summarised. In 1870, only forty-four per cent of teachers in the public schools were certificated; this had risen to sixty-two per cent in 1899, and reached ninety-seven per cent in 1914 (Anderson 1995: 177). The situation in the Catholic schools was much worse, and attempts to improve the quality of their staff proved, in the long run, to be one of the main financial pressures that induced the church to accept the transfer of its system to the state after 1918: in 1886, for example, when seventy-one per cent of female staff employed by the boards had been educated in a training college, the corresponding proportion in Catholic schools was only forty-one per cent. The proportions for men were seventy-six per cent and sixty-one per cent (Treble 1978: 117). In an attempt to resolve this, the Church established its first teacher-training college in Scotland, Notre Dame in Glasgow, in 1895;

previously, Scottish Catholic teachers had gone to Liverpool for training (Cruikshank 1970: 122).

For the country as a whole, there was a slow rise also in the proportions of teachers who were graduates of the universities, a process that continued more rapidly after World War I. For men, it was forty per cent in 1914 (Anderson 1995: 176). Regulations of 1922 required that all men entering general teaching posts (as distinct from, for example, teaching art, music or technical subjects) should be graduates (Scotland 1969: 116). The overall proportion of graduates rose rapidly thereafter, reaching seventy per cent of male teachers in 1938 (Osborne 1966: 275). There were regional variations: in 1933, eighty-seven per cent of male teachers in Aberdeenshire were graduates, compared to the national proportion of sixty-six per cent (Osborne 1966: 274). The proportions were lower among female teachers, but rose at a faster rate – eight per cent of female teachers were graduates in 1914 (Anderson 1995: 176), and this quadrupled to thirty-two per cent in 1938 (Osborne 1966: 275). The teaching force was increasingly female throughout the period: the female proportion was thirty-five per cent in 1851, seventy per cent in 1911, and – in primary schools – eighty per cent in 1927 (Corr 1983: 137; SED 1928: 43). Corr (1983: 145) attributes the feminisation to the development of more lucrative professions for men, such as in banking, the fact that female teachers earned only about half of male teachers, and so were cheaper, and the lack of progress in having teaching recognised as a profession, which had been the goal of their union, the Educational Institute of Scotland, since its foundation in 1847. Thus a career that could offer unprecedented opportunities for educated women, and which would also fit with the prevailing view that women were ideal custodians of young children, could for these very reasons seem less attractive to men. Between 1915 and 1945, though, the opportunities for women were restricted by the requirement that most of them resign upon marriage (Adams 1989).

These new teachers, housed in the new buildings, whether built by boards or by churches, were the means by which the principal aim of the Scotch Education Department was to be achieved: enforcing the regulations on attendance (Anderson 1995: 233–5). In 1871, attendance as a percentage of the age group was over eighty per cent only for ages seven to eleven. By 1901, for both boys and girls, there was over ninety per cent attendance for all ages six to twelve, and age thirteen had eighty-five per cent for girls and eighty-two per cent for boys. The attendance at age five, however, remained low, at sixty-two per cent for girls and sixty-four per cent for boys. School boards did not insist on attendance at age five: as the SED reported in 1904, there was a widespread belief that the real starting age was six (Anderson 1995: 230). The most important reform that helped increase attendance was the abolition of fees in 1891 (Lenman and Stocks 1972: 98).

The Education (Scotland) Act of 1901 attempted to raise the attendance rates over age twelve by removing the exemptions that had allowed children to leave even though the formal minimum age had been fourteen since 1883. Exemption because parents needed children's income had been common, either in the explicit form of young people entering jobs in the industrial areas, or in the hidden form of intermittent withdrawal of children in rural areas to help during busy periods in the agricultural year. Exemption could also be granted on the grounds that mothers needed help in the home. The economic necessity of this, however, should not lead us to suppose that there was popular opposition to the principle of an extended period of schooling (Jamieson and Toynbee 1992: 51). Nevertheless, even after 1901, leaving at age fourteen was still regarded as absolutely normal (Jamieson 1990: 19): in 1911, only thirteen per cent of boys and girls aged fifteen were in school (Anderson 1995: 235).

These financial and other penalties preventing parents from allowing their children to stay on were one source of the pressure for schools to assume a welfare role. However, the most immediate origins of that in official circles were in the concerns that had been raised during the Boer War about the physical fitness of army recruits. Lord Rosebery, the former prime minister, argued in a lecture he gave to students in 1900 when he was elected rector of Glasgow University that promoting children's health contributed to the efficiency of the Empire (I. Thomson 1978: 16). Henry Craik was keen on this line, and arranged for the setting up in 1902 of a Royal Commission on Physical Training in Scottish schools. He advocated military training as a moral as well as a physical exercise. The school boards, however, did not agree, and nor did the headteachers of the public schools and the inspectors (I. Thomson 1986). Some boards simply refused to let military drill take place, Glasgow arguing that such attitudes were 'opposed to the true spirit of education' (I. Thomson 1986: 115). The Commission conceded, and military drill was not enforced.

The view which did prevail was part of a much broader belief that ill-health had mainly environmental sources. This was persistently put forward by W. L. MacKenzie, medical inspector of the Local Government Board, who conducted inquiries into the medical condition of children in Aberdeen and Edinburgh. Ian Thomson (1978: 20) notes that he found that children from schools in the poorer areas were 'smaller, lighter, and in worse health than their counterparts from middle-class homes'. MacKenzie believed that the state had a duty to supervise the health of children, and that this was a necessary requirement before education could be fully effective; indeed, the very fact of compulsory attendance made it, in his view, easier for the authorities to carry this task out (Stewart 1999: 77); he recommended therefore that children should be subject to compulsory medical inspection.

There was a similar problem with nutrition, and the voluntary efforts of philanthropists in the network of Charity Organisation Societies – including one run by Flora Stevenson in Edinburgh – were not meeting the need. Some school boards, for example that in Dundee, simply defied the law and provided free meals (Stewart 1999: 80). By the time of the election of the Liberal government in 1906, and the appointment of the radical John Sinclair as Secretary for Scotland, most reforming opinion – including in the nascent Labour movement – had consolidated around the need for legislative change. Scotland was excluded from a Bill for England and Wales, partly because the opponents of state involvement had mobilised the House of Lords to reject any proposals. Prominent among these opponents over the preceding few years had been Flora Stevenson until her death in 1905. But Sinclair – aided by Craik's successor as head of the Education Department, John Struthers – then came forward with a more radical measure for Scotland, which became the 1908 Education (Scotland) Act, enforcing medical inspection, free meals and grants for clothing, free books and travel, and some bursaries. There were to be Treasury grants to the boards to help pay for these (Levitt 1988: 59; Stewart 1999: 86–7), and various disparate sources of public money for education were amalgamated into a single Education (Scotland) Fund. In the following years, the sum expended on these things grew fifteenfold, from £1,779 in 1908 to £27,404 in 1911 (SED 1913: 4).

The same measure also formalised a provision in an Act of 1906 that enabled boards to set up special schools or classes for children 'who, not being imbecile and not being merely dull and backward, are, by reason of mental and physical defect, incapable of receiving proper benefit from the instruction of the ordinary schools' (G. Thomson 1983: 235).

The SED reported that in 1912, 3,319 children were taking part in such classes. This would represent about 0.4 per cent of all those aged five to fourteen, although some of these children would have been aged fifteen or sixteen (SED 1913: 13).

EDUCATION AND THE INDIVIDUAL

Alongside these social reforms, there were also changes to the curriculum and to teaching styles. What children learnt in elementary education was gradually made less rigid and more varied, the start of a long process that continued right through the twentieth century. When Henry Craik became secretary of the SED in 1885, one of the most pressing issues was 'payment by results', by which grants to schools depended on the performance of children in tests at the six Standards that were intended to mark progress through the elementary stages from age seven to age twelve. He abolished this, thus gaining widespread admiration from teachers. In 1890 he also abolished tests in the Standards, and in 1899 abolished the Standards themselves, encouraging schools to devise their own curricula, although, as Anderson (1995: 208) comments, 'the habit of uniformity being now deeply ingrained, teachers continued to think in terms of the Standards long after they had been officially abolished'. Gradually, though, subjects other than reading, writing, arithmetic and religion appeared, for example singing, dancing and needlework. For older children, there were 'class subjects' such as English literature, geography, history and science, replacing the 'specific subjects' that had been the SED's way of maintaining the Scottish preference for offering some pupils a chance to study to a post-elementary level in the local school. Particularly controversial at this time were moves to introduce domestic science for girls, a proposal that found favour among upper-class philanthropic women, but which was resented by working-class mothers as taking time away from the more important business of academic learning (Corr 1990b; Moore 1992). For similar reasons, parents objected to boys being taught gardening in school (Jamieson 1990: 23).

At the same time as attempting to broaden the curriculum, Craik also sought to make the link between elementary education and the small but growing secondary-education sector more efficient. In 1892, he introduced a Merit Certificate to mark the end of elementary education; in 1898, this was officially recognised as being equivalent to completing Standard V. But the numbers reaching it by age eleven – to which it officially corresponded – were small. In 1901, for example, the annual report of the SED showed that of the 35,394 girls on the school registers who were aged eleven or over, only 5.7 per cent had gained the Merit Certificate; among the 37,760 boys, the proportion was even lower, at 4.8 per cent (Parliamentary Papers 1901, table 10).

Generally, though, Craik's and, later, Struthers' reforms to the curriculum were cautious. Teaching methods could not be other than formal when classes normally contained sixty children, the legal maximum from 1905 (Scotland 1969: 52). The ending of payment-by-results probably did lead to some relaxation in discipline, and the use of corporal punishment – which in Scotland was generally administered by means of the leather belt, or 'tawse' – probably declined (Bone 1968: 115–16). The inspectors began officially to discourage it. However, harsh discipline remained widespread, if some contemporary critics and some recollections of people who were schoolchildren at this time are a guide (Hendrie 1997: 90–2; Jamieson 1990: 20–2; Neill 1916; Wade 1939: 237–8): this does seem to be one of those rare instances where it is safe to infer that the absence of any mention of a practice from most official documents really does indicate its taken-for-granted ubiquity. Other contemporary claims such as that 'physical compulsion as a means of school discipline is practically obsolete' seem more likely to represent attempts by opponents of the practice to embarrass its users into abandoning it than to be based on any reliable information (Scottish Education Reform Committee 1917: 143). Child-centredness was not, in any case, a concept that was widely popular in Scotland, partly because the usual starting age for school was quite late (Roberts 1972).

There was not much official openness to ideas from elsewhere, and the purpose of the curriculum in the first couple of decades of the twentieth century was to socialise children into a morally responsible attitude to society, supportive of the Union and the Empire (Anderson 1995: 193–220).

One aspect of this was in attitudes to the Gaelic language (Smith 1978–80). The Argyll Commission in the 1860s had been sympathetic to Gaelic, and from 1872 until the end of the century official views were not systematically hostile to it. But nor was there any enthusiasm, and even those inspectors who took a keen interest in Gaelic and Celtic culture – such as the Englishman, William Jolly – regarded Gaelic as subsidiary. Typical in this regard was John L. Robertson, who became chief inspector for the northern area, and eventually head of the inspectorate as a whole. He was a member of the scholarly Gaelic Society of Inverness, came from Stornoway, and so knew the problems of the Highlands and Islands well (Smith 1978–80: 51). However, like most parents in the Gaelic-speaking areas, he saw the purpose of the new national system of schooling as being to make children literate in English. Those officials, boards, teachers and parents who did advocate teaching through the medium of Gaelic did so on the grounds of its educational effectiveness as a means to learning English, not because they had any particular desire to use education to strengthen Gaelic. Thus a survey by An Comunn Gaidhealach in 1907 reported the headteacher of Poolewe Public School telling a conference in Oban that bilingual education was desirable because it produced pupils who were 'much more intelligent, brighter, and possessed of a better knowledge of English and English composition than the uni-lingual Lowland pupils' (An Comunn Gaidhealach 1907: 32). His school was reported as providing 3.5 hours of teaching in Gaelic every week (see pp. 44–5). The survey's report in fact went out of its way to emphasise that learning Gaelic need imply no disloyalty to the Empire, and quoted a speech by the Prince of Wales at a dinner of the Highland Society in London where he acknowledged that 'the history of the Highland Society is a record not only of Scottish patriotism, but of loyalty to the British Crown'. This was at a time when the future of the language perhaps did not seem in doubt: in 1901, there were 230,806 Gaelic speakers, five per cent of the Scottish population but still over fifty per cent in most of the western and north-western Highlands and Islands. Something of the same bilingualism in education may have been found with the Scots language too: Donaldson (1986: 36–7) notes evidence from newspaper articles in Scots that, in the north-eastern rural areas especially, teachers had to use Scots if they were to be understood at all, but, for the purposes of post-elementary schooling (and for social mobility), English had to be acquired. The support for English literacy may have been – as was alleged by Gaelic activists in the late-twentieth century – the result of the national schools being used as the latest phase in a state campaign to eradicate minority languages (Mackinnon 1972), but, if so, it was popular.

Alongside and partly in opposition to these official views on the curriculum generally, however, were the beginnings of a more liberal position, and indeed the cautious changes introduced by the SED were partly a response to that. A very few of the most radical critics rejected the Scottish system as unreformable; the most famous of these, A. S. Neill, who started his teaching career in Gretna in 1914, became internationally known as a proponent of the 'new education' that emphasised child-centredness, but only after he had set up his experimental free school outside Scotland (in Lyme Regis and then in Leiston in Suffolk). In Scotland itself, there were plenty of less extreme advocates of a form of elementary teaching that would cater for the needs of the whole child. Probably most influential was Professor S. S. Laurie, who held the chair of education at Edinburgh University from 1876 until 1903. He argued in 1888 that 'the primary ... must be sacred to the humanistic in education; and ... realistic subjects should be so practically taught as to relate them to the uses and enjoyment of life' (Laurie 1901: 152).

The advocates of this approach preferred the word 'primary' to 'elementary'. The ending of payment by results was seen by them as a means of enriching the curriculum. By the end of Struthers' reign at the Scottish Education Department in 1921 it had become commonly accepted among educationalists that (in the words of Duncan MacGillivray in 1919) 'the centre of gravity in the school is fast removing from the curriculum, the subject of knowledge, to the child, the subject of training' (MacGillivray 1919: 29).

POST-WAR IDEALISM

This mood was given encouragement by the idealism that grew out of wartime disruption. The War caused a great deal of dislocation. In the annual report of the SED for 1915–16, for example, of 3,536 male teachers of military age, 2,200 were reported to have joined the forces (about one in ten of all teachers), and so the authorities were encouraging retired teachers and married women teachers to return to the schools temporarily (SED 1919a: 3). Schools were widely used for military purposes, so that neighbouring schools had to combine, often using the building in shifts.

The reaction, in contrast to the jingoism in 1914, was to look forward. The chief inspector in the Highland and Northern Division, Dr J. M. Wattie, reported in the SED's report for 1918–19 that the war had enhanced the esteem of education, and noted 'the larger expectations based on education as a main instrument for the bringing in of a new and better order' (SED 1919b: 5).

The main outcome was in the reconstruction of secondary education in the 1918 Act, as we will see in Chapter 4, and the significant changes in primary education from then until World War II mainly concerned the curriculum. A Scottish Education Reform Committee had been set up in 1916 by various advocates of change, including MacGillivray, and chaired by Alexander Morgan who headed the Edinburgh teacher-training college. For primary schooling, it commented in 1917 that there were now too many subjects in the curriculum, a theme which became known as 'getting rid of the lumber'. It proposed that more time be devoted to practical subjects (Scottish Education Reform Committee 1917: 37–8). All children would be entitled to a common curriculum.

The committee followed the normal Scottish preference for generally ignoring gender, except in those parts of the curriculum to do with practical work (discussed on pp. 38–9). On the one hand, this helped to create the sense that able girls were as entitled to gain access to a full academic curriculum as boys. However, on the other hand – in a society where gender roles were still very rigid – the apparent neutrality in effect endorsed a tendency to have lower expectations of girls than of boys. The ignoring of gender also had the unfortunate effect for historians of leaving few statistics relating to male and female differences for any sector of education: with important exceptions, such as in relation to university students and to school teaching, official statistics remained undifferentiated until well after World War II.

Throughout the 1920s and 1930s the radical campaigning for reform to curriculum and teaching methods drew inspiration from the kinds of concern expressed by the Reform Committee. Much of it emerged from the Scottish section of the New Education Fellowship which promoted child-centred education from the early 1920s. A. S. Neill was the best-known Scottish member, and attracted the praise of critics of Scottish culture and education such as the poet Hugh MacDiarmid, who (writing under his own name C. M. Grieve) praised Neill's books for 'their brilliant common sense, shrewd knowledge of life, complete integrity of attitude and simplicity of form' (Grieve 1926: 243). However, in practice, Grieve was almost as much of an outsider as Neill, despite his regular articles in the *Scottish Educational Journal*, the successor to *Educational News* as the main organ of the Educational Institute of Scotland. More relevant to understanding the impact of the ideas of the new education on teachers was the Scottish section of the Fellowship, led by William Boyd. He had founded the Glasgow University Education Department in 1907, where he remained until his retiral in 1945. He later wrote a history of the Fellowship (Boyd and Rawson 1965). At the same time, he was also an important figure in mainstream education in Scotland through his teaching on the EdB classes in the university; the largest group of students on these courses consisted of teachers in schools. He was a pioneer of child guidance, and he set up the first child-guidance clinic in Glasgow in which he established the principle that guidance should be educational, not mainly medical (Dell 1969: 33–5). Most of the children seen by the clinic were referred because of unmanageable behaviour or aggression.

By the 1930s, one practical effect of the public activities of the advocates of the new education was the slow growth of nurseries, often, like Boyd's guidance service, seen as particularly important in poor areas. One enthusiast was Agnes Muir, Scottish correspondent of the pre-school section of the World Federation of Educational Associations. She investigated Scottish nurseries in 1934 (Muir 1934), and found a total of nineteen, varying in size from twenty-six to seventy, and mostly starting at ages two to three. She found much practice that would have been approved of by the new educationalists – equipment to encourage play and music, gardens and sandpits, and staff trained in relevant methods. The nurseries also provided meals and other food, and tried to involve parents – mothers through 'sewing parties' which would be addressed by the nursery superintendent on good parenting, fathers by asking for help in mending the children's toys. But, Muir concluded, 'it is obvious that voluntary effort cannot hope to do more than touch the fringe of the great problem of the pre-school child' (see p. 479). Not all nurseries were created for these idealistic reasons, however: in Dundee, where women were the main workforce in the jute mills, they were provided by the owners, after philanthropists alleged widespread neglect of children in the city (Gordon 1991: 166).

The official response to this emerging climate was further encouragement to experiments by the new education authorities (which had replaced the boards). Even organisations that were highly critical of the SED's policies on secondary education in the 1920s praised what was being done in the primary sector. For example, the *Scottish Educational Journal* described the proposed new primary curriculum as 'elastic and doubtless educationally valuable' (Young 1986: 103). The eventual effect by the 1930s can be gauged through the results of a survey of primary teaching that was carried out in 1937 by the Scottish Council for Research in Education, which had been set up in 1928 by the EIS and the education authorities, partly in order to offer to teachers feasible means of enriching the curriculum and making their teaching more child-centred. The survey found, for example, that storytelling and history had become common, and that grammar, instead of being a formal study, had become a means to the exercise of effective composition, 'being concerned more with synthesis of sentences and word building than with analysis and parsing' (SCRE 1939: 40). There was now much more geography, history, drawing and handwork than hitherto, and indeed in the very early years (primaries 1 and 2) some schools were giving nearly eight hours per week of handwork (see p. 60). There were the beginnings of the use of electronic technology – radios were available in over one third of schools (see p. 69), and cinema projectors had begun to appear also.

Two other points about this consolidated primary system were notable by the 1930s. One was the gradual equating of age with stage. The proportion of pupils who were in the stage corresponding to their chronological age was ninety-two per cent (SCRE 1939: 22). This may be contrasted, for example, with the point we noted above, that nineteen out of twenty pupils at the turn of the century were not at Standard V or above even though aged eleven or older. Part of this change of view was the growing official attachment to the idea of the 'clean cut' – that all children should proceed to post-primary education at around the same age. This had implications for the possibility of broad access to secondary schooling, since reducing the impact of selection would be easier if all children left primary at roughly the same age (Stocks 2002: 28–30). The idea of a standardised system had, therefore, become much more widely accepted. The other point in this vein was the uniformity of provision in Scotland, which one American researcher described as 'remarkable' (Macmeeken 1939: 138), especially the fact that virtually all teachers had been formally trained in centres recognised by the SED. To this he attributed the similarity of test results among the cities, the industrial areas, and the rural areas.

Attitudes to Gaelic continued to be consistent with this. There probably was greater sympathy for its use, on the grounds that the child's starting point and interests ought to be respected. A second survey conducted by An Comunn Gaidhealach in 1936 found 284 primary schools teaching Gaelic in Sutherland, Ross and Cromarty, Inverness-shire and Argyll, out of a total of 524 (An Comunn Gaidhealach 1936: 12; SED 1936c: table I). This meant that, in principle, a total of 7,129 pupils had some opportunity to study Gaelic, or about one third of all primary pupils there. However, the survey reported that almost all this teaching was of children whose native language was Gaelic, and most of the Gaelic-medium education was at the infant stages. The goal was still mainly literacy in English. As one teacher informed them, 'the more efficiency I show in teaching Gaelic, the more I am disliked by the parents' (An Comunn Gaidhealach 1936: 8).

The radical advocacy, along with the caution of official change, continued to produce in the late 1930s strong pressure for further relaxation of what was still seen as the excessively rigid form of elementary education. A report prepared by the Educational Institute of Scotland in 1939 noted the changes, and in particular claimed historical continuity of reform, linking the new education to fulfilling what it regarded as the democratic interpretation of the previously competitive parish school tradition: 'while giving the "lad o pairts" opportunity for development, the primary school has struggled to secure justice for the boy or girl of average capacity' (EIS 1939: 4).

Therefore, the purpose of a modern primary school should be 'to provide for its pupils a stimulating environment in which their natural tendencies will develop under adult guidance into useful abilities, desirable interests and acceptable attitudes' (EIS 1939: 6).

This kind of approach did not come to fruition until the 1950s, and in some respects not until the 1960s. However, what makes this an absolutely typical statement of the Scottish interpretation of the new educational ideals is the combining of child-centredness with adult supervision and social purpose. It was a challenge to the authorities, but would not have been recognised by Neill and his allies as anywhere close to the radical ideas they propounded. The nature of the child should be respected, certainly, but in the belief that it was intrinsically social, and best guided by sympathetic but firm schoolteachers.

CHAPTER 4

Post-Elementary Education

The provision in the 1872 Act that permitted boards to establish Higher Class schools was never likely to have much effect in the absence of appropriate finance. It was, in any case, controversial even from the start, since it seemed to cut across the Scottish tradition that any parish school could offer advanced instruction that would give access to the universities. The Higher Class schools then faced competition from two sources. One was the new system of 'specific subjects' which, from 1873, were introduced into the public schools (Anderson 1983a: 110). In due course, as we will see, these were to grow into a much expanded secondary sector in the first couple of decades of the twentieth century. The other source of competition was the private schools and the independent endowed schools, which, like the Higher Class schools, served a mainly middle-class clientele. The private secondary schools were small in number, and had been founded on English models – places such as Loretto in Musselburgh, Fettes in Edinburgh and Glenalmond in Perthshire; they were joined at this time by the first girls' schools of this type, for example St Leonard's in St Andrews. Of greater numerical significance were the endowed schools that survived the reorganisation that was imposed upon them by three commissions of inquiry (in 1872, 1878 and 1882) and by Acts of 1878 and 1882. Some of the endowed schools that were subject to these inquiries were of great antiquity, for example the High School of Edinburgh. Some – for example, the academies in such burghs as Tain, Inverness, Bathgate and Dumfries – were founded in the late-eighteenth or early nineteenth centuries to extend and modernise educational opportunities. Many of the endowments were judged by the commissioners to be too small to allow a school to sustain an independent existence, and so about half of the endowed schools were closed, and a further quarter transferred to the boards, the endowments being used to provide bursaries to encourage the growth of secondary education (Anderson 1983a: 186; Scotland 1969: 64). For the three dozen mainly urban schools that remained – for example, George Heriot's and the Merchant Company schools in Edinburgh – the reorganisation of endowments caused indignation among those who believed in the public provision of educational opportunity. The funds had mostly been set up to help the children of the poor, but in these schools they were now to be used mainly for much wealthier clients, with only a concession towards their history in the provision of scholarships and free places, a requirement that equal provision be made for girls and the reservation on their governing bodies of places for representatives of the local council (Anderson 1983a: 185). Nevertheless, because of their origins, these schools liked to believe themselves to be part of the national, democratic tradition: unlike the English-style private schools, they regarded themselves as serving a local middle class, augmented (however meagrely) by bursary pupils (Anderson 1983a: 328).

Thereafter, until the end of the century, there were essentially two separate school systems in Scotland, not anything that at all resembled the end-on link between primaries and secondaries that became familiar later (Anderson 1983a: 206; Scotland 1969: 64). One system was in the public schools, and the other was in the higher-class, endowed and private schools, many of which ran their own elementary departments. The Educational Institute of Scotland campaigned to have the division in the public sector overcome, so that the Higher Class schools would receive public grants and be able to link properly with children emerging from elementary education (Anderson 1983a: 204). This strand of campaigning was also beginning to interpret the Scottish tradition of open access from the parish schools to the universities as requiring open access to secondaries (Anderson 1983a: 203). Debate about a more systematic organisation of secondary schooling had been further encouraged by the support of the Schools Inquiry Commission in 1868, mainly concerned with England but with sections on Scotland (Anderson 1983a: 109, 134). The EIS and other radical advocates of secondary education also, however, insisted that the public schools should be able to teach at a secondary level, a proposal which the SED tried to control by insisting that specific subjects be recognised only in designated 'central schools', serving a whole district (Osborne 1966: 45). Out of this debate emerged the beginnings of a belief that entry to secondary school should be based on examination, an idea that had its Scottish origins in the reorganisation of the endowed schools, and the accompanying necessity of selecting children for scholarships (McPherson 1992a: 89; H. M. Paterson 1983: 202). This interpretation of a putative national tradition of democratic education was strengthened by a committee of inquiry into secondary education established by the Conservative Scottish Secretary, Balfour of Burleigh, chaired by the Liberal MP C. S. Parker, and including Henry Craik of the SED as a member. It recommended in 1888 that secondary schools should receive state grants only in return for making free places available competitively to pupils from elementary schools (Anderson 1995: 252).

HIGHER GRADE SCHOOLS

Despite its caution and the powerful support for the selective version of the tradition, the SED's response to the pressure in the first few years of the twentieth century was an irreversible move in the direction of greater democracy. The opportunity arose in 1892 when elementary education was made free in England. Since it had already been made free in Scotland in 1890, the Liberal government persuaded Craik and the SED to transfer the resulting increase in Scottish government expenditure on education to thirty-five new secondary education committees, which were jointly formed by school boards and local authorities (Anderson 1995: 191). A category of 'Higher Grade' school was then recognised in 1899 specifically for the encouragement of scientific and technical study, one of Craik's enthusiasms. Glasgow school board had been trying to maintain a public, secondary sector with the same name since the 1880s. However, the key organisational change came in 1903, when the SED finally encouraged (and partly funded) a national network of Higher Grade schools, no longer technical but now to offer the full range of liberal studies. At the beginning of the century, there were thus two kinds of post-elementary opportunity. The full secondary course would last five years, but there would also be a truncated three-year version. Alternatively, there were mainly two-year courses offered in Advanced Departments that would be added to those public schools which were judged to be of sufficient quality to cope with post-elementary teaching; these were re-named 'supplementary courses' in 1903.

The opportunity was taken up extensively, and by 1908 there were few areas of the country without a Higher Grade school. This provision was not free or compulsory until the 1918 Act, but it was revolutionary nonetheless. By the end of the first decade, the debate between the SED and the proponents of yet wider diffusion was conducted in terms that – with the imminence of mass political democracy – could not but lead to further expansion. The Department had, in effect, been forced to abandon its original intention that the Higher Grade schools would be mostly for pupils who would leave school at age sixteen, confining university entry to the Higher Class and endowed schools: local pressure insisted that some Higher Grade schools become full secondaries (Philip 1992: 68). Typical of the argument against the SED restrictions was an article in *Educational News* in 1906 by the headteacher of Rothesay Academy, a long-established public school which had added a Higher Grade department to widen children's access to post-primary studies: if the SED's intention to confine university entry to those who had passed through the Higher Class or endowed schools prevailed, 'many children over large parts of Scotland will lose their educational birthright of equal opportunity for all' (Rose 1906: 146). A new interpretation of the democratic tradition had been established in just three years.

When the association that campaigned for further extension criticised the SED's policy in 1913, asserting that the decline of public advanced education since 1872 had caused 'broken links in Scottish education' (the title of a book by one of its members, John Smith, in that year), the secretary of the SED, John Struthers, replied by claiming that the system which the Department had been constructing was indeed truly national and democratic, and alleging that the association was more interested in promoting the teaching of classics than in encouraging wide access to a truly liberal education (Anderson 1983a: 241–2). In 1912, there were 249 secondary schools, 143 providing the five-year course and 106 the three-year one. Of these 249, the majority (179) were Higher Grade schools (Anderson 1983a: 246). The number of pupils in Higher Grade schools had grown from 3,821 in 1902 to 24,201 in 1912; as a proportion of all pupils in full secondary education (as opposed to supplementary courses) they had increased in the same period from nineteen per cent to fifty-five per cent (Anderson 1995: 310). Most towns had only one secondary school, which was usually a Higher Grade school, and in fact eighty-seven of the 143 five-year schools were Higher Grade. The Higher Grade schools were also more firmly public than the Higher Class and endowed schools: the proportion of their income that came from SED grants or local rates was respectively eighty-two per cent and forty-eight per cent, and the proportion from fees was three per cent and twenty-six per cent (Anderson 1983a: 247). In most areas of the country, therefore, the development of Higher Grade schools made secondary education available free (Anderson 1983a: 243).

The effects in the Highlands and Islands were particularly marked, for example in such foundations as Oban High School, Stromness Academy, Dingwall Academy, the Nicholson Institute in Stornoway, and the Sutherland technical school in Golspie (on which, see also Beaton 1991). Out of thirty-eight secondary schools in the region in 1912, thirty-four were Higher Grade, a much larger share than the 179 out of 249 nationally (Anderson 1983a: 247; Parliamentary Papers 1908: 635–7). Other areas which had disproportionate numbers of Higher Grade schools or departments were in the industrial parts of west-central Scotland, where the old parish-school system had never managed to cope: in Lanarkshire, for example, eighteen of the nineteen non-denominational secondaries were Higher Grade – for example, Airdrie Academy and Larkhall Academy – alongside two Catholic Higher Grade schools, for example Elmwood in Bothwell. In Renfrewshire, ten of the thirteen non-denominational secondaries were Higher Grade – for example, Shawlands Academy – and there were two Catholic Higher Grade schools, for example St Margaret's in Paisley. In Govan all six of the secondaries were Higher Grade – for example, Bellahouston Academy and the school that was attached to the Catholic teacher-training college at Dowanhill. In Glasgow itself, the Higher Grade schools extended opportunities to the working-class districts, for example in Whitehill Secondary. The north east also had a disproportionate number – thirty-five out of thirty-eight – but for a different reason: many of these were the upgraded post-elementary departments of the parish or burgh schools where there had been a long tradition of providing advanced work, financed by the endowment that had been left in 1833 by James Dick, a merchant from Forres (Anderson 1983a: 9–10, 123–4). Examples of these Higher Grade schools were Fraserburgh Academy, Aberlour school and Keith Grammar School.

The mechanism by which the SED tried to control the quality and extent of secondary education was the Leaving Certificate, but the sheer popularity of this also became a means by which pressure was exerted for further expansion and for making a academic education widely available. The secondary certificate was inaugurated in 1888, fulfilling Craik's goal of formalising the relationship between secondary schooling and the universities. It was initially awarded at three levels – Honours, Higher and Lower; Honours was dropped in 1906 as a concession to the Universities who believed it was interfering with their bursary competition (Philip 1992: 55–6, 60). The uptake of the Leaving Certificate expanded rapidly, and by 1900 there were 16,771 candidates (Philip 1992: 33). Significantly for encouraging the democratic pressure, a clear majority (sixty-one per cent) of these came from the publicly financed Higher Grade schools, and a further seven per cent were pupil teachers. This left only thirty-two per cent from private, endowed or Higher Class schools, some of which were also publicly financed. The SED introduced an Intermediate Certificate in 1902, and intended that this should become the main goal of pupils in the Higher Grade schools. They also stipulated that the full Leaving Certificate could be awarded only on completion of a designated group of courses, which at the outset had to be four passes at the Higher Grade or three Highers and two Lowers, and these had to include Higher English, Higher or Lower Mathematics, and either two languages (one of which had to be Latin) or a science and a language (Philip 1992: 43). These requirements were the means by which the SED temporarily restricted any prospects of links between most of the Higher Grade schools and the universities, although the Intermediate Certificate did reinforce the view that these schools were sources of a broad, liberal education rather than tech-nically specialist. After it became a required stage on the ·way to the Higher Grade, in 1908, the Intermediate Certificate also provided a more structured programme of study towards that university-entrance level.

Despite the growing importance of the Higher Grade schools, most post-elementary pupils were in supplementary courses. For example, in 1912, there were 49,497 pupils in the mainly two-year supplementary courses in primary schools, compared to 24,201 in the mainly three-year courses in Higher Grade schools and 19,458 in the mainly five-year courses in the Higher Class and endowed schools (Anderson 1995: 310; SED 1913: 15). It is easy to interpret the supplementary courses retrospectively as residual, but there was some real hope at the time that they could be made to inherit the parish-school tradition of providing wide access to post-elementary instruction. In 1903, there were nearly 400 Advanced Departments, and in the Schools Code of 1899 the SED had encouraged them to offer the full range of general education. After 1903, the supplementary courses were to last two or three years, and would be entered only upon passing a qualifying examination. The title Merit Certificate was now transferred to the examination at the end of the supplementary course (having previously signified the attainment of Standard V). The intention here, too, was to offer a broad education, principally through the means of the study of English literature (Anderson 1995: 255).

The net result of these extensions of post-elementary courses in the first decade of the century was to increase gradually the proportion of pupils who took them. In 1911, thirty-nine per cent of boys and thirty-eight per cent of girls aged fourteen were attending school, up from twenty-three per cent and twenty-two per cent in 1871 (Anderson 1995: 235). However, since 1901, there had been no more than a small increase in the rate of participation at ages greater than that: for girls aged sixteen, a rise from eight per cent to nine per cent, and for boys of that age a rise from five per cent to seven per cent.

A PUBLIC SYSTEM

Although World War I had been highly disruptive of elementary education, enrolments in secondary education continued to grow, especially in Higher Grade schools. In 1918, they had 30,509 pupils, which was 4,596 more than in 1914, and these represented sixty per cent of all secondary pupils (Anderson 1995: 310). The idealism in the aftermath of the War had its biggest effect on the secondary sector. Dealing with this issue was the principal aim of the 1918 Act, and the Liberal Scottish Secretary, Robert Munro, was sympathetic to the idea of wide access (a sympathy no doubt intensified by his awareness that extending secondary education was a campaigning point for the Labour Party in its threat to the Liberal dominance of Scottish politics). There were three main provisions (McPherson 1992a: 87–8) – simplifying educational administration, bringing the Catholic and other voluntary schools fully into the public sector, and – of greatest importance – creating a framework for secondary education.

The first principle of the 1918 Act was administrative. By abolishing the school boards and creating a much smaller number of much larger authorities, responsible directly for all sectors of public school education, it strengthened the basis of decision making; this was further enhanced by the recommendation that the authorities appoint professional directors of education to manage the service locally. Munro and Struthers had intended that the authorities would be the county councils and city corporations, but there was resistance to this on two grounds. The boards feared possible dilution of educational expertise. The Labour movement feared Tory domination of the county councils. But the EIS had long been in favour of a single authority for all types of school (Anderson 1983a: 204; Stocks 1970: 74). The outcome was that the authorities were ad hoc, despite Struthers' scepticism about this too: that is, they dealt only with education, and were not absorbed into the general county councils. They were to be elected by a form of proportional representation, thus helping to ensure that minorities (such as the Labour party then was) would have a fair chance of being included. The ad hoc authorities oversaw a significant expansion of secondary provision, and accepted the transfer of the voluntary schools, but by the late 1920s the arguments against absorption into the county and city councils had waned, partly because Labour's electoral positioned had generally strengthened. They were abolished in 1929–30, and thereafter (right through the remainder of the century) school education became the responsibility of general local authorities.

The second major provision of the Act has already been mentioned in Chapter 3 in connection with the Catholic elementary schools: by requiring the transfer of voluntary schools to the education authorities upon penalty of losing their public grants, it made these authorities responsible for all public-sector schools for the first time. (The small number of Episcopal schools was transferred rapidly and with no public disputes, most, although not all, of them losing their denominational character in the process.) The Catholic church was ambivalent about losing the voluntary status of its schools, especially in Glasgow where the archbishop resisted the transfer until after the Act was in place (Fitzpatrick 1986; Kenneth 1968; Rosie 2001: 216–21). There was no option that a solution resembling the English one of 1902 would be available – no chance that the voluntary schools could continue to receive public grants. In a memorandum to Munro in 1917 during the preparation of the Bill, Struthers summarised the views of the Catholic bishops in a note that Brother Kenneth, quoting it, later described as being 'as accurate as one could wish for' (Kenneth 1968: 103):

it is represented to me privately that while the Catholic Managers
would be unanimous in desiring if it could be obtained a continuation
of their absolute control of the schools with [financial] support from
one source or another ... five out of the six Bishops regard the
prospect of obtaining these terms as hopeless, and would be willing to
accept a reasonable arrangement as to public control as a reasonable
settlement of the question.

The Act allowed the church to sell or lease their schools to the education authorities, and this transfer generally went smoothly. There was initially suspicion of the education authorities as allegedly in the grip of Protestant sectarians, but, as Treble (1980: 30) points out, the expression of this suspicion was never accompanied by evidence. Professor John Phillimore, a convert to Catholicism who was a lecturer at Glasgow University, did not help matters by describing the Scottish universities as 'undefended cities' which the Catholics could 'capture' (Rosie 2001: 232). Reports of this sparked reaction from the two largest Protestant denominations, the United Free Church and the Church of Scotland, and in the second elections to the Glasgow education authority, in 1922, there was evidence of a Protestant reaction against what the *Glasgow Herald* described as the alliance between the Catholics and the Labour Party, coming at a time when events in Ireland were turning very nasty (Rosie 2001: 233). However, even in Glasgow the effects of this were short-lived.

Throughout the whole period following the Act, the SED and nearly all of the education authorities were keen to establish good relations with the church (Treble 1978), but in the large Glasgow archdiocese (which at that time included the areas that became, in 1948, the diocese of Motherwell and of Paisley) there continued to be debate within the church about whether they should lease or sell their schools (Treble 1980: 31–3). Everywhere else they were sold. One of the unresolved issues which made the Glasgow church suspicious was the question of who would be responsible for any extensions of the Catholic system, a point that was becoming urgent as post-primary education generally was expanding. An early test came in 1921, concerning the upgrading of St Mary's school in Whifflet (Lanarkshire) to Higher Grade status (Treble 1980: 31). The diocesan education board proposed to spend £8,500, but the education authority estimated that proper accommodation would require between £20,000 and £25,000, and offered to pay for the whole of this itself. The church declined this as a matter of principle. Lord Skerrington, a leading Catholic lawyer, advised the diocesan board to submit the case for the adjudication of the SED. In the end, in 1924, the Lord Advocate ruled that the board's case was stronger than the education authority's, but – as Treble points out (1980: 32) – this had been obtained at the price of recognising the supreme authority of the SED in such matters.

An even more controversial case arose in Bonnybridge in Stirlingshire in 1922, where the church had asked the education authority to build a wholly new school to cater for a growing population of Catholic children (Treble 1980: 28; Rosie 2001: 224–6). The authority noted that there was surplus accommodation in the area, and that it could not afford to pay for a new school. So the church built the school itself, but then the authority refused the subsequent transfer request under the terms of the 1918 Act (Rosie 2001: 227). This resulted in a referral to the Court of Session, which found against the church; the subsequent appeal to the House of Lords concluded the other way. This outcome, contested though it had been, resulted in the principle that the Act required that the education authorities were responsible for extending the Catholic system, not only maintaining what they had inherited.

That Bonnybridge judgement became increasingly important as the national school system expanded during the remainder of the century, and was essentially the reason why a distinct Catholic secondary system could be built up at all. The inspectors were already commenting on the inadequacies of provision in Catholic schools in the early 1920s (Treble 1978: 126). In 1923, when Catholic pupils made up about a quarter of Lanarkshire's total elementary pupil population, they were only about sixteen per cent of pupils in the first two years of post-primary education, and only nine per cent of pupils who managed to get beyond that stage (Treble 1980: 37). A second Catholic teacher-training college was opened in Edinburgh in 1919, also – like Notre Dame – for women, but that still did not meet the need for graduate secondary teachers (Treble 1978: 127). The church could not then resist the pressure to appoint some non-Catholics to teach post-primary courses (Treble 1978: 128).

In 1928, even the Glasgow archdiocese accepted that leasing was not affordable, and that the financial burden of improving and extending the Catholic system could not be borne by the church (Treble 1980: 40). By then, and into the 1930s, the transferred system began to overcome some of the problems it had inherited. For example, the ratios of pupils to teachers in the nondenominational and Catholic schools in Lanarkshire began to converge: in 1919, they had been respectively one to forty-one and one to sixty-one, but in 1931 they were one to thirty-four and one to forty (Treble 1980: 41). In 1931, too, the proportion of pupils in the Catholic sector in Lanarkshire who were in post-primary courses was 17.6 per cent, not far short of the 19.5 per cent in the non-denominational schools (Treble 1980: 41).

In the late 1920s, moreover, the religious tension had dissipated to such an extent that the church welcomed presbyterian involvement in the education authorities as a means of countering the secularists (Rosie 2001: 238). The revival of sectarian politics in parts of Edinburgh and Glasgow in the 1930s did not disrupt this, and turned out to be transient. One slightly later test of the durability of this relative harmony came during World War II, when large numbers of Catholic children were evacuated to mainly rural districts where there were no specifically Catholic schools to accommodate them (Fitzpatrick 1986: 100, note 14). The SED inspectors were alert to the risks of sectarian tensions. They did find a few, for example in Strathdon and Aboyne in

Aberdeenshire in 1939 (Lloyd 1979: 51), but even there the problem did not recur, an internal memorandum noting in 1940 that:

> fortunately a praiseworthy degree of realism and of toleration has been shown on both sides; for example, in Aberdeenshire, a stronghold of Scottish Presbyterianism, the householders, including the ministers, have given their Roman Catholic charges every encouragement to attend chapel, and in Argyll the Roman Catholics concerned have raised no objection whatever to being taught by Protestant teachers.
>
> (Lloyd 1979: 97)

The SED still went out of its way to meet the wishes of the church in this respect, despite the apparent satisfaction of Catholic parents with the situation in Argyll. The church objected to the arrangements in Dunoon, where Catholic children were being taught by Protestants, but the Glasgow and Argyll education authorities baulked at the cost of any other system, for example paying for Catholic teachers. The Scottish Office intervened at the highest level, through the parliamentary under-secretary of state, John McEwen MP (Lloyd 1979: 98–101). As Lloyd points out, the issue resolved itself when bombing began, just as the SED had hoped, and the church raised no more difficulties.

SECONDARY EDUCATION FOR ALL

In assessing the impact of the 1918 Act on the school system generally, however, the most important reform was the setting in place of a framework for the expansion of secondary education. Post-elementary education was to be free for all (although the SED would determine when that would happen). It was also to be in a unified system, though of two types: five-year secondaries, and Advanced Divisions that would last initially for two years, but would be three years for everyone when – as the Act further allowed for – the leaving age was raised to fifteen. Again, though, the SED would determine when that would happen. For pupils leaving from the Advanced Divisions, there were to be compulsory, part-time continuation classes, once more at a date to be set by the Department.

The latter never properly materialised (and are discussed in Chapter 6 below). The way in which the SED subsequently handled the question of fees for secondary education was highly controversial. The economic situation, after a brief post-war boom, was deteriorating, and in a Circular of 1920 the Department in effect relieved the education authorities of the responsibility of providing free schooling. Stocks (1995: 55) describes this as 'blatantly unconstitutional', and it certainly provoked deep controversy, becoming a focus of radical campaigning until the eventual requirement in the Education (Scotland) Act of 1936 that an adequate supply of free places must be made available. The EIS objected to the Circular, noting that, if fees were retained in the five-year secondaries, poor parents could not afford to send their children to anything other than the Advanced Divisions. Less predictable opposition came from the schools inspectors. The same J. M. Wattie who, in 1919, had noted the post-war idealism concerning education and a new social order observed that the older-established secondaries would continue to run their own primary departments. Wealthy parents who could afford to pay for the whole sequence of education from five to sixteen or eighteen would therefore have an advantage, because, as the Department noted in 1928, in such all-through schools, nearly all secondary pupils went onto the full five-year course, and very few went into an Advanced Division somewhere else (Stocks 1995: 56; 2002: 36).

Probably the most controversial recasting of the intentions of the 1918 Act concerned the actual operation of the structure of post-elementary schooling – the distinction between Advanced Divisions and five-year courses. This came in Circular 44 of 1921, which in effect instructed Education Authorities to restrict access to full secondary courses (SED 1921; Stocks 1995). The circular acquired a notoriety among radical educationalists as great as the fame that was much later accorded to Circular 600 which, in 1965, inaugurated comprehensive secondary schooling. Indeed, the two are, in a way, connected, because the 1921 prescription, in effect, prevented for many decades any interpretation of the 1918 Act as laying the basis for a truly comprehensive system, any fully democratic interpretation of the legislation's requirements that education authorities may spend money in the form of grants and bursaries in order to ensure:

> that no young person ... who is qualified for attendance at an intermediate or secondary school, and in their opinion formed after consideration of a report from the teachers concerned shows promise of profiting thereby, shall be debarred therefrom by reason of the expense involved.
>
> (Hutchison 1973: 171)

They could also offer grants to attend university. As Andrew McPherson (1992a: 88) has commented, this is the first clear statement in Scottish legislation that the public authorities may actively promote equal opportunities in education.

But Circular 44 propounded quite different views. It was the most ominous educational sign of the impact which restrictions on expenditure would have throughout the 1920s and 1930s. Its authors probably knew that the committee which the government in London had set up under Sir Eric Geddes was about to announce swingeing cuts in public expenditure, most severely in education (Simon 1974: 37–40). They had, therefore, financial reasons to limit the expansion of five-year courses, and access to the Leaving Certificate. For the same reasons, they also postponed the raising of the leaving age. The expenditure on bursaries was not immediately affected, rising from £148,239 in 1920 to a peak of £262,796 in 1926, but thereafter it fell to a low of £184,000 in 1934 (Wade 1939: 152). Allowing for inflation, this represented growth by a factor of 2.43 between 1920 and 1926, and the fall thereafter was only by a factor of 0.92. However, within this, a growing proportion was taken by students entering higher education institutions, and so the share taken by secondary pupils fell from sixty-two per cent in 1920 to forty-nine per cent in 1934.

The SED also had educational reasons to restrict access to secondary education, believing that only a small minority would indeed fulfil the Act's requirement that pupils show 'promise of profiting' from a full secondary course. The Circular did abolish the qualifying examination as a national instrument: in future, transfer arrangements from primary to secondary would be decided locally, by the education authorities (although, colloquially, the 'qualy' continued to be the name given to any tests that were used for this purpose). That, however, was an administrative change, not a change of principle, and the Circular argued against any combining of Advanced Division and secondary courses into a de facto intermediate stage. The same purpose was served by the abolition of the Intermediate Certificate, which – the SED argued – had been superseded by a more rigorous process of selecting pupils for secondary education. A philosophy from all this came from some of the proponents of scientific selection, notably Alexander Darroch, who had succeeded S. S. Laurie in the chair of education at Edinburgh University in 1903; he argued that 'common people' did not want 'book knowledge', and that educational equality was a fallacy (Darroch 1914: 33–42).

From that view – and the legacy of the debates about secondary education at the turn of the century – developed an academic and political interest in testing. The most prominent people associated with the development of testing as a means of judging whether a pupil might indeed profit from secondary education were William McClelland and Godfrey Thomson. McClelland was professor of education at St Andrews University from 1925 until 1941, and at the same time principal of the teacher-training centre in Dundee; thereafter, until 1958, he was the executive officer of the committee which oversaw teacher training (H. M. Paterson 1975; Scotland 1969: 115). His work on developing tests culminated in 1942 in his book *Selection for Secondary Education*, and so did not reach the height of its influence until after World War II, but he sought to extend interest in scientific selection in the meantime: for example, an early, unpublished version of his book informed the recommendations on transfer to secondary school which were made by the EIS in its 1939 report on primary schooling (EIS 1939: 94), and Midlothian education authority had contact with him in the late 1930s (McPherson and Raab 1988: 354). Thomson succeeded Darroch to the chair of education at Edinburgh University; he was also principal of the Edinburgh training centre at the same time, 1925–1951, and was a firm believer in the possibility of using tests to allocate children to courses efficiently and fairly (Bell 1975; Sharp 1980; Thomson 1929).

However, one of the reasons for their influence was that the politics of the matter were not as straightforward as the origin of these ideas in a restrictive definition of secondary education might lead us to expect. McClelland was convinced that selection could be made to be fair, and could be used to further the ideals of the New Education Fellowship, of which he was a member. He was in fact highly critical of the distorting effect which external examinations can have on the school curriculum, a view which he was later able to bring to bear on the operation of the sixth Advisory Council in 1947 (Duffield 1995: 42; McPherson and Raab 1988: 353). Thomson supported the omnibus school for social reasons. There would, however, be internal differentiation on meritocratic grounds, and the tests he developed were to be used for this purpose (Thomson 1929). Part of the reason why he believed in common schools of this type was that he rejected the dominant ideology of the 1920s that intelligence was one-dimensional: people, he believed, had a variety of different kinds of intelligence, and a fair education system ought to try to develop them all (Sharp 1980). These ideas of a common schooling that operated internal selection became quite influential by the 1930s, notably on the roughly one third of schools which did operate along omnibus lines, mainly in small burghs (Stocks 2002: 33–4).

Most of the discussion of the effects of testing belong later (in Chapter 8), in the evolution of that policy after World War II, but the complexity of the views of McClelland and Thomson indicates the dangers of anachronistically judging the 1920s debate by the eventual outcome in the 1960s and later. The 1918 Act, having opened up the possibility of a much wider definition of secondary education, created the space in which radical advocates of secondary education for all could challenge the most restrictive interpretations; but in the context of what had been inherited from the debates before 1914, this was bound to take the form of arguing over how to allocate children to those courses from which they would benefit the most.

The most expansive interpretation of the Act against the SED was first articulated by the Advisory Council, provision for setting up which had also been set out in the Act. That provision was itself a victory for those – Liberals, the larger school boards and the teachers – who believed that the power of the SED was an obstacle to educational democracy (Young 1986: 49–59). The Scottish Education Reform Committee had included proposals for a 'National Education Council' in its 1917 Report (Scottish Education Reform Committee 1917: 23–5). The first Council included several people who could be classified as cautious educational reformers, for example Duncan MacGillivray of the EIS, Joseph Duncan of the Scottish Farm Servants Union and the Workers Educational Association, and John Burnet, professor of Greek at St Andrews University and a noted exponent of the view that democracy meant providing access to a broad, general education (Anderson 1983a: 282; Young 1986: 79, 83; Knox 1984b). The Council worked through several specialist committees, and it was the one on the organisation of day schools which brought it into conflict with the SED. The SED had contrived to keep MacGillivray off this committee, but its convener Burnet turned out in practice to be no less radical (Young 1986: 86). The committee was of the view that the best way of promoting the equal opportunities which the Act promised was by seeing primary, intermediate and secondary education as stages, for ages five to twelve, twelve to fifteen and fifteen to eighteen. Up to age fifteen, there would be a common core curriculum, with options. This interpretation was by no means out of tune with mainstream opinion: for example, it had already been stated by earlier commentators on the Act, such as in 1919 by John Strong, rector of the High School in Edinburgh (Stocks 1995: 52).

Nevertheless, it brought the Council into conflict with the SED. George Macdonald, second secretary of the SED (and who became secretary from 1922 to 1928), put the contrast between the Council's and the official view in a memorandum to Struthers in October 1920, in which he argued that:

> the committee … have ignored the fundamental fact that the school population falls into two parts – a majority of distinctly limited intelligence, and an extremely important minority drawn from all ranks and classes who are capable of responding to a much more severe call … What the Committee seem to have done is to draw up a scheme which proceeds from the supposition that all save a few backward children are capable of profiting by the one sort of education.
>
> (Young 1986: 94)

In a clever (or devious) piece of news management, the SED persuaded the Council to postpone publication of its recommendations on school organisation until early 1922, but in the meantime issued its Circular 44 in mid-December 1921. The Council protested at this pre-emption, and received an informal apology from the Scottish Secretary Munro, but the long-term effect was to discourage it from similarly radical moves for over two decades.

Nevertheless, that these democratic ideas were not just the foibles of a few individuals was then shown by the intensity of the public response to the Circular's restrictive interpretation of secondary education (Young 1986: 102–7; Stocks 1995: 49–50; 2002: 27). Powerful opposition came from the EIS and the directors of education, notably Dr J. A. Third, director in Ayrshire, who had been a member of the wartime Reform Committee, and was later president of the Association of Directors of Education in Scotland. The growing Labour movement were also opposed – protests coming, for example, from the Scottish Socialist Teachers' Association and the Scottish section of the Independent Labour Party. There were also detailed critiques from prominent individuals such as William Boyd of Glasgow University, and John Clarke, executive officer of the Glasgow education authority. Much of this was expressed in the columns of the EIS's *Scottish Educational Journal*. Less publicly, the inspectorate made the Department aware of the very widespread dissent, and argued for the evolution of something like the Council's progressive structure (Stocks 1995: 50).

The other form of resistance may have taken encouragement from some of this debate, but was ultimately the main reason why the more restrictive interpretation had to give way. This was simply the refusal of many schools and parents to follow the SED's ideas. The SED's encouragement to centralise supplementary courses was not popular. Osborne (1966: 46) notes that in 1923, even in the cities, 172 out of 293 elementary schools had supplementary courses; the dispersal was even wider in rural areas. In 1928, of all pupils leaving schools designated as primary, although sixteen per cent had not reached the standard for entry to advanced divisions, and thirteen per cent had completed less than one full year of a post-primary course, fully seventy-one per cent were receiving at least one year of post-primary education, thirty-six per cent in an Advanced Division, and thirty-five per cent in a secondary school leading to the Leaving Certificate (SED 1928: 12–13). These proportions remained fairly stable throughout the 1930s (SED 1939a: 92). By 1938, forty-three per cent of the 2,844 elementary schools nationally had an advanced division (Osborne 1966: 70). Not only did these figures indicate a substantial proportion entering full secondary education; they also showed that the primary schools continued to provide significant amounts of post-primary teaching, and so attested to the widespread demand for it.

They suggest also that the main reason why demand was not even higher was simply financial. At a time of acute economic recession, keeping children at school until they were older than fourteen was beyond many families' means. This was exacerbated by some schools' insistence that parents pledge themselves to five years of secondary education right from the start at age twelve. Stocks (2002: 35) notes that in Glasgow in 1932, only sixty per cent of pupils whose attainment would have entitled them to enter a full secondary course actually did so; in rural Perthshire, where the cost of travelling was an added disincentive, the proportion was as low as forty per cent. Although most of the education authorities – even the Labour-controlled ones – did not follow through their opposition to Circular 44 with much of an attempt to subvert the SED's policies, that too may have had as much to do with financial restrictions as with principle (Stocks 2002: 35).

The SED could not but respond, especially since part of their case was that the Advanced Divisions could offer a worthwhile education. They introduced a Day School Certificate in 1923. There was a Higher version, based on a national examination set by the SED, that was to mark the end of three years of post-primary work. The Lower version was set by education authorities, and was to mark the successful completion of two years' work. The Higher Certificate had some social standing, partly because it was available also in secondary schools. It proved attractive as a way of recognising good-quality post-primary work, just as the abolished Intermediate Certificate had been, and the Department bemoaned the schools' insistence on using it to offer an academic secondary education to a growing number of children (Wade 1939: 210–12). The proportion of primary schools with courses approved for the Higher Certificate was around seventeen to eighteen per cent in the late 1920s and early 1930s (Wade 1939: 207). The number of Higher Certificates awarded rose from 2,615 in 1925 to 4,999 in 1936, falling back to 4,149 in 1938 as the school population as a whole declined (Wade 1939: 224; SED 1939a: 14). All students taking such courses studied English, which included history and geography, and nearly all studied mathematics (including over eighty per cent studying algebra and geometry). Around eighty per cent or more studied science, and two thirds or more studied French. Only one fifth or fewer took Latin, technical subjects and commercial subjects, and one in ten studied domestic subjects (Wade 1939: 213). This was very definitely an academic course, but not a classical one.

These Advanced Divisions, however, were still regarded as providing an inferior education, being conducted according to different regulations and staffing standards from those in secondary schools. H. M. Paterson summarises the evidence on this from SED files:

> the lowest building cost per pupil for secondary schools was almost double that for Advanced Divisions (£30 as against £16), and the average size of class in Advanced Divisions was appreciably greater than the average for secondary schools (30.3 pupils as against 23.75 pupils nationally; 36.6 pupils as against 26.5 in Glasgow).
>
> (H. M. Paterson 1983: 211)

The teachers in the secondary schools were probably more highly qualified than those in the Advanced Divisions (Wade 1939: 193–4).

Moreover, however respectable the Higher Certificate was, it catered for only a small minority of Advanced Division pupils: when, in 1936, nearly 5,000 pupils were gaining the Higher Certificate, there were over 87,000 pupils in the Advanced Divisions (Wade 1939: 158). Around two thirds of pupils who gained the Higher Certificate actually did so in the secondary schools (Wade 1939: 224), and so in 1934 there were only 1,649 Higher Certificates awarded to pupils in Advanced Divisions, or about two per cent of pupils entering the Advanced Divisions (Wade 1939: 161). The provision for the remainder in the Advanced Divisions – leading to the Lower certificate, or to no formally recognised certificate at all – was much poorer. The Lower Certificate courses tended not to be well-defined, but rather to be the first two years of a three-year or five-year course (Wade 1939: 227). In some respects this did have the potential to open up opportunities to pupils, insofar as it postponed segregation, and was somewhat in the spirit of the recommendations of the Advisory Council, but it did lead to a lack of serious curriculum development. In any case, even as late as 1936, fifty-one per cent of pupils who embarked on a post-primary course did not complete two years of it (Wade 1939: 241). In the late 1930s, just under a quarter of those entering Advanced Divisions eventually received the Lower Certificate (SED 1939a: 92).

There was, therefore, also growing pressure to create a unified, truly secondary sector, and there was growing participation in courses that were conducted under the secondary regulations. Most of the Higher Grade schools had been converted into full secondaries in 1923, giving a secondary sector of some 250 schools (McPherson 1992a: 88). Thereafter until the eve of World War II, despite SED preferences, in every year an actual majority of pupils in post-primary education was attending secondary schools (Anderson 1985: 475). In 1924, the share was fifty-two per cent in secondaries, and the remainder in Advanced Divisions. In 1938, the proportion was the same, but the total in any kind of post-primary course had grown from 146,123 to 173,764 (and had reached a peak of 186,562 in 1934). Because the secondary courses were generally longer than the Advanced Division ones, these figures are consistent with a majority of primary pupils not entering secondary schools. Nevertheless, the maintenance of the secondary proportion over a period of educational expansion indicates an extension of opportunity: Scotland had 13.5 pupils in secondary school per thousand total population at the time of the census in 1921, and 16.8 per thousand at the census in 1931 (Anderson 1985: 475). The fall in absolute numbers after 1934 probably represented the effect of emigration and of a fall in the birth rate overtaking the effects of expansion: there was around half a million net loss of population by migration in the 1920s and 1930s (Lindsay 1992: 155), and – although the total population fell by less than one per cent between 1921 and 1931 – the number of children aged five to fourteen fell by nearly nine per cent. One consequence of the expansion was that the numbers entering for and gaining the Leaving Certificate rose steadily, after having fallen sharply with the abolition of the Intermediate Certificate in 1924. In 1925, there were 5,099 candidates, 3,064 of whom gained the Group Certificate. In 1939, there were 7,898, of whom 4,086 gained the Group (Philip 1992: 84).

Nevertheless, this still meant that the total number gaining the Group Certificate or the Day School Certificate (Higher) in the last year in which the latter was awarded and for which data are recorded (1938) was less than the total gaining the Group Award or the Intermediate Certificate in 1924: 9,179 compared to 11,868, a fall of twenty-three per cent (Philip 1992: 72, 78, 84). As proportions of the rising total number of post-primary pupils, the contrast was even sharper – from 8.5 per cent to 5.3 per cent (Anderson 1985: 475; Wade 1939: 157). One investigation by the Scottish Council for Research in Education of pupils passing through full secondary schools in the 1920s found that only twelve per cent of each year cohort gained the Leaving Certificate (Wade 1939: 240). This disjunction between growing participation in post-primary courses, including in secondary courses, and a lack of official recognition of these pupils' attainments was uncontainable: in due course, the pupil, parental and teacher insistence on a broadening definition of secondary education was bound to prevail.

The curriculum into which parents and teachers wanted to direct pupils entering secondary education was as firmly academic as that for the Day School Certificate (Higher). Craik and Struthers had repeatedly tried to mould it in utilitarian directions (Anderson 1983a: 238), but at no point in the first four decades of the century did there seem any prospect that technical courses in any kind of post-primary school would be widely acceptable as a form of truly secondary education. Working-class parents insisted on using secondary courses – even if only for one or two years – rather than courses which the SED described in 1927 as being 'designed expressly for their needs' (Anderson 1985: 473). The point, in other words, was that educational democracy was in the process of being defined as gaining wide access to the academic tradition. The Higher Grade schools, after their initial, brief designation as technical schools, never sought to differentiate their curriculum from that of the Higher Class and endowed schools, and the democratic pressure within them was to gain equal access to the highly academic Leaving Certificate.

This was not a curriculum based on Latin and Greek, although it included at least the former; it was the characteristic curriculum demanded by the growing professional middle class, recruiting new members from the upwardly mobile members of the working class (Anderson 1985: 480, note 39). Just as with the Day School Certificate (Higher), the typical Leaving Certificate course in 1938 consisted of compulsory English – which included geography and history – mathematics or arithmetic, and, for almost all candidates, French (Osborne 1966: 172). The proportion of candidates taking Latin was just over half, the same as the proportion taking science. Only six per cent took commercial subjects, four per cent took domestic subjects, and 0.3 per cent took technical subjects. Altogether, the Leaving Certificate on which secondary courses in general were modelled provided a liberal academic course, neither technical nor overwhelmingly classical.

In both the Advanced Division courses and in the Leaving Certificate, the role of English in this general education was central, an introduction to liberal citizenship. It was the main inheritor at the school level of the nineteenth-century Scottish university predilection for philosophy. It was also the main focus of education for citizenship in a democratic community. The subject, notably, always included the study of both literature and language, and through literature it sought to address questions of moral philosophy. The literature to be studied was to represent the core of European culture: as the standard requirements for the Higher Leaving Certificate examination were put in an SED circular of 1936:

> candidates may be expected to have some acquaintance with the authorship and period of the leading masterpieces of our literature . . . Knowledge of literary history should in all cases be based upon a first-hand acquaintance with literature itself . . . [Such] answers as show independent reading, careful and methodical instruction, or intelligent criticism, will be accorded full weight in the adjudgement of marks.
>
> (SED 1936d: 11–12)

The general purpose of this was summed up well in the recommendations on the curriculum for the Advanced Divisions which the Scottish Council for Research in Education made in 1931: 'to teach English to pupils of any age is to help them to satisfy . . . the need to understand others and to be understood by them' (SCRE 1931: 27). Although these views could be seen as resembling the emerging idea in England that 'the great tradition' of English literature was the main instrument of cultural transmission – the idea which such writers as F. R. Leavis and T. S. Eliot developed from Matthew Arnold – the Scottish version was more thoroughly democratic, perhaps rather more resembling Raymond Williams's reinterpretation of the Leavisite approach (Williams 1963). This was not the initiation into a priesthood of literary taste, but a modernised expression of the tenets of Scottish common sense philosophy: good-quality works of imaginative literature 'enlarge the discipline of life by supplementing, refining, and correcting it' (SCRE 1931: 51).

G. S. Osborne, in the systematic comparison of Scottish and English schools
which he wrote in 1966, summarised the popular view of the twentieth-century
Scottish tradition as it was emerging between the wars in this way:

> there was no fear in Scotland that the academic type of secondary
> course would lead to over-production of intellectuals ... On the
> contrary, few Scots appear to have believed that mental power might be
> fostered in some children through work with their hands rather than
> with their brains ... All this was as foreign to Scottish ways of thinking
> before the war as was the feeling that different kinds of children
> needed to be taught in different kinds of schools. Mental growth was
> fostered by the traditional academic subjects.
>
> (Osborne 1966: 170)

R. D. Anderson, likewise, notes that the history of Scottish post-primary
schooling in this period showed that, in contrast to other systems, including
that in England, 'the transmission of the classical tradition did not necessarily
depend on the ideal of the gentleman or the influence of "aristocratic" schools
but could equally well have democratic roots' (Anderson 1985: 472).

Democracy of this sort was not the SED preference, but it was probably
that of a majority of parents, of teachers and perhaps of inspectors, seeking
to realise the expansionist potential of the 1918 Act in the teeth of official
reluctance.

The gradual increase in participation in post-primary provision, the
persisting preference within that for what was seen as a proper, academic
secondary education, and the resulting frustration with the inequity of funding and staffing standards between the Advanced Divisions and the secondary
schools eventually forced the SED to recognise all this as secondary, in the
Education (Scotland) Act of 1936 and in a revised Code, covering all post-
primary courses, in 1939. The leaving age was to be finally raised to fifteen in
1939, but that was postponed again because of the outbreak of war. There
would be two kinds of secondary course – junior and senior – allocation
between which had to be the subject of formal schemes drawn up by the
education authorities. In the postwar period this would increasingly mean
selection based partly on intelligence tests. The junior course would be three
years long once the leaving age had been raised, and was intended to culminate
in a Junior School Certificate; this course was modelled on that leading to the
Day School Certificate (Higher), and so represented official approval of the
sort of academic respectability for all pupils towards which the democratic
pressure had been pushing policy (Osborne 1966: 172; SED 1939b: 17–20;
Stocks 2002). The senior course would last five years and would lead to the
Leaving Certificate. There had to be an adequate supply of free places in each

area, although education authorities were permitted to charge fees for places over and above that; a few did so, at very low levels, until 1965.

The SED insisted that these two routes should have 'parity of esteem', and be distinguished by length only, and also insisted that the legislation defined kinds of course, not types of school. However – as the ILP MP James Maxton pointed out – even if that were feasible, it would have required much greater funding than was likely to be made available by the conservative National Government of the time, and, in urban areas especially, the two kinds of courses did tend to end up in different kinds of school (H. M. Paterson 1983: 211).

Officials in the SED also claimed that this new structure was an authentic fulfilment of the Scottish democratic tradition. For example, the most senior of the chief inspectors, George Andrew, wrote in the SED reports for the years 1933–6 that the change would come to be regarded as a 'landmark':

> It is in line with the democratic spirit of our tradition, for in effect it admits the right of the individual to the type of post-primary education most suited to his needs, without involving him in any terminological discrimination. In the school commonwealth all citizens are equal.
>
> (SED 1937: 17)

Whether that would be possible in a system that continued to be divided – and how the popular pressure for universal secondary education would interpret the new opportunities – would not be evident until a couple of decades later.

CHAPTER 5

University Education

Scotland had four universities in the second half of the nineteenth century, following the amalgamation of King's and Marischal Colleges in Aberdeen in 1860. King's, St Andrews and Glasgow dated from the fifteenth century, and Marischal and Edinburgh from the late-sixteenth. A university college had been set up in Dundee in 1883, and it was affiliated to St Andrews in 1901. The founding statutes for the universities in the first half of the twentieth century were the Universities (Scotland) Act of 1889 and the enactments of the Executive Commission which it set up. The framers of the Act and the commissioners proceeded with the standard Scottish assumption that the universities were public institutions, and that they should be reformed by legislation in a manner that applied uniformly to all four of them.

Just as the 1872 Education Act had arisen out of the Argyll Commission, so this arose out of the extensive inquiry into the condition of the universities that had been conducted between 1876 and 1878 by the Commission chaired by John Inglis, who had been rector of King's College, Aberdeen and who had also chaired the executive commissioners which had given effect to the previous Universities Act of 1858. Two main issues faced the 1876 Commission (Anderson 1983a: 92–102). One was curricular: should students be given greater freedom of choice of subjects? The Scottish practice until then had been to prescribe the subjects that were needed for completing the Master of Arts course, as a means of enforcing breadth, although it was a particular conception of breadth that related primarily to preparation for work as a minister of religion. These six traditional subjects were Humanity (the term used for Latin), Greek, Mathematics, Logic, Moral Philosophy and Natural Philosophy (the term for physics) (Anderson 1983a: 30). This list paid little attention to emerging subjects such as English, which only in Edinburgh University had evolved as a fully separate subject from its origins as part of Logic. It paid no attention at all to the applied subjects that might be needed by an industrial economy – such as engineering and commercial studies. It was a broad introduction to liberal arts, and the aspiring professional would have to take further specialist training before being fully qualified – as a minister, a lawyer or a teacher, for example. Moreover, because few students went as far as graduation, few followed the full prescribed course (Anderson 1983a: 75–6): the 1876 Commission estimated, for example, that at Glasgow University only one in six or seven arts students ever took a degree (Scotland 1969: 146). On this matter, that Commission attempted a compromise. Degree studies would rest on a 'First Examination' in Latin, Greek, Mathematics, English and science, in order to provide a 'foundation of general culture' (Anderson 1983a: 99); the survival of compulsory Greek was, as Anderson notes, a remarkably conservative feature. Beyond that there would be various lines of study leading to the MA – the traditional one, and five specialisms in literature, philosophy, law and history, mathematics and natural science.

The proposed First Examination, as well as recognising the foundation course, was also the 1876 Commission's attempted solution to the second main issue – whether there should be an entrance examination. The supporters of an entrance examination said it would raise standards, an issue that had become acute when Scottish graduates did poorly in the examination for entry to the Indian Civil Service when it was introduced in 1855. The First Examination was not to be an entrance requirement, but it could be taken in school, and so this proposal in some respects anticipated the growth of the school Leaving Certificate in the early years of the twentieth century. The opponents of an entrance examination claimed that it would restrict the route from parish school to university which was believed to be the basis of the success of the Scottish school and university system as a whole. It would also, they claimed, make it more difficult for older students to attend – the person who worked for several years after leaving school in order to accumulate some savings.

In seeking to implement the principles of the 1876 Commission, the 1889 Act left most of the strictly educational issues to a new executive commission, chaired by Lord Kinnear. This Commission went much further than its predecessor following the 1858 Act. It introduced a compulsory entrance examination at last and, from 1888, the universities also accepted the Leaving Certificate as being equivalent to an entrance examination; so the expanding and democratising secondary sector gradually became the main embodiment of the old practice of access directly from the parish school. For example, by 1910, the proportion of male Scottish entrants to Edinburgh University who came from a secondary school was over eighty per cent, up from two thirds in the 1870s, with a further five per cent coming from Higher Grade schools. The parish-school tradition had in fact died half a century earlier: even in 1870, the proportion coming directly from an elementary school was one fifth

(Anderson 1983a: 304). For Scottish women, secondaries in 1910 supplied seventy per cent of entrants, and Higher Grade schools a further fifth.

The 1889 Commission encouraged new chairs in non-traditional subjects, and encouraged the appointment of non-professorial staff. Faculties of Science were established, along with a new BSc degree and mechanisms for recognising research degrees. Probably the most significant change in the long run, however, was the introduction of separate Honours degrees; the old MA was henceforth called the Ordinary degree. The 1858 Commission had allowed for Honours study, but only as a supplement to work on the standard curriculum; there was no Honours degree in the sense of a curriculum designed over three or four years. The Ordinary degree continued the traditional curriculum, but with significantly extended choice: students had to choose seven subjects, and the prescription was now only that at least one had to be taken from each of four departments – language and literature, mental philosophy, science, and history and law (Anderson 1983a: 270). The Honours courses were indeed more specialised, but student choice was still highly circumscribed: they still had to take Latin or Greek, a philosophical subject and a science (Anderson 1983a: 271).

The 1889 Act also formalised the administrative structure of the universities. The 1858 Act had established the university court, and the position of rector elected by current students. The rector was nominally chair of the court, but, because of the practice of electing prominent politicians to the post, the actual work was usually undertaken by the assessor whom he nominated. The three main officers after 1858 were the principal, the chancellor – elected by a new General Council of graduates – and the rector. The 1889 Act made the court the supreme governing body. It was elected by the General Council and by the senate, the body which governed educational matters. The principal ran daily affairs, and – being chair of the senate – was potentially very powerful. This system was seen as more democratic than the previous one where the senate had the greater power, because the court represented opinion outside the university.

These changes to curriculum, examination and administration not only laid the basis for the universities in the twentieth century; they also have been the source of persisting controversy as to their significance for Scottish educational democracy. The elements of that claimed tradition, as confirmed by the 1858 Act, were that university should provide a broad general education, that it should be accountable to its community and that it retained links to the community through its students, who did not live in secluded colleges but at home or in lodgings (Neave and Cowper 1979: 10–11). For these community roles, the urban situation of the universities was also significant: they were not monastic institutions, but had been founded on the mainstream European model of the civic university, exemplified in Bologna, Paris and Leyden.

It has been claimed since at least the 1920s that the 1889 Act led to the under-mining of all these elements – by introducing specialisation, by encouraging the view that universities were primarily about research and preparation of an elite, and – through the entrance examination – by reducing the opportunities for poor students to attend. The best-known exponent of these views in the second half of the twentieth century was George Davie, whose book of 1961 – *The Democratic Intellect* – has shaped the discussion of Scottish universities since. He in turn was renewing a criticism that had been made by such advo-cates of a particular interpretation of the Scottish tradition as Herbert Grierson, who argued in his 1936 rectorial address at Edinburgh University that the effect of the 1889 reforms was to 'smash [the] uniform . . . curriculum and to introduce the blessed principle of options', the effect of which, he alleged, was 'vocationalism, the direction of all one's studies towards a money-making profession', 'the quest for the easiest path towards something that can be called a degree' and 'purely fanciful combinations' of subjects (Grierson 1937: 11–12). Davie got his title from this same milieu of 1930s discussion about Scottish identity. In 1932, Walter Elliot, later to be Conservative Secretary of State for Scotland, described what he called Scotland's 'demo-cratic intellectualism':

> it is a heritage wherein discipline is rigidly and ruthlessly enforced, but where criticism and attack are unflinching, continuous, and salt with a bitter and jealous humour. It is a heritage wherein intellect, speech and, above all, argument are the passports to the highest eminence in the land.
>
> (Elliot 1932: 64)

The full significance of Davie's work really belongs to the period when he published it – because it was as much an intervention in a contemporary debate as a work of history – but the question of the significance of the 1889 reforms for the tradition of educational democracy remains.

BROADENING ACCESS

There were three aspects to this alleged threat to the democratic university. One was sociological: who gained access? Here the evidence is quite clear: partly because of the accompanying expansion of secondary schooling, in most respects access became wider in the half century following the 1889 Act, not narrower as was alleged by later critics.

The first point is that the universities remained closely linked with their various communities right up to World War II. They were overwhelmingly Scottish, and also firmly regional. In 1910, the proportion of students who were born in Scotland was eighty-nine per cent in Aberdeen, sixty-nine per cent in Edinburgh, eighty-one per cent in Glasgow, and seventy-four per cent in St Andrews (Anderson 1983a: 296–8). In that same year, the proportion of the Scottish students who came from the corresponding catchment areas was almost equally high. In Aberdeen, eighty per cent came from the north east (and a further twelve per cent from the Highlands); in Edinburgh, seventy per cent came from the Lothians, the Borders and the east-central region; in Glasgow, seventy-four per cent came from the west (and a further four per cent from the south west); in St Andrews, sixty-nine per cent came from the east-central region (Anderson 1983a: 296–8).

In many respects the universities remained even more local than these figures indicate (UGC 1921: 257–87). In 1919, the proportion of full-time students at Aberdeen University who came from within thirty miles of the university was fifty-three per cent; in Edinburgh, it was fifty-six per cent; in Glasgow, it was fifty per cent; in St Andrews, it was seventy-nine per cent (higher than might be expected given the population of north-east Fife, because this included the college in Dundee). The proportions had not changed much by the mid-1930s in Aberdeen and Edinburgh (UGC 1936: 65): in 1934–5, sixty-one per cent in Aberdeen and fifty-four per cent in Edinburgh. St Andrews was somewhat less local than in 1919, with sixty-one per cent, but Glasgow was much more so, with seventy-one per cent.

Large proportions of students actually lived at home, and the incidence of this grew when economic conditions deteriorated in the late 1920s, as Table 5.1 shows. The balance were mostly in lodgings, not hostels. Most of the change between 1919 and the mid-1930s was in Glasgow, where the proportion living at home rose from thirty-nine per cent to seventy-eight per cent for men and from fifty-eight per cent to eighty-one per cent for women. The other main departure from the national proportions was for women at St Andrews, where hostels for women were much more common: thirty-seven per cent already in 1919, and forty per cent in 1934. But even that latter figure was no more than equal to the proportion living at home. In all these respects, the four old universities remained attached to their communities in complex ways, even if

Table 5.1 Place of Residence of University Students, 1919 and 1934 (%)

	1919		1934	
	Male	Female	Male	Female
Home	42	49	61	63
Lodgings	57	37	34	21
Hostel	1	14	5	17

Sources: UGC (1921: 257–87; 1936: 65).

in some of them there were the beginnings of a resident student population who began to develop a more inward-looking student culture (Anderson 1983a: 328–34).

It is perhaps, then, not surprising to find that opportunities for access did not narrow, and indeed in many respects widened. Partly this was because of sheer expansion, but that was entirely accounted for by the most numerically significant extension of access in this period – the admission of women to formal graduation for the first time in 1892. The number of male students in 1911 was actually below that for 1891 – 5,924 compared to 6,604 (Anderson 1985: 467). However, the number of women had, by 1911, reached 1,846, giving a total student population that was eighteen per cent larger than twenty years earlier. Although that combined figure still represented only just over 1.6 per thousand population, compared to about 2.3 a decade later in 1921, that was still roughly a sixteen per cent increase on the 1.4 per thousand in 1901.

Women had been attending university classes for a couple of decades before 1892. The most developed programme was at St Andrews, which had pioneered a formal diploma for women in 1877, the Licentiate in Arts. It was referred to after 1882 as the 'LLA', even though the first 'L' was never explained, and the founder of the Licentiate, William Knight who was professor of moral philosophy, denied that it stood for what he regarded as the patronising term 'Lady' (Bell and Tight 1993: 78). Between 1877 and its abolition in 1931, it was taken by 36,008 candidates, and the full LLA had been awarded to 5,118 of them (Bell and Tight 1993: 79). It was intended to be of MA standard, and was normally taken by what would now be called distance learning; thus the university made a substantial profit out of it. Encouraged by this, St Andrews achieved after 1892 a relatively high ratio of female to male students: in 1913, some forty-three per cent of under-graduates were female, when the Scottish average was about one quarter (Bell and Tight 1993: 82; Anderson 1985: 467).

Other universities had similar, though less formal and less successful, schemes – for example, Edinburgh had a Certificate in Arts for women from 1872 – and in all four universities women could attend university-type classes taught by professors, but not university classes themselves (Anderson 1983a: 255). However, the expansion after 1892 was encouraged as much by the new openings for professional women as by the sort of proto-feminist campaigning that lay behind the LLA. The new girls' secondary schools provided comparatively well-paid, secure and respectable posts for female graduates, and indeed one of them – St George's in Edinburgh – became a centre for training female secondary teachers (Anderson 1983a: 256). There were also campaigns to gain access for women to medical careers, and that led by Sophia Jex-Blake in the 1860s to have women admitted to Edinburgh University's medical courses attracted widespread publicity because of the violent opposition by which it was met from some male students and professors (Corr 1990a: 301).

The numbers of both male and female students rose sharply after the war – part of the mood of democratic reform – so that the total reached 11,746 in 1921 (Anderson 1985: 477). The female proportion peaked at thirty-four per cent in 1926. By 1931, in the depths of recession, total numbers had fallen back again to 11,150, and by 1939 to 10,034, and again the changes were almost entirely accounted for by changing numbers of women – 3,323 in 1926, 3,536 in 1931, and 2,710 in 1939. The female proportion therefore fell, being thirty-two per cent in 1931 and twenty-seven per cent in 1939.

But the overall, though fluctuating, expansion of female enrolment was not the only way in which access was at least not harmed in the half century following the 1889 Act when compared to the period around that Act. In Glasgow University the proportion of working-class students may in fact have risen: twenty-four per cent of male students belonged to a broad working-class group in 1910 (including farm workers as well as the industrial working class), compared to fourteen per cent in 1870, although five out of six of these were sons of artisans and other skilled workers (Anderson 1983a: 310–11). For women between 1900 and 1910, around one in five had working-class fathers (see pp. 312–13). Between 1927 and 1935, about thirty-seven per cent of male students at Glasgow University had fathers who were artisans, or were in unskilled employment, or were unemployed; among female students, the proportion was about thirty-five per cent (Collier 1938: 177; McDonald 1967). Both of these were higher than in the pre-war years. The working-class entrants were heavily concentrated in the MA courses, especially the Ordinary degree, as is shown in Table 5.2. By comparing the numbers of students with the birthrate at appropriate dates in each social class in the catchment area of the university, Collier (1938: 174) calculated that, between 1911 and 1931, opportunity had risen most for working-class groups: in 1911, sons and daughters of professional fathers were seventy-one times more likely to enter than those of fathers in unskilled occupations, but by 1931 this ratio had fallen to fifty-one to one. This is consistent with the growth in the proportion living at home, which we noted earlier.

Table 5.2 Percentage of Students at Glasgow University who were Working Class, 1927–35

	Male	Female
Law	24	11
Medicine	20	7
Theology	36	0
MA Honours	44	29
MA Ordinary	49	38

Source: Collier (1938: 177).

Such detailed information is not available for the other universities, although something like it can be calculated for Aberdeen. There, the proportion of graduates whose father was in a working-class occupation was about ten per cent in the 1880s, nineteen per cent in the 1900s, thirty-one per cent in the 1910s, twenty-eight per cent in the 1920s and twenty-six per cent in the 1930s (Forsyth and Mercer 1970: 455). Again, despite the contraction in the 1930s, the working-class share remained higher than in the 1880s.

Finally on the sociological aspects of access, there is the question of age. This is the one respect in which the social base of the universities did narrow, but the concentration into an age range of roughly seventeen to twenty had already begun to happen long before the 1889 reforms (Anderson 1983a: 301). Thus, in 1890, sixty-three per cent of male students at the Scottish universities were between these ages. By 1910, this had increased to seventy-seven per cent. For women, the figure was then eighty-eight per cent, up from sixty-seven per cent a decade earlier. The real decline for men had been among sixteen-year-olds, an effect of the reforms in secondary education: from twenty-three per cent in 1870 to fourteen per cent in 1890 and two per cent in 1910. The figures for the period between the wars were not compiled in the same way, and so direct comparison for ages over twenty is not possible, but the trend for the under-17s continued: that proportion never rose above five per cent in any of the universities (UGC 1921: 257–87; 1936: 66).

One reason why the social base of the universities did not narrow, and in significant respects became wider, were bursaries, especially from the Carnegie Trust. Andrew Carnegie, from Dunfermline, had made a fortune in the US steel industry, and in 1901 established a trust fund to help the Scottish universities. That part of it which was directed to helping students stipulated that any person whom the universities accepted for entrance was entitled to apply for payment of about one half of their fees. There was no means test, but – as Anderson (1983a: 309) notes – the better-off students tended not to apply because of the stigma attached to a subsidy that did not depend on success in a competitive examination, unlike the older-established university bursaries. By 1904, one half of all students received some Carnegie money (Anderson 1983a: 288). In the 1920s and 1930s, the Trust was paying the fees of around 4,000 students each year, about forty per cent of all full-time students at the universities (Carnegie Trust 1926: 7; 1936: 7). This rather under-states the significance, however, since only students from Scotland were eligible, and the Trust also by then applied a minimum threshold of prior educational attainment: in 1925, the Trust itself estimated that around seventy per cent of eligible students over the previous six years had had their fees paid. The proportion of all students was higher in the more working-class universities of Aberdeen (forty-nine per cent in 1935) and Glasgow (forty-eight per cent) than in St Andrews (forty per cent) and Edinburgh (thirty per cent). The proportion was highest in the Arts faculties (forty-six per cent in 1935), and lowest in Medicine (thirty per cent). There were almost no gender differences.

The changing social base of the universities was supplemented also by a new sector of higher education college which the SED created in 1901 – the central institutions. They were established as exceptions to a new code governing continuation classes: the code recognised colleges that would provide, from a central location in each region, classes which it described as 'of the very highest kind in applied science and art to selected students who will devote their whole time to study' (Cowper 1970: 48). By 1908, there were sixteen of them, a further three being added up to 1950. These included the three agricultural colleges and two veterinary colleges, which were taken over by the SED from the Board of Agriculture in 1896, and from 1912 were run by the new Department of Agriculture for Scotland (Cowper 1970: 101). Most of the work of the central institutions was probably not at university level – the term 'higher education' then frequently being used to refer to anything beyond the elementary level – despite the aspiration of the SED in 1906 that they should become 'industrial universities' (Anderson 1995: 277). Their story, therefore, mostly belongs to Chapter 6. Nevertheless, in the Glasgow and West of Scotland Technical College and in Heriot Watt College in Edinburgh, the aspiration did come close to being realised (Cowper 1970: 62). The agricultural colleges also tended to work closely with neighbouring universities, Edinburgh University in fact having had a chair in agriculture since 1790. By 1938 probably about 2,500 of the students in the various central institutions were working at university level (Osborne 1966: 184), and from 1919 the central institution in Glasgow – by then called the Royal Technical College – received grants from the same source as the universities, the University Grants Committee.

To arrive at a total of university-level students in the 1930s, we also have to add the approximately 900 non-graduate students training to be teachers (Cruikshank 1970: 237). As is discussed more fully below, these courses could be classed by then as being at a university level, whereas at the beginning of the century all trainee teachers who were at university level would have been counted among the students at the universities, because they would have been taking courses there. So – with about 10,000 university students (Anderson 1985: 477) – we reach a total university-level under-graduate population of around 13,500, making about 2.7 per thousand, nearly double what it had been before the central institutions had been inaugurated. Altogether, then, university-type education was not less open in the 1930s than in the period before the 1889 reforms.

PUBLIC UNIVERSITIES

The second aspect of the threat which the 1889 reforms seemed to pose to university democracy concerned the matter of political control. The Scottish universities had been receiving some state grants since the early nineteenth century, but this was made more systematic and regular after 1889. The Act of that year gave them £42,000 annually, although only £9,000 of this was available for new developments (Anderson 1983a: 273). It also ended the practice whereby students paid individual fees for each class they attended: henceforth, there would be a general fee fund in each university, which could be used more effectively for institutional development. From 1892 these new sources were supplemented by £30,000 from the same source as was used to build up secondary schooling – the grant following the decision to make elementary schooling free in England. The 1908 Education (Scotland) Act also permitted the Scottish Secretary to make grants to universities. By then, state grants were providing around a third of university income, the remainder being mostly from fees and endowments (Anderson 1983a: 289). The Carnegie Trust provided capital grants and grants for research: the annual capital grant of £40,000 after 1901 meant that the Trust was giving more to the universities than the state, and so – as Anderson (1983a: 288) comments – it became, in effect, a ministry for the Scottish universities, requiring them to draw up plans for development.

The state grants after 1919 were mostly paid through the new University Grants Committee, a body answerable to the Treasury in London and dealing with universities throughout Britain. One reason it became involved was the severe contraction of the universities during the war. Student numbers at Glasgow, for example, fell from 2,916 in 1913–14 to 1,662 in 1916–17, and the total loss of fee income during the war was over £50,000 (Moss et al. 2000: 134, 138). In Aberdeen, numbers fell from 1,069 to 612 in the same period, and the loss of income was over £22,000 (Hutchison 1993: 44). The universities themselves took the initiative in approaching the Treasury for help, temporary at first but then permanent after the war was over. In its first year, it provided twenty-nine per cent of the income of the four universities, but only eighteen per cent of the income of the Royal Technical College, which continued to receive a further fifteen per cent from the SED (UGC 1921: 257–89). In session 1934–5, the four universities received thirty-eight per cent of their income from the state, nearly all of it from the UGC; the Royal Technical College received forty-five per cent, but half of that continued to be from the SED (UGC 1936: 76–7).

Nevertheless, although this growth of state funding from London did represent the beginnings of a process of shifting the universities into a more British frame of reference, it was not pronounced by the late 1930s. The sociology of the entrants, if nothing else, ensured that, but so also did the character of the UGC. Its money was provided as grant-in-aid, and so there was no detailed scrutiny of university expenditure. The UGC was made up mainly of academics, and so was insistent that universities ought to be autonomous of direct state interference (Shattock 1994: 1–5). Its first chairman was Sir William McCormick, who had been secretary of the Carnegie Trust (Anderson 1983a: 288).

That the universities could operate in this autonomous way was due in part to the administrative reforms which the 1889 Act had put in place. Although these reforms did recognise the status of 'lecturer', it did not give security of tenure, and so in practice the professors remained powerful (Anderson 1983a: 275). Despite a slow growth in the proportion of professors who came from outside Scotland, the Scots-born remained the majority: seventy-one per cent in the 1890s, sixty-four per cent between 1900 and 1920, fifty-eight per cent in the 1920s, and back up to seventy-two per cent in the 1930s (Anderson 1987: 39). By the 1930s, however, the majority of new appointments were of people who had not been born in Scotland (Anderson 1987: 45). The Scots-born came disproportionately from the eastern lowlands and the north east, with the Highlands and the western lowlands under-represented. The large majority of them came from professional families – fifty-four per cent in the late-nineteenth century, fifty-one per cent in the first four decades of the twentieth century (Anderson 1987: 48) – and a further quarter or so came from other middle-class backgrounds. That left only around fifteen per cent from working-class or farming families, and Anderson summarises that this composition of the professoriate did not reflect the democratisation of the wider educational system that was then taking place (Anderson 1987: 50). The period after 1889 was, therefore, transitional. It probably consolidated the control which the professoriate exercised, partly because of the growing ideology of academic autonomy – a real change from the mid-nineteenth century. Because that professoriate remained mostly Scottish, the autonomy was exercised in ways that had been inherited from their Scottish past. The beginnings of a British career structure for academics, and the inevitably greater British political interest in the Scottish universities through the UGC system, ensured that, by the second half of the twentieth century, the Scottishness of higher education would be a matter of controversy. But to attribute this to the 1889 reforms would be to pre-date it by five or six decades.

BROAD CURRICULUM

The third and final aspect of the controversies over the democratic tradition was curricular – the topic of the debates leading up to the work of the 1889 Commission. The 1889 reforms did not abandon the generalist tradition, rather ensuring that the rapidly expanding Scottish professional class of the twentieth century would continue to have a respect for academic knowledge. In fact, despite George Davie's main allegation, the place of philosophy was actually strengthened in the end: Logic or Moral Philosophy were prescribed again in all the universities by the 1920s.

It is true, however, that the character of university learning was changing. Precisely because the universities were social institutions, not secluded colleges, they had to pay attention to the changing character of the economy and the changing structure of employment. There were widespread doubts as to whether a curriculum designed primarily for educating ministers of religion and schoolteachers was effective in the development of entrepreneurs or in the specialist technical training which modern industry required (Sanderson 1972: 157). Attention to science, modern languages and commercial subjects was bound to be added. The proportion of full-time students taking science or technology degrees in the universities rose threefold between 1900 and the 1920s, as Table 5.3 shows. Particularly strong in the period from about the middle of the nineteenth century were natural philosophy and engineering (Sanderson 1972: 159–62). Medicine continued to provide a large share of the remainder, but that still left a substantial proportion in the traditional faculties of Arts, Divinity and Law. These were even more important for female students: for example, in 1935, no fewer than seventy-three per cent of them were in these faculties. This whole process, then, was not a turning away from the traditional curriculum, but a supplementing of it. The sciences took their place in a faculty structure that remained broad, and so were institutionally absorbed into a modernised version of general education (Robertson 1984: 50).

This is probably also the best way to interpret the slow decline in the proportion of arts faculty students who took the Ordinary degree – not a replacement of a general course by specialist ones, but the modernisation of general education through the still broad requirements for Honours degrees. In any case, the change was very slow, as Table 5.4 shows, so that even by the 1930s over two thirds of graduates were still taking Ordinary degrees.

Table 5.3 Broad Area of Study of Full-Time University Students, 1900, 1919 and 1935 (%)

	1900	1919	1935
Arts, Law, Divinity	53	33	52
Science, Technology	7	22	17
Medicine	40	45	31

Sources: Anderson (1983a: 352–6); UGC (1921: 257–8; 1936: 70–1).

Table 5.4 Percentage of First Degrees that were Honours, 1900, 1913 and 1935

University	1900 (arts graduates)	1913 (arts graduates)	1935 (all graduates)
Aberdeen	35	31	23
Edinburgh	22	40	21
Glasgow	14	21	31
St Andrews	not available	not available	31

Sources: Anderson (1983a: 284); UGC (1936: 72).

Much the same point about the role of general education could be said for the developing central institutions, in the main more concerned with applied science than were the universities, but aspiring under SED guidance to a university-type role. That view of their function could be shared by such advocates of a democratised liberal education as Professor S. S. Laurie, who in 1901 welcomed their foundation as potentially spreading higher education to the working class (Cowper 1970: 51). Henry Craik, secretary of the SED, argued in 1895 that a proper system of technical education should have 'as its special duty' the aim of showing 'that industrial capacity has an intellectual side' (Cowper 1970: 51). The Scottish Education Reform Committee (1917: 113) that reported at the end of World War I was highly critical of merely utilitarian education, and recommended that the central institutions be affiliated to local universities, a move that took place only between some courses at the Royal Technical College and Glasgow University (Moss et al. 2000: 179).

These persisting curricular themes ensured that the university in Scotland in the first few decades of the twentieth century became central to any idea of educational democracy, even when only small numbers of people entered it: it provided the model of knowledge on which were based the Leaving Certificate, the attempts to provide a broad general education in the Advanced Divisions in the 1920s and 1930s, and the training of teachers. The 1889 Commissioners in fact tried to reconcile the conflicting pressures from within the tradition: they introduced the entrance examination, but retained the junior classes, and then abolished them after a few years. They encouraged specialisation, but also required that all students – even for Honours – had to follow a broad curriculum in their first two years. They also encouraged a trend that was already underway – the growth in the proportion of students who graduated, probably to at least four fifths of entrants (Anderson 1983a: 283).

The entrance examination and the recognition of the Leaving Certificate helped to encourage schools to see general education in the same way as the universities did, especially after the Group Certificate was enforced from 1902. From 1927 the universities also imposed what was in effect their own grouping requirements, in the form of an 'attestation of fitness' which was similar to the Group certificate but could be partly met by sitting the universities' own Preliminary Examination as well as by means of individual passes in the Leaving Certificate (Philip 1992: 70, 83).

However important this emulation may have been, the most important route by which the university definition of general education affected the whole education system was through the training of teachers, and the universities' own academic study of education. The universities aspired to a role in teacher training, and for a couple of decades after the 1890s the main way in which this happened was through training students attending concurrent classes at neighbouring universities or central institutions. By the end of the first decade of the century, around one half of all students in the arts faculties were from the training colleges (Anderson 1983a: 276), and the EIS's *Educational News* could comment in 1911 that 'deep seated in the heart of every Scottish teacher is the affection for a University connection' (Stocks 1986: 110). Relations with the SED, however, were acrimonious, largely over the extent of university autonomy in providing teacher-training courses (Bell 1983; Stocks 1986). Craik regarded the beliefs about open access as nothing more than nostalgia. Craik's successor, Struthers, believed that the universities were incapable of modernising their conception of general education in a manner that would best serve the needs of the teachers trying to create opportunities for a much wider range of school pupils. He wrote in private in 1907 that the universities were inclined to produce teachers 'whose aim would be to turn out pupils for the bursary exam and regard all the rest of his pupils and their future destiny as matters scarcely deserving his serious consideration' (Hutchison 1993: 40; Scotland 1975).

The SED inevitably won, and took teacher training away from the universities by the 1920s (Hutchison 1992). George Davie (1986) has interpreted this as a sign that the tradition of general education was being destroyed by the bureaucrats in the Department. That criticism, however, ignores the point about a modernised tradition, in aspiration much more democratic than before because of the changing character of the schools to which the new kinds of teacher would go. The new system of four regional centres of training – in Aberdeen, Dundee, Edinburgh and Glasgow – continued to pay attention to general education. Partly this was because increasing proportions of their students were graduates, and because even those female trainees who were not graduates had to have passed the full Group Leaving Certificate and therefore had much the same foundation in general education as their male predecessors would have had from their university studies half a century earlier. The training centres aspired to operate at university level, more successfully than the central institutions insofar as psychology and philosophy were the foundations of all their courses. Removing teacher training from the universities was not a guarantee of a new kind of theory – for the non-graduate female students, the links between theory and practice remaining under-developed – but the main point for understanding the kinds of educational experience which these young female students went through was that it was quite definitely an intellectual one (Cruikshank 1970: 177–8).

The route through university into teaching was a means by which large numbers of working-class boys and girls entered a profession. Working-class graduates from Aberdeen, for example, were much more likely to become schoolteachers than their middle-class peers: in the 1920s and the 1930s, around one half of working-class graduates did so, compared to around forty per cent of graduates whose father was in a lower-middle-class job, and only about a third of graduates whose father was in a professional or managerial post (Mercer and Forsyth 1975: 65). The intellectual preparation which these working-class teachers went through, and their return to some of the same communities from which they had come, helped to disseminate the old ideas of academic learning to an unprecedented extent.

The connection between teacher training and general education was also maintained through staff (Cruikshank 1970: 178–84). Godfrey Thomson in Edinburgh and William McClelland in Dundee held university chairs in education at the same time as they ran the regional centres, and William Boyd at Glasgow had extensive contacts with teachers through his EdB classes. These three were also involved in the flourishing of educational research that followed on the setting up of the Scottish Council for Research in Education in 1928, under the auspices of the EIS and the directors of education (Craigie 1972; Morris 1994; Nisbet 1978, 1999; Wake 1988). It aimed to fill a gap left by the intellectual timidity into which the Advisory Council had retreated following the controversies over the 1918 Act (Young 1986: 133–44). The Research Council then became the main source of authoritative research on Scottish education, especially in its pioneering surveys of schoolchildren between the 1930s and the 1960s (Hope 1978).

The state of university-type education in the 1930s was, therefore, not nearly so atrophied as the romantic critics of the 1889 reforms have alleged – quite the opposite. For the emerging professional class, recruited from a wider base than hitherto through the expanded and somewhat democratised secondary schools, the touchstone of a general education would no longer be philosophy in the way that it had been for ministers, lawyers and teachers half a century earlier. This was not an attachment to classical knowledge at all, but to general education. It was academic in the sense that it was thoroughly meritocratic: the Leaving Certificate became the only gateway through which entry could be gained to higher learning. It was far from being scholastic, however. It was knowledge for a useful, social purpose, a modernisation of that very old Scottish idea that the purpose of learning was to clarify and purify the 'common sense' of the community.

CHAPTER 6

Technical and Adult Education

The puzzle about adult education in Scotland throughout the twentieth
century is summed up well by R. D. Anderson:

> The SED's concentration on school-leavers at one end of the spectrum
> and Central Institutions at the other meant that technical education for
> the ordinary worker was neglected – as was 'liberal' education for
> adults, left to bodies like the Workers' Educational Association, which
> was slow to catch on in Scotland.
>
> (Anderson 1995: 282)

Why was this? Why was a country with an apparent commitment to a national
tradition of democratic education so resistant to education outside formal
institutions? Some tentative answers are offered at the end of this chapter, but
the main point about the period is that the relative failure of adult education
was not through lack of trying.

The concept of technical education can be dated in Scotland from well
back – such as the founding in 1821 of the first Mechanics' Institution as the
Edinburgh School of Arts by Leonard Horner (the institution which later
became Heriot Watt College), and the attempts in the Highlands after the 1745
rising to use education to modernise the economy and society (Thompson
1972–4). However, the twentieth-century growth has its origins in two linked
developments. One was the Technical Schools Act of 1887, which arose out of
the same movement as was yielding the development of secondary education
at the same time: in the views of many, the two purposes were inseparable,
since secondary schools were intended to raise the technical competence of
skilled workers (Cowper 1970: 25). The other was the source of that Act –
a UK commission that had been set up in 1881, in response to fears that
France and Germany were becoming more successful economically because of

a better system of technical education. It was chaired by Sir Bernhard Samuelson and reported in 1884, when it recommended that the best preparation for technological study was a good secondary education. The commissioners were impressed by technical education in Scotland, though mostly from afar: they visited only briefly, and spent most of their time in Allan Glen's secondary school, an isolated example of technical specialisation, and in the Glasgow College of Science and Art, part of what later became the Royal Technical College. The 1887 Scottish Act was a direct outcome of the reports of this Commission, but – in the absence of substantial funding – the encouragement which the Act sought to give to technical education came to little.

At the same time, the rather scattered beginnings of adult education in the university extension movement had petered out in Scotland, which Marwick (1937: 233) and Kelly (1992: 223) attribute to a lack of demand: because entry to the mainstream university courses was (compared to England) so readily available, and because there was no requirement to graduate, there was no need for different forms of provision in the cities, and the population elsewhere was too scattered to be able to take advantage of centralised classes. During the debates about reforming the secondary-school endowments in the 1880s, radical proponents of wider access suggested that they be used to provide evening classes, but again this came to little, although part of the Heriot's endowment in Edinburgh went to the School of Arts (Anderson 1995: 269).

TECHNICAL EDUCATION

The real beginnings of technical education lie, therefore, with the 1901 Code governing continuation classes. These classes were to be funded by money which the SED had taken over in 1890 from the Department of Science and Arts in London, and the new regulations were intended to clarify what the resulting grants were to be spent on. Technical education was defined as 'instruction which aims at communicating to the pupils knowledge and facilities which have a *direct* bearing upon some special occupation, industrial or commercial' (Cowper 1970: 47; emphasis in original). The local continuation classes for pupils who had left school at fourteen were intended to feed into the central institutions that were established by the same Code. The 1908 Education (Scotland) Act obliged school boards to provide continuation classes. Some places took their responsibilities more seriously than others. In Edinburgh in 1910, a quarter of people aged fourteen to eighteen were in evening classes and a further quarter were still in schools; one of these, the new Tynecastle in 1912, was deliberately designed to provide technical education for the children of the skilled working class (Anderson 1995: 280). Glasgow tried to make continuation classes compulsory (as was permitted by the Act), but came up against the reluctance of employers to let their young workers attend. Generally, the provision was uneven, and, after the initial impetus given to these classes by the 1908 Act, there was at best modest growth over the next three decades: numbers of enrolments were 78,171 in 1901, 144,815 in 1911, 145,774 in 1926 and 163,605 in 1938 (SED 1913: 21; SED 1928: 16; SED 1945: 9). The failure to implement that part of the 1918 Act which allowed for compulsory continuation classes up to age eighteen represented a real loss of opportunity: in the 1920s, only about one in seven of the fifteen to eighteen age group were in these classes.

The continuation classes, despite the intentions, were never exclusively concerned with work, because the SED also interpreted them as a way of prolonging the general education of adolescents (Anderson 1995: 264). Henry Craik had little enthusiasm for a technical education that ignored general education (see p. 266), and S. S. Laurie, although a member of the organisation that campaigned for the greater availability of technical education, had argued in 1884 that a nation's success is ensured by 'moral energy and intellectual vigour' (Anderson 1995: 266).

A similar view pervaded another experiment in the education of young adults in the 1920s and 1930s – the schools which provided courses for young unemployed people, officially called Juvenile Unemployment Centres in the 1920s and Junior Instruction Centres after 1930, but in Scotland colloquially known as 'buroo schools' (Elliott 1979). These were funded by the Ministry of Labour, and run by the education authorities. By the early 1930s, they had about 4,000 students aged between fourteen and eighteen, and by the mid-1930s there were about 6,000, and so they were about a tenth of the size of the continuation classes for that age group (Elliott 1979: 14; SED 1936a: 52). Because, for many students, contact was intermittent, the numbers spending any time in the classes were much larger: in 1934–5, for example, the SED reported that around 29,000 had spent some time in the Centres. Only some of the border counties and some counties in the far north did not make some such provision. Their intention was never purely vocational: it was always to supplement their students' general education as well as to improve their physical fitness and to develop their practical skills (Elliott 1979: 17). Because these young people tended to have left school at the first opportunity precisely because they were not interested in academic study, this aspect of the Centres' work caused particular difficulties. The EIS, in a report on them in 1935, recommended that the only way to develop general education there was by project work, using newspapers, quizzes and the arithmetic of everyday life (Elliott 1979: 18).

A similar concern with general education could be found in the central institutions. As we have seen, the SED intended them to operate at university level, and although this was not realised except in the Royal Technical College and in Heriot Watt College, the aspiration pushed them in the direction of interpreting technical education as including general education. The central institutions (including the agriculture colleges) grew rapidly at first but then stabilised: the numbers of evening-class students quickly reached around 12,000 (by 1904), and – with an interruption during the war years – fluctuated around that figure until the end of the 1930s (Cowper 1970: 185–6). The number of day students rose more markedly, from 1,537 in 1904 to 5,890 in 1914 and 9,870 in 1920. It remained at roughly that figure until the late 1930s. This was modest, not spectacular, progress, especially compared to the much greater expansion of secondary education, and even to the growth of university-level education.

One reason why the central institutions were never just technical colleges was their diversity (Cowper 1970: 103–50). They included art colleges in Aberdeen, Glasgow and Edinburgh. The fame of the Glasgow college was associated particularly with the name of Charles Rennie Mackintosh, whose view of design was certainly not merely utilitarian. Likewise, the Scottish Academy of Music, also in Glasgow, had its origins in the Glasgow Athenaeum which was a cultural rather than a vocational institution. The Scottish College of Commerce in Glasgow offered classes in general culture as well as in specifically vocational work. The Edinburgh Cookery School intended to improve the knowledge which mothers had of nutrition and health; one of the pioneers there in the first decade of the century was Helen MacKenzie, the wife of W. L. MacKenzie, who – as we saw in Chapter 3 – pioneered surveys of children's health at about the same time (Begg 1994: 79–80). Dundee College of Technology insisted that its purpose was to instil in young men 'a knowledge of the principles of their trade' – that is, an intellectual understanding, not just technical dexterity (Cowper 1970: 115). The course offered at Heriot Watt College in telegraphy and telephony in 1902 was advertised explicitly as going beyond mechanical skills: it invited people who might 'wish to rise above the position of being mere machines performing certain mechanical and routine operations', to which end they must 'acquire a fair knowledge of the fundamental laws underlying the science to which they owe their livelihood' (Cowper 1970: 162).

LIBERAL ADULT EDUCATION

The Scottish predilection for general education is seen most clearly, however, in the work of the various voluntary movements which sought to provide education for the working class, with or without state aid – notably the Workers' Educational Association and the Marxist Labour Colleges. The WEA had its origins in England in 1903, under the leadership of Albert Mansbridge (Kelly 1992; Simon 1965). The aim was to provide non-partisan liberal education, achieving social reform through education. The key was the three-year tutorial class, aspiring to university standard. There were no Scottish branches before World War I, although there were Scots activists in the movement, such as Tom Jones, a lecturer at Glasgow university, and J. M. Mactavish, who took over from Mansbridge as general secretary in 1915. While still working as a docker in 1907, he argued for working-class education on these grounds:

> I am not here as a supplicant for my class. I decline to sit at the rich
> man's gate, praying for crumbs. I claim for my class the best that
> Oxford has to give. I claim it as a right – wrongfully withheld – wrong
> not only to us but to Oxford.
>
> (Creighton 1984: 29)

This encapsulates the themes that dominated the WEA's work: the claim to gain access to general culture, the self-consciously class base of that claim, but also the assertion that general culture itself would benefit from being spread more widely.

There were attempts in Scotland in 1913 to establish WEA classes under the auspices of school boards, and some classes did run in Glasgow in 1916, but the movement was not properly established until 1919 (Duncan 1999: 109; Marwick 1953: 11). Just as the English WEA had attracted the support of academics such as R. H. Tawney, so the Scottish movement was aided by William Boyd of Glasgow University, and also Alexander Darroch of Edinburgh University, a believer in working-class general education despite his rather strict views on selection for secondary school (noted in Chapter 4 above). Between 1920 and 1931, the Scottish WEA employed a full-time tutor-organiser, W. H. Marwick, but his post had to be discontinued because of financial difficulties, and he moved to a lecturing job in the extra-mural department at Edinburgh University (Marwick 1953: 11; Roberts 1970: 133). A key teacher in the Edinburgh WEA classes until about 1924 was the philosopher Norman Kemp Smith, who was driven by the principle, which he derived from the common-sense philosophical tradition, that 'all men are equal in intellect, and differ only in character' (Davie 1986: 53). Like many of the other professors who became involved in WEA work, he believed that providing an intellectually stimulating general education for workers was necessary to dissuade them from revolutionary Marxism.

By 1926-7, there were sixteen branches in Scotland, with 818 members, but the movement remained much weaker than in England: Scotland had only six per cent of the 30,000 enrolments in WEA classes in Britain as a whole in that year (Bryant 1984: 11) at a time when its population was about eleven per cent. One of the obstacles to the advance of the WEA was that it was not permitted to receive grants directly from the state, unlike in England and Wales (technically, this was known as 'responsible body' status): in Scotland it was thus dependent on voluntary effort and cooperation with the education authorities, who ran their own evening classes and so would be inclined to use the WEA to supplement these rather than replace them. Thus it is even difficult to say precisely which classes were WEA classes and which were education authority ones (Marwick 1953: 11). Until 1934, there were no regulations specifically governing adult education, all these classes being run under the code for continuation classes (Kelly 1992: 300). The SED, despite the aspirations of the likes of Mactavish and Mansbridge, refused also to recognise WEA work as being even potentially equivalent to university studies (Wiltshire et al. 1980: 198). Furthermore, residential adult education simply did not exist in Scotland before World War II: the one initiative that was taken, the setting up of Newbattle College, did not come until 1936, and so its story belongs to the post-war period (Ducklin and Wallace 2000).

Therefore, even in 1938–9, the first thorough survey of adult education in Scotland (aiming to cover all types of provision apart from that by the Labour Colleges) could conclude that 'there is no highly organised system of adult education such as exists in England' (Cochrane and Stewart 1944: 4). They noted that, because all the SED money went via the education authorities, there were no grants to universities that would help establish joint provision between them and voluntary organisations. Moreover, because the SED did nothing to encourage the three-year tutorial classes of the WEA, there was no official way of distinguishing between different levels of adult education.

Not surprisingly, then, the survey found that provision of adult education was dominated by education authorities, which ran 189 courses. There was also evidence of the revival of the university extension movement that had started in the 1920s, with forty-seven courses run by the university extra-mural departments and thirty by university settlements. Instrumental in that revival was A. D. Lindsay who, as professor of moral philosophy at Glasgow University, established the extra-mural department there in 1924; his work was sustained by his successor in that chair, Hector Hetherington, and by Robert Rait, professor of Scottish history; both of them were later principals of the university (Marwick 1974: 37). Similar developments were led in Edinburgh in 1928 by Alexander Morgan, who had been head of the teacher-training centre there, and in Aberdeen by Norman Walker, lecturer in education. In contrast, the 1938–9 survey found only five courses run directly by the WEA.

These classes in 1938–9 accounted for 9,300 enrolments, from about 4,500 students, about half of whom were women. They were mainly in liberal, general education, nearly one half of student hours being spent on foreign languages and literature, English and Scottish language and literature, and psychology (Cochrane and Stewart 1944: 8). Students' motivation was mainly not vocational: only thirteen per cent of men and eight per cent of women gave that reason for attending (see p. 27). Around three quarters of men and women gave what the researchers classified as reasons of 'personal culture'. However, only about a fifth of the classes were progressive – that is, part of a programme that lasted more than one year (see p. 11).

The classes were concentrated in the four large cities, which had sixty-four per cent of the classes even though they contained only thirty-nine per cent of the Scottish population (see p. 9). Large and small burghs had classes roughly in proportion to their share of the population, but the landward areas were under-represented, with thirty per cent of the population but only eight per cent of classes. People aged over fifty-five were under-represented compared to their share of the general population (about seven per cent in the classes compared to about twenty-two per cent of the population); the only age group that was over-represented was people aged between twenty-five and thirty-four, who made up thirty-eight per cent of the students but only about a quarter of the population (see p. 13).

This form of adult education was not, however, fully compensating for the social class and other inequalities in access to schooling (see p. 22). Among the students, a fifth of men and a third of women had attended at least five years of a secondary course or university, at a time when only around five per cent of the population had done so. By contrast, only fifty-four per cent of male students and thirty-eight per cent of female ones had left school at fourteen, compared to eighty-six per cent of people in the general population. The proportions of respondents who were in paid work were eighty-eight per cent among the men and sixty-eight per cent among the women; twenty per cent of women were full-time housewives. For those who were in paid employment, forty-four per cent of the men and twenty-five per cent of the women were in skilled working-class jobs; eight per cent of the men and six per cent of the women were in semi-skilled or unskilled working class jobs. This would indicate that the skilled working class was represented in these classes roughly in proportion to their share of the general population (thirty-one per cent: see McCrone 1992: 139). The semi-skilled and unskilled, however, were under-represented, since they made up twenty-eight per cent of the general population. For men, the adult education classes were somewhat more socially open than even the most open of the universities, Glasgow, where, as we saw, probably around a third of students came from a working-class family. For women, however, the adult education classes had no higher a proportion of working-class students than that university: thirty-one per cent as against about one third.

Even though that survey sought to cover all types of adult education apart from that taking place in the Labour colleges, undoubtedly this does not represent everything that was taking place, since most large-membership organisations would have had some kind of educational programme in those days before mass broadcasting. For example, the only branch of British adult education that quickly did gain a significant presence in Scotland was the Women's Institutes, the first Scottish branch of which, in Longniddry in 1917, came two years after the movement's founding in Wales (Kelly 1992: 302). As early as 1925, there were 460 local institutes in Scotland with 27,500 members; by 1938–9, there were more than 1,000 institutes with 50,000 members. Women would travel many miles to hear lectures on such practical matters as housing, water supplies, sanitation, diet and child welfare. One of the early lecturers was the same Helen MacKenzie who had been involved in developing the Edinburgh School of Cookery. The institutes were particularly important in bringing adult education to women in the Highlands and the north east (Scott 1925: 228).

In the urban areas, a somewhat similar role was played by the Scottish Cooperative Women's Guild, founded in 1892 by the Cooperative movement. It grew from fourteen branches and 1,491 members in that year to 270 branches and 28,746 members in 1920, and to 421 branches and 32,854 members in 1938 (Callen 1952: 31–2). Its educational activities did have a vaguely political flavour – on the principles of cooperation, for example – but the topics of lectures and classes were broadly the same as in the Women's Institutes, dealing with such matters as the medical inspection of children, the role of school boards, and home management (Gordon 1991: 267–8). The aims were not dissimilar, in fact, to those of the WEA – the self-improvement of workers.

Another example of voluntary provision that was of enormous significance was the Sunday Schools of the presbyterian churches. They had been founded in 1787 in Aberdeen, and by 1891 included as many as fifty-two per cent of all children aged five to fifteen (Brown 1997: 64). The numbers declined slightly in the first few decades of the century, but still stood at thirty-eight per cent in 1931, which meant that as a proportion of the total population of the country, the Sunday School attenders were about eighty people in every thousand (see p. 62). That was at a time when, as we have noted in earlier chapters, attendance at secondary school was 16.8 per thousand, and at university-level courses was at most about 2.7 per thousand. The demographic reach of Sunday Schools was approaching that of primary schools, where enrolment was 137 per thousand in 1931 (SED 1939a: 88).

Probably also best thought of as part of voluntary provision were the public libraries, insofar as participation in them was not usually organised in any formal sense (Aitken 1971). The first public library in Scotland had opened in 1853, in Airdrie, as a result of the 1850 Public Libraries Act. The growth until 1918 was mainly in cities and small burghs: by 1900, forty-four burghs or parishes had adopted the provision of this Act or its successors, and by 1919 there were a further thirty-five (Aitken 1971: 349). The most important source of finance for building libraries came, again, from Carnegie, who funded fifty-six of these seventy-nine libraries (the first in 1883 being in his native Dunfermline), including twenty-eight of the thirty-five between 1901 and 1918 (Aitken 1971: 349). The 1918 Education (Scotland) Act empowered the new education authorities to establish library services, and this extended them to rural areas, still with Carnegie's help. By 1926, all but one of the then thirty-seven authorities had established a service, and Argyll followed in 1946 (Aitken 1971: 349–50). When Carnegie gave his first grant in 1883, only ten per cent of the population were living in areas with a library service. This rose to forty-six per cent in 1903, fifty per cent in 1913, eighty per cent in 1923 and 100 per cent in 1946 (Aitken 1971: 348). The public libraries gave ordinary people access to informal learning in a much more thorough way than ever before. The educational role of libraries in Scotland was probably enhanced by the relevant power's being vested in the education authorities by the 1918 Act, and some librarians reported having to work hard to overcome a perception that the libraries were primarily for schools (Aitken 1971: 104).

LABOUR COLLEGES

Beyond the education authorities, the universities, the WEA and the voluntary organisations, the only substantial providers of adult education were the Labour Colleges, quite a different sort of organisation altogether (Duncan 1992; Roberts 1970). Again, the origins were in England, at a meeting in 1908 in Oxford organised by students who formed the Plebs League after objecting to the curriculum of Ruskin College. Scottish developments followed quite soon, however. A series of meetings was held in Glasgow during 1915 and 1916 with the aim of setting up a Scottish Labour College, culminating in a conference in February 1916 that was attended by 496 delegates from 412 working-class organisations such as trades unions, trades councils, the Independent Labour Party, the British Socialist Party (predecessor of the Communist Party) and the Women's Labour League (Duncan 1992: 108). Most of the key radical figures in the Labour movement were involved, notably Helen Crawford, J. D. MacDougall, James Maxton and Willie Gallacher, but the best-known was John MacLean, whose speech to that meeting had to be read by MacDougall because MacLean was in jail for sedition. The meeting resolved to set up a College, which was opened in September 1919 in Glasgow (Roberts 1970: 52).

There were essentially three key principles. One was independence: any association with the capitalist state would corrupt the integrity of a truly working-class education. This principle was, from the beginning, a direct rejoinder to the WEA, and relations between them over the following two decades were poor. The second principle was that state education was wholly inadequate. The flavour can be had from a circular which had invited people to a planning meeting in 1915:

> the universities and other institutions for higher education have for their object the training of men and women to run capitalist society in the interests of the wealthy. We think the time has come for an independent college, financed and controlled by the working class, in which workers might be trained for the battle against the masters.
>
> (Duncan 1992: 109)

The third principle was then the response to that perception – that any working-class education worthy of the name had to be a Marxist education.

The organisational objectives included a full-time day college, but that proved impossible to organise. This failure was probably mainly due to a lack of finance rather than a lack of interest. Although only nine students were ever able to take part, one of these, John McArthur, much later recalled sitting an examination along with fifty-six other Fife miners, before being selected as one of the three students whose attendance would be paid for by their union (MacDougall 1981: 31–2). Most of the classes were therefore run in the evenings, with John MacLean's and J. D. MacDougall's being legendary (Duncan 1992: 115). MacLean, especially, seems to have been a charismatic lecturer, attracting 500 students to his economics classes in Glasgow City Halls and a further 100 to those in Govan. In 1919–20, there were Labour College classes in Aberdeen, Ayrshire, Dumbarton, Dundee, Edinburgh, Fife, Lanarkshire and Stirlingshire (Duncan 1992: 120).

Nevertheless, this movement was prone to the same kinds of schisms as affected the revolutionary left in general. MacLean's type of Marxism was increasingly at odds with the leadership, whose only hope of raising enough money was to remain on good terms with the trades unions. He was marginalised in the Labour College by 1921, and the leadership then took the decision to merge with the National Council of Labour Colleges, based at that time in Glasgow but dominated by its English branches. As it was, the unions which did give most support were from the skilled trades, and so tended to be reformist rather than revolutionary (Roberts 1970: Appendix iv–v).

The Scottish Colleges continued to grow until 1926–7, when they reached a peak in student numbers of 6,598 (Roberts 1970: Appendix ii). They then started a long process of decline, reaching 2,202 students in 1932–3. They received a brief boost in 1936 when the Scottish Trades Union Congress narrowly voted to withdraw support from the WEA, but by 1938–9 the numbers were still only 2,469, even though the STUC did not reverse its decision until 1944.

The Colleges were hampered not only by political sectarianism but also by their refusal to accept university lecturers as tutors, and by the reluctance of most school teachers to take part for fear of running into political trouble with their employers (Roberts 1970: 99). The result was a generally poor quality of teaching, one anonymous letter to *The Plebs* (magazine of the Plebs League) in 1924 alleging that there were too many 'denunciatory tirades against some monstrosity called capitalism, with oratory that descended to the commonplace and grammar that gave one the creeps' (Roberts 1970: 146). The historian of the Scottish Colleges, J. H. Roberts (1970: 188), comments that 'mastery of a subject at adult level was virtually impossible when it was considered feasible to deal, in one lecture, with the theories of Plato, Bacon, More, Hobbes, Rousseau, Comte and Spencer'.

The Labour Colleges were not the only educational organisation founded by the radical segments of the Labour movement. Another was the Socialist Sunday Schools, representatives of which attended some of the planning meetings of the Labour Colleges (Roberts 1970: 42). They had been started in Glasgow in 1896, and received the support of early socialists such as Keir Hardie MP, Bruce Glasier, later president of the Independent Labour Party, Margaret MacMillan, a child-welfare reformer, and Archie McArthur, one of Hardie's friends who became highly influential on the development of the whole Socialist Sunday School movement (Fisher 1999; Reid 1966: 23, 30). By 1900, there were seven schools in Glasgow, one in Paisley and one in Edinburgh, and in 1912 there were fifteen in Glasgow and eight in Edinburgh. Their aims were what Reid calls 'disciplined class consciousness', but that was to be achieved by moral exhortation rather than by Marxist economics, agnostic rather than militantly atheist. Therefore, as Fisher (1999: 140–1) notes, the curriculum of the schools was revolutionary only in the sense that it sought to extend to workers' children the benefits of Western culture, 'the Bible, the Greek and Roman myths, Shakespeare – as well as the Victorian "standards" such as Tennyson, Longfellow and Dickens'.

EXPLANATIONS

The picture for adult education in Scotland is patchy, then, and nearly all the various segments we have looked at here struggled to achieve their aims. The only exceptions were those voluntary organisations, such as the Women's Institutes, the Cooperative Women's Guild and the Presbyterian Sunday Schools, whose educational work was part of a wider mission. We may return, therefore, to the question we asked at the beginning of the chapter: why?

The first point to note is that technical and adult education was able to achieve more of its aims where it was most formal. In that sense, the central institutions were more successful than the continuation classes – despite potentially radical proposals such as in the 1918 Act – and both were far more successful than the WEA or the Labour Colleges. The usual interpretation, as we have seen in connection with the university extension movement, is that this was because other opportunities were available, in the degree classes of the universities and in the schools. But saying that options were available does not explain why they were preferred. There seem to be two possible explanations. One is something we have touched on frequently in connection with elementary, secondary and university education: the Scots preferred to define real education as what took place in formal institutions, and even more specifically as education in the mainstream culture of Western Europe. That did seem to be in the process of becoming more widely available through its traditional purveyors, the schools and universities, and in the most socially open of the universities, Glasgow, the proportion of working-class students was not much lower than the proportion of working-class students in the mainstream adult-education classes. Directing energies towards getting access to secondary schooling and the universities would seem therefore more attractive than experimenting with novel institutions such as the WEA or adult classes run by the universities or the education authorities, and quite definitely to be preferred to the revolutionary rhetoric of the Labour Colleges.

The other reason lies in the general cultural and educational outlook of the only political force that might have tried to create something fundamentally different, the Labour movement (Knox 1984a). Its leaders came mainly from the skilled working class (see p. 17). From that milieu they acquired a culture of respectability. They mostly favoured temperance (see p. 23). They saw their socialism in religious terms, many taking that from the United Free Church. Above all, though, they had a deep respect for a traditional conception of Scottish education, even though about two thirds of them had never attended university (see pp. 35–6). Morris (1983: 13) notes that the educational influence went deeper, through the strong presence of teachers among these socialist activists. Teachers, he points out, had many of the skills that the infant Labour movement needed – organisational, oratorical, but above all intellectual. From this set of educational views came the kind of attitude towards popular culture that was expressed elsewhere by such communist intellectuals as Antonio Gramsci: a belief that, without the refinement which could come from education, popular culture was not up to the task of creating a better society. Along with this went a very traditional kind of morality, that was, for example, much more sexist than would ever have been tolerated by the middle-class campaigners for female access to secondary schooling and university (Gordon 1991: 278). The outlook of most of these leaders made it highly unlikely that any alternative conception of adult education would prevail over the inherited tradition. They, like most other Scots, respected it, believed in its democratic potential and saw in the slow extension of access to secondary and university education the apparent confirmation that such faith was justified.

PART II

Welfare and Individualism, 1940s–1990s

The Effects of War

The effects of World War II on Scottish education were much more severe than those of the first war, but they also led to the most searching discussions of the future of education that the century had yet seen, raising hopes that all the dreams of the democratising reformers could be realised.

Lloyd (1979), concluding his definitive study of the wartime experience, describes the immediate impact as 'disastrous' (see p. 465), not only in the postponement of the reforms to secondary schooling that were to have accompanied a raising of the school leaving age in 1939, but – more importantly in the short term – through what he calls 'the trauma of evacuation', which – along with bombing – brought the impact of war into the lives of Scottish pupils to an unprecedented extent. Evacuation started at the end of August 1939, and, in its first three days alone, no fewer than 101,774 children were moved, accompanied by teachers and other helpers (Lloyd 1979: 43). By the end of September the numbers had reached 175,812. The sending areas were the cities, the towns on the lower Clyde and the towns around the naval port at Rosyth (Lloyd 1979: 83). The receiving areas were the landward parts and small burghs in the mainly rural counties, such as the north east, Argyll, the rural south west, Stirlingshire and the central Highlands.

Nevertheless, despite the size of this operation, the majority of school-children stayed behind in the cities: the proportions evacuated were forty-two per cent in Glasgow, thirty-seven per cent in Dundee and twenty-eight per cent in Edinburgh. This lack of universal evacuation in itself was divisive, as was the preference of the Scottish authorities – in the Department of Health of the Scottish Office – for moving whole families together rather than (as in England) whole schools (Lloyd 1979: 47). It is true that this was probably more humane, since few evacuees were moved on their own. A survey by William Boyd of Glasgow University found that eighty-three per cent of the children who were evacuated from Glasgow and Clydebank went with at least one other family member: forty-nine per cent went with siblings only and a further thirty-four per cent went with their mother (Boyd 1944: 91). It was educationally far more difficult, however, as we saw in Chapter 4 in connection with the problems which the education authorities faced in providing Catholic teachers for Catholic children. The concern which Catholic parents may have felt about the possible reception of their children is perhaps one reason why Boyd found that the Catholics among the children in his Clydebank survey were more likely to be accompanied by their mother (forty-two per cent) than the Protestants (thirty-three per cent), and why fifty-eight per cent of Clydebank Catholic children were not evacuated at all, as against fifty per cent of Protestant children in the town (see p. 80). Nevertheless, he also found that among Clydebank Catholic parents who chose not to send their children away, only four per cent cited religious reasons, the same as among Protestant parents (see p. 87).

Boyd also found that the reasons why some parents declined to have their children evacuated had little to do with disregarding risks from air raids (Boyd 1944: 87): only a quarter of parents who took such a decision in Glasgow and Dundee discounted these risks, and only one in ten did so in the obviously vulnerable Clydebank (with its proximity to the Clyde shipyards). The main reasons were simple reluctance to part with children or the inability of the mother to accompany them. Parents were somewhat more likely to send girls away than boys: in Clydebank and Glasgow, fifty-five per cent of girls were evacuated, as against forty-five per cent of boys (see p. 85). They were also much more willing to have older children evacuated than younger ones: in Clydebank, Glasgow and Dundee combined, forty-three per cent of children aged eleven to fourteen were evacuated, but only thirty-one per cent of those aged eight to ten, and twenty-five per cent of those aged five to seven (see p. 85).

These figures show the reluctance with which parents allowed their children to take part, and so it was not surprising that when no bombs did fall in the autumn and winter of 1939–40 children started drifting back home. By June 1940, in Dundee, Edinburgh and Glasgow, no more than about one in eight children remained away (Lloyd 1979: 53). As Boyd (1944: 77) commented, 'in a voluntary scheme of evacuation the most important single factor determining success or failure is the judgement of the parents'. However, the position changed abruptly again when Clydebank was bombed on the nights of 13–15 March 1941: by July, there were 142,000 evacuees, although this time only a minority (58,000) were children (Lloyd 1979: 119). The rolls of Glasgow schools fell from 152,000 to 113,000 between February and May. From then until the end of the war, however, the numbers of evacuees gradually fell: in June 1944, there remained only 22,238 evacuees in the whole of Scotland, 12,653 of them children (Lloyd 1979: 119).

Schools in the sending areas were severely disrupted. In December 1939, there were hardly any primary schools open in the sending areas at all, and the secondaries were managing to provide only a third of their normal classes (Lloyd 1979: 86). In March 1940, matters had improved but were far from being back to normal: a third of the primary pupils and a fifth of the secondary pupils remaining in the sending areas were not attending school, and only five per cent of primary pupils and twenty-nine per cent of secondary pupils were attending full-time (see p. 87). Things got steadily better from summer 1940 onwards: in June 1940, twenty-two per cent of all school-age children in the sending areas were in full-time education, but a year later that had grown to seventy-five per cent (Lloyd 1979: 128–30). Many schools, if they had not been disrupted by bombing, were occupied for military purposes, or simply for the purpose of providing shelter to families made homeless by the same bombing. There was an attempt, therefore, to organise home instruction schemes, mainly for pupils preparing for the Leaving Certificate (Boyd 1944: 211–19; Lloyd 1979: 55, 88, 157). The receiving areas, by contrast, coped remarkably well, with over ninety per cent of children receiving full-time education even in 1939–40, despite the arrival of evacuees (Lloyd 1979: 86).

As a proportion of all pupils in the country, the proportion receiving full-time education was seventy-three per cent in June 1940, eighty-six per cent in June 1941, and an average of around ninety-eight per cent throughout 1942 and subsequent years (Lloyd 1979: 128, 130–1). Indeed, as in World War I, the proportion taking part in secondary schooling actually rose after a slight fall in 1939–40 – from 9.3 per cent of pupils aged fifteen in 1939 to 11.3 per cent in 1945, and from 6.4 per cent of pupils aged sixteen in 1939 to 8.0 per cent in 1945 (Lloyd 1979: 203). The numbers of candidates for the Leaving Certificate also rose – from 6.3 per cent of the age cohort in 1938–9 to 7.5 per cent in 1944–5, the total number of certificates growing from 4,086 to 5,233 (see p. 204).

There was also, of course, a general sense of anxiety. An inspector commented in 1943 that:

> much of the restlessness and inattention shown by pupils of all ages
> and of all areas is hardly a matter of discipline ... [It] is a manifestation
> of the anxiety and excitement of the times. The child who knows his
> father to be in constant danger or the child who is bravely concealing
> his apprehension of air-raids may not unnaturally fail, at times, to keep
> his mind on grammar or on sums.
>
> (Lloyd 1979: 161)

Nevertheless, by the second half of the war, the inspectors were reporting that there was no evidence of long-term educational damage from evacuation, and the results of a survey conducted after the war by the Scottish Council for

Research in Education reported that there was no discernible difference in educational progress between those who had been evacuated and those who had not, or among children who had been evacuated for different lengths of time (SCRE 1958: 37). More generally, children's health almost certainly improved as a result of rationing and the maintenance of the meals and milk services in the schools: the SED reported later that, in Glasgow, the proportion of children with no physical impairments had risen from eighteen per cent in 1939 to thirty-six per cent in 1948 (Lloyd 1979: 291). Over the country as a whole, the proportion of pupils taking milk in school rose from twenty-four per cent in 1939 to sixty-four per cent in 1945 (Lloyd 1979: 297–9), and in the cities the proportion was even higher (over two thirds in all of them, and over four fifths in Glasgow).

In the universities, central institutions and colleges, the effects of the war may in fact have been somewhat less disruptive than in World War I, perhaps because, as Anderson (1988: 115) notes of the students in Aberdeen, 'in 1939, unlike in 1914, the mood was one of anxiety and dissent rather than unquestioning patriotism'. Glasgow University suffered less of a drop in student numbers than it had done in the first war – a decline of twenty per cent compared to one of thirty-three per cent (Moss et al. 2000: 199). That was partly because the student recruits were almost wholly from the Arts faculty, which was relatively smaller in 1939 that it had been in 1914; science and medical students could have their military service deferred until they graduated, on the grounds that the war effort would be better served if they had the chance to develop fully their technological skills (Moss et al. 2000: 200). For similar reasons, many local technical colleges – which were beginning to come into existence towards the end of the war – provided courses in furtherance of the war effort, such as evening class in physical optics for aircraft spotters (Cormack 1972: 417); likewise, the Workers' Educational Association provided adult education services for the armed forces (Marwick 1953: 12).

On the other hand, Glasgow University suffered directly from war in a way that it had not in 1914–18, although to a minor extent compared to some of the Clydeside schools: a bomb fell in nearby Kelvingrove Park (Moss et al. 2000: 201). In Glasgow, as elsewhere, students were recruited as fire-watchers and fire-fighters. That did include female students, but a more extensive female commitment was found in the colleges of cookery and related matters. In the Edinburgh School of Cookery, the students took part in Ministry of Labour schemes to cook for emergency harvest workers, Home Guard members, casualties in the military hospitals and ordinary citizens who had been bombed out of their homes (Begg 1994: 117). The staff were also heavily involved in providing public training in large-scale cookery (see p. 113).

All this, then, prepared the way for a mood of educational reform. The schoolteachers had begun to take on a wider, social role through necessity, and the experience of war in general, and evacuation in particular, brought different social classes into contact with each other through education as never before. The Research Council's survey in 1947 found that there were almost no social class differences in the rate of evacuation: over Scotland as a whole, the proportion of children having experienced evacuation was sixteen per cent in working-class families and fifteen per cent in middle-class families, and in the cities the proportions were, respectively, twenty-nine per cent and thirty-two per cent. The researchers commented that 'modern war is no respector of social distinctions' (SCRE 1953: 190, 356).

The initial reaction to the emerging political mood for reform by the rather conservative secretary of the SED, John Mackay Thomson, was highly cautious. For example, in January 1941 Arthur Greenwood, a member of Churchill's coalition Cabinet, circulated a memo on post-war reconstruction which included amongst its many aims 'equality of opportunity and reform of the educational system' (Addison 1975: 167). Mackay Thomson commented: 'I hope to be able to show that the Act of 1918 did nearly all that legislation can be expected to do to secure equality of educational opportunity in Scotland' (Lloyd 1979: 319).

That, however, rather disingenuously ignored the controversies which had surrounded the SED's interpretation of the Act, and so it is hardly surprising that this cautious official line could not resist the popular pressure for a new era of reform. The Secretary of State, Tom Johnston, although not particularly interested in or knowledgeable about education, saw a revived Advisory Council as the means by which he could circumvent the SED officials. In October 1942, he managed to have the sixth council appointed with a remit that gave them greater freedom from SED interference than any of their predecessors, and – as we noted in Chapter 1 – including in its membership several people who would be intellectually and politically resistant to Mackay Thomson's conservatism. During the next five years, but especially between 1945 and 1947, this council became the forum in which debate about reform could be expressed, and its reports became reference points for reformers for the following three decades or more.

The details of these post-war debates, recommendations and reforms are dealt with throughout this part of the book. Primary education (Chapter 7) continued the process of becoming gradually more child-centred, but in a cautious way that never really challenged the dominance of the teacher or of academic study. Secondary education (Chapter 8) was radically reconstructed after the mid-1960s, but then raised in an even more acute form than ever before the question of whether educational democracy needed a rethinking of what education was, or whether it could be defined as providing wide access to a tradition of general, academic learning. The universities (Chapter 9) were transformed from the 1960s onwards, shifting from an elite to a mass role, and – in a parallel to the inclusion of the Higher Grade schools in the secondary sector after 1923 – absorbed the central institutions in 1992: so, by the end of the century, the question of democracy and general education as much concerned higher education as it did the schools. Repeated attempts were made to give technical education (Chapter 10) proper recognition, most notably by the founding of a network of local technical colleges from the early 1950s onwards. They were more democratically accessible than the universities, and partly as a result they, like the central institutions before them, moved slowly in the direction of providing courses in higher education. The question of repeating a further step in the secondary reforms arose, then, for post-school education too: should colleges, former central institutions, universities and liberal adult education be recognised as a common though differentiated system of lifelong learning, just as there emerged a common system of secondary schooling after the 1930s?

All of this remained controversial, however, because the various democratic reforms, although widely accepted, continued to provoke minority dissent, most notably comprehensive secondary schooling. They were controversial, too, because of the inherited belief that true education was academic and general. That provoked opposition from the vocationalists, for whom academic education was a diversion from the needs of industry. However, it also was unattractive to a particular style of radicalism, influenced by thinking in England and America, in which academic education was little better than a middle-class, male, white conspiracy against oppressed social groups. No wonder, then, that Scottish education at the end of the century was in just as much turmoil as it had been throughout.

The main question for the second half of our period, then, is in deciding just how much of the radical vision was realised, and by what means. Summing up the work of the Council, Lloyd says that 'the remarkable birth, life and work of the Sixth Advisory Council were the unique products of the pressures of total war on a society that, in exchange for unprecedented sacrifice, required a vision of a better future' (Lloyd 1984: 113).

But, he added, 'the war ended, the vision faded, Johnston left office but the SED remained'. That pessimistic verdict is the common one that has been offered on the post-war period in writing during the last two or three decades. Whether it is fair is something which we will assess in the book's final chapter.

CHAPTER 7

Primary Education

Even though the structure of primary schooling was not in question after World War II, there was a great deal of debate about its character. The immediate occasion was the decision by the sixth Advisory Council right at the start of its proceedings in 1943 to inquire into primary education (Young 1986: 227). However, the thinking which this stimulated had a background to draw on dating from the pre-war sense that the primary school remained too rigid – a background in which several of the members of the Council had been active. William McClelland, for example, had contributed an article to the journal of the New Education Fellowship in which he argued that democracy required critical, thoughtful and self-reliant citizens, and that schools could help to achieve these ends:

> one of the social dangers of our time is the prevalence of certain qualities, for whose propagation our schools are not exempt from a measure of responsibility – qualities like submissiveness, blind receptiveness, taking one's views on trust or from tradition, susceptibility to suggestion.
>
> (McClelland 1936: 92)

If education could thus help to ensure that people would not accept totalitarian rule of any form, then the post-war era seemed the time to make the necessary reforms. As early as November 1941, the *Scottish Educational Journal* carried a series of articles, probably by Robert Rusk, director of the Scottish Council for Research in Education (Young 1986: 169). Among the ideas he proposed were the abolition of the inspectorate, in order to loosen the central control of Scottish schools, the running of individual schools along democratic lines, the erosion of the distinction among subjects, and the adopting in their place of one of the standard elements of the new educational programme – cross-curricular project work (Young 1986: 170). The EIS subsequently published a pamphlet on educational reconstruction which continued to endorse the 1939 report discussed in Chapter 3. Noting that 'psychological experiment shows that children develop by virtue of their own activity', they recommended that 'it is upon the activities of children that the school should build, offering more varied and ordered opportunities for activity than have been enjoyed in the past' (EIS 1943: 4).

POST-WAR REFORM

The report of the Council was drafted by the convener of its committee on primary education, W. D. Ritchie, who was director of education for Ayrshire (Young 1986: 252). Also on the committee were McClelland and James Robertson, who was the main author of the report on secondary education (to be discussed in Chapter 8). On the one hand, its recommendations were wholly in keeping with the pre-war debates and the wartime reforming mood (SED 1946). They criticised 'mass production' education (see p. 18), and encouraged nurseries as a 'model' for primaries (see p. 14). The report suggested that only classes which contained the 'whole normal range of ability' could allow the system to respect the individuality of all children. Such mixed-ability classes would then be grouped internally, with the teacher moving children among the groups to suit their pace of development (see p. 19). It criticised the existing curriculum as too rigid: 'the hard division between "subjects" is a logical and adult conception that is justified neither by life experience nor as a natural way of learning' (see p. 20). The atmosphere of schools was too 'academic', too 'verbal rather than real', too passive: 'children are required to sit still, listen, accept, and reproduce either orally or on paper' (see p. 20). The curriculum, then, should 'follow the child's natural line of development' (see p. 21). Accordingly, the report asserted that it was no more than a 'half truth' to claim that reading, writing and arithmetic are the foundation of the primary curriculum. The real basis ought to be 'physical education, handwork, and speech' (see p. 29).

On the other hand, firmly rooted in the ideas of the new education though this was, it was more attached to Scottish educational traditions than it claimed itself to be. The best teaching method may have been child-centred, but the aim was to socialise children into a common cultural inheritance: 'the richest of all gifts it is in our power to bestow' on a child is 'a literary education that will give him the power of communication not only with the whole of the present world but with the past and the future' (see p. 21). The allegation that there was too much 'lumber' in the curriculum was less serious than the use of inappropriate teaching methods (see p. 27). Above all, the teacher was to remain central, the guide that enabled young minds to be freed. In the study of literature, for example, the means should be more child-centred: 'the teacher should [not] try to get the cheap satisfaction of trying to "mould" character' (see p. 58). But the end should be the learning of a culture. The committee included a whole chapter on 'Scottish traditions' – both on defining them and on suggesting how they should be taught, and recommending that children understand the richness and complexity of Scottish culture, rejecting the caricature of Scottishness as 'meanness, smugness or maudlin sentimentality' (see p. 74). To this and other ends of educating children to exercise their judgement, one of the main tools would be the study and discussion of literature. 'By inducing the children to talk freely and frankly', the teacher leads them to 'sound thought and imagination', and to 'delicacy in the valuing of words, in the appreciation of things, in their own thinking and emotions, in their acts and utterances' (see pp. 58–9). For the primary school, this is the social use of English that – as we saw in Chapter 4 – had come to be the main source of the principles of moral philosophy in the secondary curriculum too.

If it would be quite inaccurate, therefore, to portray this report as a manifesto for educational liberation, it is also misleading to describe the official response as only conservative. The SED in fact endorsed the report in its Circular 122 of 1947, noting that most of the recommendations were for teachers, schools and education authorities, rather than for national policy-making (Young 1986: 353). In response to the report, the inspectorate did, however, produce in 1950 its first-ever unified set of recommendations on the primary curriculum; this became the guiding policy until the late 1960s (SED 1950). It is true that the inspectors re-asserted the fundamental importance of reading, writing and arithmetic (see p. 7), but that was immediately followed by a recognition and implicit endorsement of two radical changes. 'It is now increasingly recognised that the school should be "child centred" and not "curriculum centred"', so that the means by which children learn may be as important as what they learn. The other change was that 'it is recognised that the school is not concerned solely with preparing children for adult life, but must also make its contribution to their well-being and happiness as children' (see p. 7). Likewise, although the 1950 report placed the teacher and the curriculum at the centre of the school's activities, the manner in which that should happen was different only in emphasis from that which was recommended by the Advisory Council: for example, 'the teacher should contrive situations in which the pupil will learn from experience' (see p. 22), a view which was close to the Council's recommendations about fostering delicacy of judgement. In several respects, the differences between the two documents were rhetorical rather than real. Thus, on arithmetic, the inspectors recommended that 'accuracy is the prime essential' (see p. 62), whereas the Advisory Council seemed to give much greater prominence to its cultural significance: 'the development of Arithmetic is an essential part of the story of civilisation'

(SED 1946: 35). But, in fact, the Council also said that 'accuracy is the crux of success in Arithmetic' (see p. 38), and the inspectors acknowledged a cultural significance for the subject too: 'arithmetic is the basis of all human activities that involve any form of quantitative measurement' (SED 1950: 62). They, like the Council, also saw the goal of arithmetic teaching as being understanding, not just mechanical dexterity: 'long and laborious sums should not be given', and the teacher's practice in correcting errors should ensure 'that the pupil understands how to avoid making them in future' (SED 1950: 71–2). The inspectorate's document also managed both to endorse corporal punishment and to discourage its use: although the teacher 'should serve as a model in behaviour' and should encourage 'self-respect and self-discipline', corporal punishment 'may be salutory in its effects' (see pp. 97, 98, 110).

As a result, the primary school in the 1950s and 1960s represented a mixture of progressivism and the academic tradition. Perhaps the strongest evidence of the persistence of traditional attitudes was in the growing use of formal tests of attainment. In fact, that, too, had been recommended by the Advisory Council, although with the caveat that tests should be developed to measure achievement in handwork and physical activities (SED 1946: 121–2). In its annual reports throughout the 1950s, the SED commended the use of tests to enable the efficient transfer of pupils from primary to secondary. Thus, as Bain (1995: 147–8) notes, in 1952 written tests in English composition were regarded as 'entirely salutary' (SED 1953: 28), and cautious concern was expressed in 1958 that some parts of the country were moving away from such tests (SED 1959: 12).

One aspect of this was the continuing dominance of the written word, a matter over which the inspectors expressed recurrent concern. In 1955, they noted that 'in English, ... oral work is not sufficiently emphasised' (SED 1956: 11). In 1959, they noted that 'teachers are finding that their pupils enjoy [the] opportunity for self-expression unhampered by premature insistence on the niceties of spelling and grammar' (SED 1960: 14), and in 1962 they welcomed 'a growing realisation of the importance of oral English', but 'in oral and in written work there are still not enough opportunities of using English as a medium of expression and the stimulus which comes from the child's own desire to convey information' (SED 1963: 15–16).

The inspectors' aim, however, was to have oral and imaginative work recognised as being part of academic education, not a challenge to it. For example, their criticism of arithmetic teaching in their 1962 report was of its excessively mechanical character, not of the intellectual principles which they had laid down in their 1950 recommendations: 'the teaching of arithmetic continues to suffer from over-emphasis on mechanical perfection to the detriment of understanding of the processes involved and of the subject's relevance to practical situations' (SED 1963: 16).

Developing group work was part of this process of modifying the curriculum. In 1954, the inspectors suggested that the full benefits of the 1950 policy would not be realised 'until group and individual methods are used more extensively' (SED 1955a: 21), and by 1959 they were reporting that group work had become more common (SED 1960: 14). In that year, they also noted that group work improved the academic performance of pupils, preparing more of them for entry to the main programmes of the junior and senior secondary courses (as discussed on p. 14). They also complained, however, about a lack of adequate stimulation for the most able pupils: 'the difference between their work and that of the average pupils is too often one of quantity rather than one of quality' (also on p. 14).

The general response from education authorities was to encourage freedom guided by teachers. One report, in Glasgow, endorsed the 'activity curriculum' and proposed that the characteristics of the child should determine the working of the school (Jardine 1955: 5). However, it also continued to give the teacher and the curriculum the leading role in enabling the child to flourish. Central to this was the 'scheme of work', which would guide the teacher in 'organising the work of the class' (Jardine 1955: 7). The role of the teacher was 'to draw together and reduce to order by set lessons the knowledge, incomplete and unorganised, acquired by pupils through the study of different topics, and thus to ensure assimilation and a high standard of work' (Jardine 1955: 8).

The evidence we have about these policy developments suggests that they did lead to an overall improvement in the learning that went on in primary schools. The Scottish Council for Research in Education carried out surveys of the whole age-ten cohort of primary pupils in 1953 (about 76,000 in all), and about 5,000 pupils aged ten in 1963, and found a gain in all four domains they measured – mechanical arithmetic, arithmetical reasoning, English usage and English comprehension (SCRE 1968: 53). The gains could be expressed as the number of months of learning by which the average pupil aged ten had advanced in the decade: 3.9 in mechanical arithmetic, 5.2 in arithmetical reasoning, 7.6 in English usage and 6.2 in English comprehension (see p. 57). Boys and girls made similar gains (see p. 61). There were gains at all levels of measured prior attainment. For English, the greatest gains were for those whose attainment was lowest initially: for the bottom third of that distribution, the improvement over the decade was equivalent to around one whole year of schooling (see p. 61). For arithmetic, however, the greatest gains were made by those at around the middle of the distribution of prior attainment. Gains were similar in different areas of the country (see p. 62). Although the report did not record gains by social class, the spatial similarities and the extension of gains to all levels of prior attainment suggest that the most disadvantaged social classes benefited at least equally.

In the light of all the various pieces of official advice, and of the research evidence of rising attainment, it was hardly surprising, then, that teachers and the inspectorate inferred that a combination of child-centredness with maintaining the authority of the teacher and the coherence of the curriculum could lead to significant gains for all kinds of pupil.

SCOTTISH CHILD-CENTREDNESS IN THEORY

The apparent revolution that was inaugurated in 1965 was therefore much less real than it was supposed at the time, or than its detractors and supporters have claimed since. In that year, the SED issued *Primary Education in Scotland*, a document that has ever since been referred to as simply the Primary Memorandum. This was undoubtedly a great novelty in at least one respect: as Farquharson (1985: 24–5) notes, it was 'the first time that a document of this kind was not produced entirely and anonymously by the Inspectorate'. The committee had a majority of inspectors and teachers (as opposed to SED officials and academics), some of the latter with long experience of trying to put student-centred ideas into practice. For example, Ian Morris, an inspector on the committee, recalled that one of the teacher members, Jack Smith, had started his teaching career in a Juvenile Instruction Centre in Glasgow, and through that had come to support student-centredness as a way of engaging disaffected young people with education (Morris 1994: 92–3). On the other hand, although there were only nine inspectors out of a total membership of twenty, all the other members had been selected by the inspectorate (Morris 1990: 25), and the inspectors dominated proceedings (Farquharson 1985: 25).

The Memorandum was described at the time as revolutionary also in its content (Osborne 1966: 120), and certainly some of its language was quite radically different from the tone of its 1950 predecessor. The child entering the primary school at age five was now thought of as being naturally active, as already an individual, and as having play as his or her 'characteristic mode of learning' (SED 1965a: 5). The child also had a 'curiosity about the world', and a 'desire to learn'. The detailed recommendations in specific areas of the curriculum also seeemed revolutionary. Mathematics, for example, was placed under the heading of 'environmental studies', and was seen as providing understanding of those aspects of the environment 'which are best expressed in terms of number or which show qualities of regularity, order, pattern, structure or form' (see p. 145). Likewise, English – which was under 'language arts' – was first 'to encourage fluent self-expression in speech and in writing'.

So the least that can be said is that the Memorandum sanctioned many new ways of talking about the primary curriculum. On the other hand, we would be quite mistaken to see it as the eventual implementation of the most radical ideas on child-centredness that the new educationalists were advocating in the 1930s. Ian Morris noted that in its work, 'the concept of child-centred education ... had to be tempered with effective learning' (Morris 1990: 26). Much of the dicussion inside the committee seems to have been not about the autonomy of the child but about what Farquharson (1985: 27) calls 'the compatibility or otherwise of the needs of the child and the needs of society'. There could, then, be no question of the child being given complete freedom: in the words of D. M. Whyte, a member who was a primary head teacher in Forfar, the belief was that 'the child-centred approach works best when it is carefully programmed – structured, if you like' (Farquharson 1985: 29).

The outcome of this tension in the document was as evident as the support for child-centredness. The child of age five would continue to be governed by 'emotion' rather than 'intellect', and so the school had to provide the discipline without which effective education could not happen. That was the main justification for pupil autonomy offered by the Memorandum – not as a moral good in itself, but as a means to the end of sound learning, and indeed sound citizenship:

> where children have an active part in their own learning, where they feel secure in the knowledge that they can achieve success and have a particular place in class and school activities, where they understand the routine and rules which order their lives, where the school is an interesting place to come to and they can accept the teachers as their friends, they readily develop not only the qualities of character which they need as individuals but also the qualities of conduct which living with others demands.
>
> (SED 1965a: 90)

This was to be fostered not only by fair systems of discipline in the sense of behaviour, but also – for all the interest in projects and cross-curricular themes – by the continuing importance of discipline in the academic sense. Thus, although self-expression may now have been seen as the first objective of English, that was the means to effective communication, intelligent listening and reading thoughtfully and critically (SED 1965a: 97). Likewise, although 'corporal punishment should not be necessary in the modern primary school', the document does not argue for its being abandoned altogether: 'the use of this sanction ... is a matter essentially for the professional judgment of teachers' (see p. 91).

The committee was therefore grappling with concerns that would have been familiar to the Advisory Council in its work on its 1946 report. One of the standard criticisms of the Memorandum therefore seemed to miss the Scottish historical point. For example, McEnroe argued in 1983 that the radicalism of the document was merely rhetorical, since in fact, despite 'frequent references to liberal sentiments, [it] envisages education as an instrument for promoting the value-system of a reified society' (McEnroe 1983: 244). It was precisely because the Memorandum was not as thorough a revolution as its language sometimes might appear to imply that it may be understood as a growth from the prior thinking in the earlier SED document of 1950, in the 1946 report and in the EIS's 1939 recommendations for reforming the primary school. All of these were attempts to reconcile the ideas of child-centredness with the very Scottish belief in the value of structured learning, acquired in institutions under the guidance of academically respectable teachers. The tensions between the individual and tradition in all these reports are, then, the historical products of the tensions within a national tradition, not the ideological obfuscation of which they are accused by their detractors.

SCOTTISH CHILD-CENTREDNESS IN PRACTICE

The simultaneous presence in the 1965 memorandum of new educationalist ideas and quite traditional respect for the teacher and the curriculum then helps to explain the peculiarly Scottish version of child-centredness that emerged over the following two decades.

There seems little doubt, on the one hand, that the Memorandum encouraged the process that was already underway of making the primary classroom less rigid. The inspectors reported in their 1970 review that the Memorandum had had a 'significant' influence on primary education, 'and the work of the schools has been informed and enlivened as a result of its suggestions' (SED 1971a: 11). The report of the following year described the situation as 'consolidation' (SED 1972a: 7), and from then until the end of the decade the SED annual reports make no mention of the topic (and these reports themselves were discontinued after 1979).

On the other hand, the continuity with tradition comes across more clearly than any sense of radical change. The definitive inspectorate summary was published a decade and a half after the Memorandum (SED 1980). Teachers, they reported, were inclined to narrow the curriculum rather than broaden it (as discussed on p. 46), partly because of what the inspectors claim was 'public concern about standards', and partly because of 'Scotland's traditional success in teaching "the basics"' (see p. 47). There was 'little evidence of activity learning' (see p. 45), and most teachers were 'reluctant to foster too much pupil independence and responsibility' (see p. 49). The inspectors then presented a vignette of what they saw as a typical Scottish primary teacher, which included this:

> she works extremely hard, seeing her task as being to interpose
> herself between her pupils and what they ought to be learning ...
> [She] expounds knowledge with care and precision, maintaining a
> stable if at times soporific atmosphere through her direct control of
> events.
>
> (SED 1980: 45)

Other surveys were coming to similar conclusions. One was carried out in 1975 by T. R. Bone, the principal of Jordanhill College of Education, and T. D. Morrow, a lecturer there, and was reported in the *Times Educational Supplement Scotland*, which – just as the EIS's *Scottish Educational Journal* had been in the first half of the century – was becoming the main forum in which Scottish educational policy was publicly discussed (Bone and Morrow 1975a,b,c). They rejected what they saw as a false dichotomy between traditional and child-centred education, and described the emerging Scottish approach as a 'third style'. As they pointed out, the traditional style had been frequently caricatured by its critics, and in reality 'very few traditionally minded teachers have ever forgotten that they were dealing with children, even if differences between them were minimally recognised in practice' (Bone and Morrow 1975a). As we have seen, this is probably an accurate description of the Scottish primary school as it developed between the 1930s and the 1960s. They also suggested that Scottish teachers would be resistant to 'excessive individualisation of the curriculum', and that 'extreme instances of the progressive approach have proved intellectually offensive to the Scots in general'. That is certainly consistent with the results of the inspectors' 1980 survey. The emerging Scottish approach, they said, provided a 'balance between the requirements of society and the needs of children' (Bone and Morrow 1975b). The child-centred movement had brought great gains, they agreed, especially in understanding how children learn (Bone and Morrow 1975c). However, the teacher must retain an important shaping role,

> to provide opportunities for active learning by children, with areas
> of freedom for them to explore in accordance with their own interests
> and abilities, but within an organised framework, with a planned
> sequence of experience which is progressively more taxing of their
> skills.
>
> (Bone and Morrow 1975c)

None of this should really have come as a surprise to anyone who was aware of the Scottish context. Farquharson (1990: 32) quotes Bourdieu's comment (1971: 204) that:

> the educational system ... is deeply marked by its particular history
> and capable of moulding the minds of those who are taught and those
> who teach both through the content and spirit of the culture it conveys
> and through the methods by which it conveys it.

She was not enthusiastic about this, and saw the only partial adoption of the child-centred approach as a symptom of Scotland's 'subordinate' position in capitalism and in the Union with England (see pp. 34–5), but whatever the validity of that, the point about the shaping effect of history seems the best way of understanding how Scotland came to its compromised adoption of child-centredness.

COMMON CURRICULUM

This ambivalence also then helps to explain the development of the primary school in the 1980s and 1990s. The largely uninterrupted Scottish inclination to support a planned curriculum and an attention to academic learning laid the ground for ideas about a national curriculum, even though these were coming from a Conservative government that was seen as being out of step with Scottish educational principles. But, at the same time, the very fact that Scottish child-centredness had been adopted in such a partial way probably made it resistant to the onslaught from the New Right.

The politicisation of these debates was itself new, since – in contrast to events in secondary education, as we will see in Chapter 8 – primary schooling was largely not a matter of political controversy until the 1980s. The idea of a 'balanced' curriculum in Scotland did not, in fact, have its roots in Conservative thinking at all. One of the earliest proposals was for the secondary sector, in the Munn report of 1977 (something which, again, we discuss in the next chapter). For primaries, the SED-sponsored National Committee on Primary Education proposed in 1983 a balance of subjects and also a balance of 'skills, activities, social experiences' (CCC 1983: 19). Similarly, in 1986, another official committee had proposed a common curriculum for ages ten to fourteen (thus spanning the divide between primary and secondary), recommending what Brian Boyd called 'autonomy within guidelines' (Boyd 1994: 21; CCC 1986b). The government, however, found this too consensual, and so tried to introduce a stronger prescribed curriculum for the full age range five to fourteen, and, controversially, with a requirement that pupils be tested in standard ways at ages eight and twelve (Adams 1997, 1999; Kirk and Glaister 1994).

The reaction to the policy – both politically and educationally – had two aspects, and illustrates the precarious co-existence of pupil autonomy and constraints in the Scottish tradition here. On the one hand, and most politically visible, there was resistance, culminating in the most widespread educational rebellion since the refusal of parents and teachers in the 1920s to accept the SED's narrow interpretation of the implications of the 1918 Act (see Chapter 4 above). The source of the dissatisfaction lay in a perception that the government's imposed changes were unnecessary precisely because Scottish reforms in earlier decades had been cautious. As it was put by a former inspector, and former senior adviser in Lothian Region, Bill Gatherer, Scottish teachers and parents 'share the "classical" educationist's desire for structure, and so they welcome conformity and the tightly organised system of curriculum control which is characteristic of Scottish education' (Gatherer 1990: 69).

The objections focused on the testing proposals (Brown 1990). In a cleverly orchestrated campaign in the late 1980s, the EIS and various organisations representing parents argued that Scotland had never abandoned the regular assessment of pupils, and that these proposals would be intrusive on good educational practice in which the teacher ought to decide how and when to assess. During the first period in which the tests were supposed to run, spring 1991, the coalition opposed to the tests organised a boycott. In a survey by the *Times Educational Supplement Scotland* (21 June 1991: 1), it was reported that only about forty-eight per cent of the 120,000 children who were eligible to sit the tests had in fact done so. Near complete testing happened only in a few places: for example in Borders, the authority had threatened to discipline teachers if they refused to take part. In Grampian, a small majority (fifty-two per cent) was tested. Elsewhere, the proportions tested were small – thirty-three per cent in the large Strathclyde Region, thirty per cent in Highland Region, twenty-nine per cent in Central, twenty-one per cent in Lothian and sixteen per cent in Fife. Although part of this was because teachers were boycotting the tests, it seems clear that they had parents on their side. Particularly important were the school boards which the government had set up after 1989, elected by parents of current pupils and by teachers, with parents in the majority. Not for the first time in the century, Scottish parents were not very impressed by the intentions of national government, and parental members of boards turned out in general to be respectful of teachers' judgement (Munn 1993: 91–5). The *Times Educational Supplement Scotland* (10 May 1991: 3) reported that eighty-five per cent of the primary-school boards in Lothian Region objected to the tests, and that a survey of parents of eligible children conducted by Highland Region had found that sixty-one per cent objected.

The EIS's own survey of Glasgow parents concluded that some eighty-five per cent had withdrawn their children from the tests, and that across Strathclyde as a whole the figure was sixty-eight per cent (*Scottish Educational Journal* May 1991). The result of all this was that the tests were withdrawn after the 1992 general election, being replaced by a form of testing in which teachers would chose when to test a child.

On the other hand, despite the controversy, the curriculum – described emolliently as the 5–14 'guidelines' rather than a national curriculum – was accepted with little fuss. As Adams (1999: 358) notes, the document which launched it in 1987 (SED 1987) did not criticise teaching methods. It was mainly concerned with arguing for a broad curriculum that would be fairly standard across the country, and that would stipulate ways in which children's progress could be assessed by teachers and communicated to parents. The main elements of the curriculum would be English, mathematics and 'environmental studies', a vast area that included science and social subjects. Later there were policies on religious and moral education, the only area in which the Catholic schools developed their own distinctive approach.

By the early 1990s, most schools were reporting that the policy had led to their changing the content of what was taught (Adams 1997: 69–71). This relative smoothness of implementation was partly because of the relative autonomy of the policy process in Scotland, able to modify the intentions of the Conservative government in ways that would be acceptable to Scottish teachers and parents. As a former director of education in Tayside Region, David Robertson, forecast in 1990, much would depend on how the political instructions were interpreted by the specialist committees and the professionals, 'how it is translated into regulations and advisory circulars, and how all this guidance is reacted to and translated into action by teachers in schools' (Robertson 1990: 94). There was also a great deal of continuing emphasis on the teacher's role in encouraging children's self-belief (SCCC 1996: 4), security (see p. 7) and independent and group learning (see pp. 8, 10), and there was advice that teachers had to maintain order and establish an effective climate for learning:

> there is also a need to maintain consistency so that learners know what they are doing and what is expected of them, but to allow for spontaneity so that they feel able to take risks, to explore and to think creatively.
>
> (SCCC 1996: 19)

Much the same approach could be found in the guidelines on how schools could help children's personal and social development (SCCC 1995).

In practice, research did indeed find resistance to those aspects of the guidelines that teachers judged not to be consistent with their conventional practice: thus Swann and Brown (1997: 91) concluded that the policy was modified in practice to fit with teachers' 'existing ideas about their day-to-day teaching and the extent to which they regard the new policy as desirable and practical'. Despite their earlier enthusiasm for child-centredness, the inspectorate never really dissented from this compromise, and certainly did not do so by the 1990s. It found between 1992 and 1995 that a majority of Scottish primary schools 'encouraged pupils to be increasingly independent in their learning', but also that this was achieved by the schools' providing 'a purposeful working environment which encouraged varied teaching methods' and 'well-chosen learning activities' (SOEID 1996a: 7). Bourdieu's comment about the force of history seems as apposite here as it was in describing Scottish reaction to the most radical versions of the ideas of child-centredness.

Probably another reason why the curricular changes were accepted during the 1990s with little demur was some evidence that the academic attainment of primary pupils might no longer have been as satisfactory as it apparently had been until the 1960s. The main source of this was a series of surveys collectively known as the Assessment of Achievement Programme (Stark et al. 1997). Although most of the weaknesses which they found were in the first two years of secondary, in some areas of the curriculum, such as mathematics, there seemed to be evidence of decline compared to earlier years, or at least a halting of previously upward trends in attainment (Maclellan 1999: 375). The doubts were then reinforced by the results of the Third International Mathematics and Science Study, reporting in 1997, which seemed to find that Scottish pupils were no better than average when compared to other developed countries – out of twenty-one countries, thirteenth in mathematics and eleventh in science (Maclellan 1999: 376; SOEID 1997c). The validity was disputed: for example, the Scottish children in the samples were, on average, almost two years younger than the children in some of the countries that came near the top of the list, even though the same test was given in every country. When the performance of children who were all aged nine was compared, Scotland appeared in a much better position: in mathematics it came eighth out of twenty-one, and in science it was fifth. Scotland's ranking varied across particular aspects of mathematics (although not science): it was relatively poor in whole numbers (sixteenth) but very good in geometry (second). The importance of age was seen also in the fact that the gain in performance by Scottish children between primaries four and five was above the average gain in the other countries (Maclellan 1999: 376). Nevertheless, the criticisms received widespread publicity, and the sense was reinforced that a more formal organisation of the curriculum was required.

STRUCTURED INDIVIDUALISM

Developments in the 1980s and 1990s may therefore be understood as an evolution of the dominant Scottish tradition of autonomy within firm social constraints, rather than as a distortion of pure child-centredness by the New Right. This interpretation is confirmed by the further growth through the 1980s and 1990s of attention to individual learning, even though usually in an ambiguous way: if the Conservative government really had fundamentally displaced Scottish practice, then this kind of growing individualism could never have happened. Six topics may illustrate this – on teaching methods, discipline, gender, special educational needs, Gaelic and nurseries.

The child-centred approach was actually given new support by research from the USA and elsewhere on how children learn, notably Howard Gardner's work on 'multiple intelligences', recognising forms of intelligence other than the linguistic and the mathematical (SCCC 1996: 5). Such ideas had been commonplace in the thinking of the new educationalists earlier in the century, but the basis of Gardner's and others' conclusions in research gave new rhetorical force to them. Similar views were found in the official advice on child guidance (Macbeath 1988; SCCC 1995). However, there were then many suggestions that radical reform to pedagogy and the curriculum was required before these ideas would be taken seriously (for example, Bloomer 2001). As well as the attention to emotional development in the 1980s and 1990s, schools began to use a more varied set of teaching materials, for example through broadcast programmes, computers and (eventually) the Internet. In 1982–3, for example, ninety-two per cent of primary schools had a colour television (Macintyre 1984: 69). By the end of the century, around half of primaries had computers that were less than four years old, and about half had access to the Internet (Scottish Executive 2000: 3, 6).

This more sympathetic treatment of children accompanied the final ending of corporal punishment in the early 1980s, the second topic. As encouraged by the 1965 Memorandum, there had been a slow movement towards abolition. Thus its 'gradual elimination' was recommended by a new code of principles on discipline drawn up by the SED, the headteachers and the directors of education in 1968 (McNally 1982: 28). For the first time, systematic evidence was gathered on the extent of corporal punishment: in research carried out for the EIS, eighty-four per cent of boys and fifty-seven per cent of girls at secondary school said that they had been belted when they were in primary school (Pollock et al. 1977: 20). Phasing out was endorsed by the EIS (McNally 1982: 32) and by an SED committee on discipline (SED 1977c: 53–5). The eventual legal ban, however, came as the result of a challenge to the practice by parents of children in Strathclyde Region, whose case was endorsed by the European Court of Human Rights in 1982 (*Western European Education* 1985).

That Region had in fact banned corporal punishment just before the ruling, as had Lothian Region, and legislation followed in 1986 (Darling 1999: 35–6; McNally 1982: 31).

On gender – the third topic – a slow and ambivalent transformation began to take place in official attitudes. The curricular recommendations during the 1940s, 1950s and 1960s had maintained the Scottish practice (which we noted first in Chapter 3) of largely ignoring gender. The 1946 report of the Advisory Council, for example, started with the usual injunction to the reader to interpret the male pronouns as including primary pupils of both sexes (SED 1946: 1). Occasionally it noted in passing that men and women had common require-ments from education: for example, 'what is needed by the ordinary man or woman is . . .', followed by a list of the principles of arithmetic teaching (see p. 36). In those parts of the report which dealt with the central purposes of education – for example, on reading comprehension – no differentiation was made at all (pp. 56–9). Only in relation to subjects which Scottish society would have expected to have been segregated was there any explicit comment: for example, it was suggested that boys and girls could be taught needlework together until age nine (see p. 34). Much the same general ignoring of gender in relation to the core aspects of the curriculum was true of the SED's 1950 recommendations on the primary curriculum and the 1965 Memorandum, although on the periphery of academic work there was still seen to be a need to treat boys and girls differently (SED 1965a: 170). In contrast to all this, the 5–14 programme did include attention to gender issues for the first time, although in ways which Turner et al. (1995: 9) described as add-ons. The Sex Discrimination Act of 1975 outlawed deliberate segregation by gender, and may have helped to change the climate slowly. Nevertheless, although these were real changes, the traditions remained strong. As Turner et al. (1995: 147) conclude on gender in primaries: 'the belief in tailoring provision to the individual child in ways described as "gender blind" diverted thinking from political and structural features'.

This only reluctant attention to gender in the curriculum may partly have been because men continued to occupy disproportionately the highest-status posts. By the 1950s, women already made up over four-fifths of primary teach-ers, and this grew even further – eighty-four per cent in 1956 (the year after equal pay for men and women had, in principle, been accepted by the SED), eighty-eight per cent in 1971, ninety-two per cent in education authority schools in 1994 (SED 1957: 141; 1972c: 150; SOEID 1996c: 5). Even by 1994, however, the proportion of women among headteachers of education authority primary schools was only seventy-three per cent.

The mood of the 1970s and 1980s also encouraged a growth in proper provi-sion for children with special educational needs, the fourth topic concerning child-centredness. The SED had set up four working parties to consider the

matter in the 1960s (Petrie 1978: 9), and in an Act of 1969 education authorities were required to assess the needs of such children periodically and with
techniques that were not only medical (as discussed on p. 11). They were
required also to establish child guidance clinics. Most importantly, as Petrie
(1978: 11) notes, the Act redefined special education, moving away from the
notion of dealing with a fixed disability, to what it called 'education by special
means appropriate to the requirements of pupils whose physical, intellectual,
emotional or social development cannot . . . be adequately promoted by ordinary methods of education'. The SED abolished the category 'remedial
teacher', replacing it with 'learning support', and there began to emerge the
view that these teachers might be involved in the education of a wide range of
children, not only those with specific disabilities. The 1980 Education
(Scotland) Act maintained this momentum, by requiring that education
authorities develop a 'record of needs' for children with 'pronounced, specific
or complex special educational needs', and by 1993 the number of children
whose needs were recorded in this way had grown by a quarter (Closs 2000:
202). Since the proportion of children who were educated in special schools
did not change much – being between one and two per cent from 1950 to
1995 – the growth was mainly of pupils who were in mainstream schools
(Closs 2000: 203). In 1995, there were almost equal numbers of special schools
(201) and specialist units in mainstream schools (210), providing, in all, for
some 9,000 pupils (Closs 2000: 203).

Developments in Gaelic-medium education – the fifth topic – can also be
interpreted as indicating a growing respect for the learner. All the post-1945
official reports had expressed support for Gaelic, and thus had continued in the
spirit of the 1918 Act. The 1965 Memorandum, while continuing to insist that
'children have to be taught English' and that teaching in the medium of Gaelic
was therefore an aspect of respecting 'the needs and interests of the pupils',
also recognised the value of Gaelic itself, and encouraged schools to foster its
health (SED 1965a: 199, 201). A survey by the Scottish Council for Research
in Education in 1958 found the language to be dying out as a medium of
expression among children on the mainland (SCRE 1961): the only mainland
districts with more than one in twenty primary-age children having Gaelic as
their first language were Ardnamurchan (twenty per cent) and Lochcarron
(thirteen per cent). On the islands, however, the proportions were higher: over
eighty per cent in the southern Outer Hebrides, sixty-six per cent in Lewis,
fifty-one per cent in Skye, forty per cent in Coll and Tiree and seventeen per
cent in Islay (see pp. 70–1). In all the islands and northern counties, a total of
4,848 primary children were being taught Gaelic, in 211 schools, down from
5,234 in 1951 and 6,944 in 1935 (see p. 74). As a proportion of all primary-age
pupils in the counties (see p. 72), this meant that twenty per cent were studying
Gaelic, probably fewer than the third or so in the 1930s (see Chapter 3 above).

In 1958, 1,257 children, or about five per cent in these counties, were being taught other subjects through the medium of Gaelic. In the first two years of primary in the Gaelic-speaking areas, over two thirds of classes were taught mainly in English (discussed on p. 73).

Only when the language went into apparently precipitious decline in the 1970s and 1980s did the movement to extend Gaelic-medium education get going, and only from the late-1980s did it receive government financial support (Robertson 1999). The main political change was the setting up in 1975 of a separate local government unit covering the whole of the Outer Hebrides, Comhairle nan Eilean. It launched a Gaelic-medium project, and was followed in 1978 by a Highland Regional Council project in Skye. In 1993–4, there were forty-five Gaelic-medium primary schools, teaching 1,080 children, although a few of these were in the Lowlands where enthusiasm for learning the language had begun to grow; this had increased to fifty-nine schools and 1,831 pupils in 1999–2000 (Scottish Executive 2002). Gaelic-medium nurseries had also expanded, from three catering for fifty-four pupils in 1993–4 to thirty-three with 276 pupils in 1999–2000: the national Gaelic guidelines that had been issued as part of the 5–14 programme expressed concern at the erosion of children's fluency in Gaelic in English-language environments (Robertson 1999: 246).

In contrast to the attention given to Gaelic, however, there was very little encouragement given to the development of bilingual education in the other minority languages that had, by the 1990s, become quite widespread (SCCC 1994). The school census of 1990 found that around three per cent of school-age children had a home language other than English (Mackinnon 1995–6: 117a). Of these the main language of the home was Gaelic for only sixteen per cent of primary-age children. It was Punjabi for twenty-eight per cent, Urdu for thirteen per cent, Cantonese for nine per cent, Arabic for five per cent and English for nine per cent. The situation was similar for secondary pupils, although many more of them (thirty-nine per cent) used English as the main language at home because speakers of languages other than the Asian ones had, by that age, come to use English. The persistence of the Asian languages into the secondary stages suggested that these language communities had become sufficiently strong in the cities to sustain an independent existence.

The final example of the ways in which ideas on a cautious child-centredness were strengthened was the growth of nurseries. The sheer scale of this was striking, as we summarised in Chapter 2, from under ten per cent of four-year-olds in 1970 to ninety-seven per cent in 2001. Part of the reason was a wider change in gender roles, especially the growing proportion of mothers who were taking up paid employment after having children. This growth, then, did not represent straightforwardly a growing enthusiasm for a changed view of how young children should be educated. There remained a widespread belief that proper nurseries should be structured and preparatory to education. This caused controversy during the 1980s, especially in Strathclyde, where more radical advocates of nurseries as providing play and nurturing found themselves frustrated by what they saw as educational conservativism. Helen Penn, who led that section of Strathclyde education authority, invoked Robert Owen in support of the view that the purpose of nurseries was to foster 'the intellectual, emotional and moral development of children, and the liberation of women' (Penn 1992: 2). However, she concluded pessimistically that Scottish nurseries tended to be structured, children's activities being directed by staff, and suspicious of, as she put it, children running wild (see p. 86). She was probably correct that this view was widely held. For example, the spokeswoman of Strathclyde nursery teachers was reported in the *Times Educational Supplement Scotland* on 14 June, 1991 (on p. 1) as saying that 'in areas [of social deprivation], children need firm foundations to give them a head start', a view that received official encouragement in the 1990s by the growth of programmes of 'early intervention' – concentrating attention in the early years on teaching children to read and write (Scottish Executive 1999). This was believed to be particularly effective for children who had little parental support for their learning at home, a belief that received some support from research (Fraser et al. 2001: 43–4).

Thus the official view of teaching and learning for ages three to about seven remained that structure was necessary in order to encourage children's creativity. In the guidance on the nursery curriculum for children aged three to five, there was a great deal of child-centredness: for example, young children coming to nursery are 'active, experienced learners with a natural curiosity ... unique individuals eager to make sense of their world, to develop relationships and to extend their skills' (SCCC 1999: 3). However, all this was to happen under adult guidance: 'adults should support or extend the learning experience, increase its level of challenge or channel children's interests into a broader or more balanced set of learning experiences' (see p. 44). This was freedom, but very definitely licensed freedom.

These developments concerning teaching styles, discipline, gender, special education, Gaelic and nurseries show that, alongside the common curriculum, there continued to grow – partially but quite definitely – some of the attention to individual learning that had been an interest of reformers throughout the century. The main implication of the new education in Scotland, therefore, was to reform schools, not to end them. The outcome was what could be called structured individualism, freedom constrained by the needs of socialisation. This all may seem an odd mixture if the individualism of the new education early in the century is contrasted with the market individualism that was promulgated by the New Right (Hartley 1987). However, it is doubtful if Scots ever saw it that way. Scottish primary education was more individualistic than ever before, and – in the 1980s and 1990s – Scots had little difficulty in reconciling Conservative government intentions with the trends that were already well underway. However, they also had little difficulty in accepting that this freedom should be guided by adults and by policy, especially if that policy were made by professionals rather than by politicians. The very fact that the rebellion over primary-school testing led to a modification of the policy probably reinforced the legitimacy of the primary-school curriculum and teaching methods as a whole, the sense that the policy was not an imposition at all but an outgrowth of Scottish traditions. In the last decade of the century, however modified by respect for the individual learner, the aspiration was still to socialise children into responsible adulthood.

CHAPTER 8

Secondary Education

As with primary education, the origins of post-war thinking about secondary education lie in the 1930s, specifically with the 1936 Education (Scotland) Act which brought about secondary education for all, but left it divided into junior and senior versions. As we saw in Chapter 4, the most radical campaigners for universal secondary education had always been open to the possibility that it would not be structurally divided, and by the mid-1940s some more influential opinion had come over to their side. One particularly noteworthy series of articles was by Sir William McKechnie in the *Scottish Educational Journal* in 1944 (McKechnie 1944); he had retired as secretary of the SED in 1936 (having followed George Macdonald into the post in 1929). McKechnie had been impressed by some experiments in 'multilateral' schools in London, called 'omnibus' schools in Scotland. As early as 1931, he had come privately to see these as offering a model for the modern expression of the Scottish tradition as it had been evolving during the preceding half century (Stocks 2002: 28), and he now wrote that:

> the present position . . . appears to me to demand the concentration in
> comprehensive post-primary or secondary schools of all the pupils who
> have reached the appropriate stage, wiping out all the various
> distinctions that have been tried and found inadequate.
>
> (McKechnie 1944: 492)

The Council heard much support for this position when it took evidence in the mid-1940s, for example from such influential bodies as the Association of Head Masters of Senior Secondary Schools, the Scottish branch of the Association of Headmistresses, the Association of Directors of Education in Scotland, and the Educational Institute of Scotland, although all of these acknowledged that a comprehensive system could not be introduced immediately

(Young 1986: 264–9). Individual headteachers also contributed to the debate, for example Frank Earle, headteacher of Kirkcaldy High School, who wrote a book in 1944 arguing that common educational aims for all pupils could only be realised by educating them in common schools, and also that this was the only way to recognise the individuality of all pupils (Earle 1944: 72). Kirkcaldy had been running as an omnibus school since 1930, and he explained in detail how it had overcome some of the practical difficulties of organisation (discussed on pp. 108–16).

The Council's report of 1947 accepted these arguments, and recommended that the only way of fulfilling the democratic potential of the 1918 Act was by re-organising most secondary education in omnibus schools (SED 1947: 32). There would be a core curriculum for all pupils to age sixteen (see pp. 59–61). The leaving age should be raised to sixteen, at which point all pupils would sit an examination for a nationally recognised School Certificate (see pp. 52–7). This would not be centrally controlled, but would be set and marked by individual schools (drawing on experience which had been gained during the war, when, for practical reasons, the running of the Leaving Certificate had been devolved to schools). National standards of assessment would be maintained by means of a uniform test taken by all pupils in every school, and then using that as the basis of an elaborate statistical procedure for adjusting the marks of teachers in the tests they set themselves (a procedure that was devised by William McClelland). The pupils themselves were not to be judged by the uniform test: that was solely for the purpose of giving guidance to teachers on the standards expected. The aim of all this would be to extend 'initiative, variety, experiment' (see p. 59), because 'the end of education is individual excellence' (see p. 10). These emphatically child-centred ideas were interpreted, in characteristically Scottish fashion, as social: although 'selves can develop only in accordance with their own nature', 'their nature is social' (also on p. 10).

POLICY AND PRACTICE, 1947–1965

The SED's immediate response was cautious; indeed, it said nothing much at all until 1951, when it suggested that the comments on examination and curricula were more relevant to junior than to senior secondary courses, thus ignoring the point about structural re-organisation (Young 1986: 369). In fact, many of the Council's ideas on the curriculum did become policy in the inspectorate's 1955 report on junior secondary education, a sustained attempt to provide a coherent philosophy for that sector that was not just a diluted version of the senior-secondary curriculum; this is discussed further below.

The system which was consolidated in the 1950s therefore remained structurally divided. There were senior courses providing five years of education, culminating in the Leaving Certificate, and there were junior secondary courses which (after the leaving age was raised to fifteen in 1947) lasted three years. The crucial policy issue was then how to allocate children to different courses at the end of their primary schooling. The responsibility for this lay with the education authorities, and in the late 1940s few of them were yet using standardised tests (Macpherson 1958: 12). The Education (Scotland) Act of 1946 encouraged greater consistency, and many authorities were then influenced by McClelland's book on selection for secondary education (McClelland 1942). McClelland had argued (pp. 104, 214) that the fairest principle would be that any pupil who had a better than fifty per cent chance of passing the Leaving Certificate should be admitted to senior-secondary courses. Using data from a survey of pupils in Dundee, he estimated that around thirty per cent of pupils 'had the ability and attainment necessary for success in a senior secondary course' (see p. 219), but to achieve that from the actual success rate of eleven per cent would require 'far-reaching improvement in social and environmental conditions' and 'an increase in the variety and attractiveness of the senior secondary courses' (see p. 220). In practice, throughout the 1950s, education authorities allocated pupils to five-year courses on the basis of a mixture of attainment tests, intelligence tests, recommendations from primary teachers and parental preferences (SED 1961b: 8–16). The proportion of pupils who took at least part of a five-year course was around one third: in 1952, thirty-one per cent of all school leavers left from a five-year course, and in 1960 this figure had risen to thirty-three per cent (SED 1953a: 87; 1961a: 118–19).

Two controversial issues then arose. One was for the authorities – 'wastage', since only around one in eight of all pupils actually completed the full five-year course. Thus, in 1952, only twelve per cent of pupils leaving school had stayed on beyond third year; in 1960 this was still only seventeen per cent. The proportions gaining the Leaving Certificate were even smaller: the number of certificates awarded was 8.5 per cent of all school leavers in 1952, and 13.1 per cent in 1960 (SED 1953a: 89; SED 1961a: 120). Even among those who entered five-year courses, only a minority completed them: twenty-six per cent in 1952, rising to thirty-five per cent in 1960 (Philip 1992: 110). It was also found in research that many able pupils were not completing the five-year course. Of a sample of children who were born in 1936, and who thus mostly left school between 1951 and 1954, among those with high ability (in the sense of an IQ of 130 or above), only sixty-seven per cent of boys completed any kind of five-year course; the proportion for girls was fifty-four per cent (Macpherson 1958: 43–4). Much the same was true of progression to higher education among the same sample – about sixty-three per cent of boys and fifty-three per cent of girls (Maxwell 1969: 38). The official view was that pupils were wasting their time taking part in courses which they did not complete or which they did not use properly.

The problem was that, despite all the attempts to refine the selection procedure, it never proved possible to make it infallible. That then led to the second controversial issue: what happened to people who did not do well in the selection tests? The corollary of the 'wastage' among high attainers was that these same surveys also found significant amounts of academic success among people who had only moderate performance in formal tests: fourteen per cent of boys and fifteen per cent of girls with IQs between 100 and 129 successfully completed a five-year course in the 1950s (Macpherson 1958: 43–4). Since only forty per cent of boys and forty-four per cent of girls with IQ in this range were given the opportunity to enter a five-year course, the success rate was about one third (Macpherson 1958: 32, 34). This raised issues of fairness: those who were not allocated to five-year courses were denied the chance to succeed in them. It also raised different questions of wastage: if the other approximately sixty per cent of pupils with moderate IQs had been given the chance to enter five-year courses, and if one third of them had indeed succeeded, then the proportion among all such pupils who would have completed such a course would have risen to around one third from the fourteen to fifteen per cent that was actually achieved. Since pupils of moderate IQ in this sense made up forty-eight per cent of boys and thirty-eight per cent of girls, those affected were a large minority of all pupils.

Doubts were also cast on whether even McClelland's attempts at rigorous testing were measuring what secondary schooling was supposed to be for. For example, Nisbet (1957) found among university students that the correlation between test scores at the end of primary and eventual success in university examinations was very moderate indeed (correlations between 0.07 and 0.26). Likewise, Nisbet et al. (1972: 236) found that among children who left primary school in 1963, tests at age eleven were only moderately good predictors of success in the Higher Grade examination (correlations at best of only about 0.5).

Of particular concern to radical campaigners for a system of common schooling was the further evidence that the pupils who suffered by the unfairness of the allocation decisions were disproportionately working class. One study of pupils born in 1946, who mostly transferred to secondary in 1958, found evidence that the system was operating meritocratically at the extremes of the distribution of attainment at the end of primary: pupils with very high scores in a test administered at age eleven by the researchers were almost certain to be in a five-year course, regardless of social class, and pupils with very low scores were likewise almost certain not to be in such a course. However, in the middle two-thirds of the distribution of scores, sixty-six per cent of middle-class pupils were in five-year courses but only thirty-seven per cent of working-class pupils (Douglas et al. 1966: 155). These calculations thus discounted the fact that, by age eleven, there were already differences of social class in test scores: the unfairness was operating among pupils who ought, in a meritocratic sense, to have had the same chance of making progress. Putting the two sources of class difference together – the differences in test scores and the different chances accorded to children with the same test score – resulted in stark class differences in the proportions of children on senior-secondary courses. A survey by the Research Council of children aged fifteen in 1960–1 who had attended public schools found that around sixty-nine per cent of the children of professional fathers were in such courses. In the intermediate non-manual class the figure was forty-nine per cent. In the skilled manual class it was twenty-nine per cent, and in the semi-skilled and unskilled classes about fifteen per cent. In each class, the proportions were similar for boys and girls (SCRE 1970: 114–15).

The SED's first attempt to deal with the problems of wastage was to reform the Leaving Certificate. The first major change was in 1950, when the Group Certificate was abolished: thereafter, the certificate would simply record the results which candidates had attained in individual subjects (Philip 1992: 106–7). This led over the following decade to a doubling of the number of candidates, from 8,444 in 1949 to 18,562 in 1961 (see p. 110). Much more significant, however, was the introduction of an Ordinary Grade in 1962; the Lower Grade was abolished. To cope with the expected extra administrative work, responsibility for the new examination and for the Higher Grade was transferred in 1965 from the inspectorate to a new semi-independent body, the Scottish Certificate of Education Examination Board. The O grade was normally to be taken at age sixteen, and so was a belated acceptance of part of the Advisory Council's case on examinations; it also represented the final acceptance by the SED that the Intermediate Certificate that had been abolished in 1924 had fulfilled a role in enabling pupils of moderate ability to make gradual progress.

The new examination was almost immediately very much more popular than the SED had planned. The SED intended it for the most able thirty per cent of pupils, provided they had 'satisfactory teaching' and had expended 'adequate effort' (McIntosh and Walker 1970: 181). By 1968, twenty-nine per cent of the year-group were passing at least three O grades, but thirty-eight per cent were being presented for at least one, indicating that interest in it was much broader than was officially expected (Gray et al. 1983: 57). By 1974, that wider demand for access had broken through any barriers which the SED sought to impose: around three quarters of the age group attempted at least one O grade, beyond even the seventy per cent which the EIS had suggested in 1967 (Scotland 1969: 205). Sixty per cent of the age group were achieving one or more passes, and forty per cent were achieving three or more (Gray et al. 1983: 58). An investigation in 1970 found that this expansion was being achieved without any change in the standard of the new examination (McIntosh and Walker 1970): by relating O grade performance to measures of general intelligence, the researchers concluded that the increase in uptake was because pupils of below-average ability (IQ under 100) now had the stimulus of a worthwhile goal for which to aim.

That teachers and pupils were able to take advantage of this new examination was the consequence of the popular reaction to the perceived unfairness of selection. One response was to insist that the junior secondary courses were in fact able to offer the general education which Scottish popular opinion had always seen as the only type of real education. A survey reported in the *Scottish Educational Journal* in 1944 that claimed to have been constructed to be representative of the Scottish population with respect to 'age, sex, occupation and place of abode' had found that, when asked what the aim of education should be, most people mentioned 'to encourage intellectual development', the same level as supported 'to make good citizens' (SEJ, 12 May 1944: 254). Whatever the validity of that evidence, it was certainly consistent with the ways in which many of the teachers in those schools that provided only junior secondary courses sought to develop them, aided by the inspectors. The 1955 report on their curriculum followed the Advisory Council's 1947 report in recommending that all pupils study 'English, mathematics, geography, history, science, art, music and physical education' (SED 1955: 14). As in earlier decades, English was central. 'English has a universality and a comprehensiveness that distinguish it from other subjects' (see p. 70), both in the sense that 'every teacher is a teacher of English' (a principle that had also been cited by the Advisory Council) and in the sense that English may deal with every kind of human activity: the English teacher could 'help to lay the foundations of a philosophy of life without which no education is complete' (see p. 71). Even when the SED eventually did, in 1963, produce a set of recommendations on vocational education, in the report of a working party chaired by John Brunton, head of the inspectorate, it still endorsed the idea that 'the traditional Scottish secondary school course was one designed to provide a broad general education ... and this tradition was to a large extent continued in the expanded secondary education of the years after the war' (SED 1963b: 7).

The practice in the junior secondary courses in this respect was variable, but better than in the Advanced Divisions in the 1920s and 1930s. In his survey of the secondary-school experience of pupils who had left primary in about 1948, Macpherson (1958: 32, 34) found that only eight per cent of boys and fifteen per cent of girls in three-year courses were studying a language other than English, which was often taken as an indicator of a general course. Nevertheless, this did mean that, of all pupils (including those entering five-year courses), thirty-six per cent of boys and forty per cent of girls were receiving at least some kind of general education. A survey (of directors of education) reported in the *Scottish Educational Journal* in 1957 found that 129 of the 556 schools that provided junior secondary courses were offering academic courses (Russell 1957: 724). This figure of 556 is close to the SED's 597 of schools providing only three-year courses (SED 1957: 145). Since the SED reported a further 206 schools offering five-year courses, it would seem that the 335 secondaries offering academic courses (whether for three years or for five) were about forty-two per cent of all secondaries. Russell commented that the academic junior secondary course was the model that should be followed, and that junior secondary courses that were not academic or did not take place in an omnibus school were 'the weakest link in the secondary chain'. That Russell's assessment of the academic type of junior secondary school was not inaccurate was shown a few years later when the O grade was introduced: in 1963, fifty-one per cent of the 744 secondary schools were providing courses leading to O grades or Highers, at a time when only about thirteen per cent of secondaries were offering only four-year or five-year courses: thus only forty-nine per cent offered only three-year courses (SED 1964: 115, 149). Another way of putting this is that the common description of the selective system as being organised into separate types of school is accurate for under two thirds of schools: for thirty-eight per cent of them (those offering three-, four- and five-year courses), selection was operated by organising pupils into separate streams, not into separate institutions.

Some of the junior-secondary provision may then indeed have fulfilled one of the other aspirations of the Advisory Council – that, in the interim, they should bring some kind of secondary education to districts where provision had been sparse before. An example was Lanarkshire, where a mixture of five-year, four-year and three-year schools had emerged by the mid-1960s; in such a context, the four-year schools were a distinct improvement on the three-year ones (Gray et al. 1983: 237). But, however many of the junior secondaries attempted to provide a general, liberal education, the standard against which most parents judged a proper education continued to be the five-year senior-secondary courses. In this respect, demand certainly outstripped supply: in 1963 in Fife, about a third of the parents were denied their wish that their children should attend senior secondary courses (McIntosh 1963: 145).

Within the five-year course itself, the paradigm remained as it had been in the pre-war years – English, mathematics, a science and a language. Here, too, English was at the centre. The Advisory Council had referred to the 'civilising work of English teaching', and to great literature as 'a source not of pleasure and recreation alone but of comfort, counsel and enlightenment' (SED 1947: 62, 70), while also warning against 'vulgarisms' and corruption by Hollywood (see p. 63). The aspiration to provide wide access to this kind of course became another form of pressure towards expansion, not only in connection with the question of allocation between junior and senior secondary courses, but also because – as we have seen – only a minority of pupils on the five-year courses in the early 1950s actually completed them. Even a decade later, among those who attempted at least one Higher in 1962 or 1963 (a reasonable indicator of having embarked on a five-year course), the proportion passing at least four was forty-two per cent – forty-seven per cent of males and thirty-seven per cent of females (calculated from Scottish School Leavers Survey; see also Gray et al. 1983: 76).

On the other hand, the proportion of those engaging on a five-year course who passed Higher English was always high. In 1956, there were 5,901 passes in the subject, which corresponded to eighty-five per cent of people who left school at the end of a five-year course (SED 1957: 60, 145). In 1962–3, eighty-three per cent of pupils who had attempted at least one Higher passed Higher English (from the Schools Leavers Survey); the proportion for males was eighty-one per cent and for females was eighty-seven per cent. Therefore, although the full breadth was not as widely available as was officially and popularly intended, a central component of that liberal education was the normal experience of pupils completing the senior secondary courses. Moreover, the senior secondary courses, although biased in their recruitment from different social classes, seem to have operated more or less merito-cratically for people who did manage to get there. Thus, in 1962, among those who attempted at least one Higher, the proportion passing at least four was forty-eight per cent in the middle class and forty per cent in the working class. Among the same group, the proportion passing Higher English was eighty-seven per cent in the middle class and eighty-one per cent in the working class. These are small differences compared to the differences in gaining access to such courses. Nisbet et al. (1972: 237) similarly found in the mid-1960s that 'staying on at school [beyond age 15] is a function of ability rather than of social class'. They reached this conclusion by calculating the average scores in an intelligence test taken at age eleven among pupils who stayed on beyond age fifteen. These scores did not vary by social class: in other words, there was no evidence that a working-class child had to be more able than a middle-class child before he or she could stay on. The normal interpretation of such evidence was that it showed that working-class pupils were as able to take advantage of a full secondary education as their middle-class peers, when given the chance.

DEMOCRATIC REFORM, 1965–1980s

The imperfections of the divided system, along with the popular aspirations to a broad general education, provided the political impetus for reform. The opportunity came with the election of the Labour government in 1964, and in some respects the main pressure for change came from England, where disputes about selection were much fiercer. It was often alleged at the time in Scotland that ending selection was unnecessary and was a form of anglicisation

(MacKenzie 1967: 30; McPherson and Raab 1988: 373). However, in two important respects that was inaccurate. The first was the popular pressure we have been noting. As with the movement towards secondary education for all in the 1920s and 1930s, the push towards a common type of secondary education was evident in the popular respect for general, academic education, in the attempts by a significant minority of junior secondary schools to provide that, and in the perception from research that allocation to senior-secondary courses was often unfair in meritocratic terms.

The other source of Scottish thinking on ending selection was that which emerged around the sixth Advisory Council, the 1947 report of which had not been forgotten. In 1957, for example, Sir James Robertson reiterated its principles, including ending selection (Robertson 1957). As we have seen, the report was not as uninfluential on the SED's thinking about the curriculum as might have seemed, and indeed the inspectors acknowledged as much in 1966 (Bone 1967: 48). In any case, the report had also been cited by English campaigners for ending selection, such as Sheena Simon in an influential book in 1948 (B. Simon 1991: 148, 332). She was impressed by Frank Earle's omnibus school in Kirkcaldy (S. Simon 1948: 48–9), holding it up as an example of how the Advisory Council's principles could be operated in practice. There were also several Scottish activists on the Labour Party committee which persuaded the annual conference in 1950 to support the ending of selection – notably Margaret Herbison, MP for North Lanark, and William Ross, MP for Kilmarnock (Pedley 1971: 94). Herbison praised the Advisory Council report in a debate in Parliament when it was published, claiming that Labour members 'have always felt that it was altogether wrong to segregate children at the tender age of eleven into junior and senior secondary schools' (Parliamentary Debates 1947). Whether or not the main enthusiasm for reform lay in England, such a view had come to permeate the Scottish Labour Party by the 1960s.

The key Scottish politician in practice in the 1960s was Ross, who became Secretary of State for Scotland in Wilson's government, instructing the SED to issue Circular 600 in 1965. McPherson and Willms (1987: 510–11) summarise the main purposes. The first was to end selection. The second was to establish just one type of secondary school, providing for all ages between twelve and eighteen, and, as it put it, 'a full range of courses for all pupils from a particular district who would attend it throughout their secondary career' (SED 1965a: 3). The only exception would be in sparsely populated rural areas where this form of organisation would not be economical. There was confirmation of the SED's intention to raise the leaving age to sixteen, which in fact happened in session 1972–3. The fourth aim was to reduce the segregation of social classes into different kinds of school: for example, the small remaining element of fee-charging in education authority schools was abolished.

All of this, fifth, was to the further purpose of increasing and widening access to certification.

Gray et al. (1983: 231–3) note that this caused the educational debate to be politicised as never before, introducing a controversy that has never gone away. In some respects, however, the reorganisation went smoothly in Scotland (McPherson and Willms 1987: 511). In 1965, about one fifth of all secondary schools were already six-year omnibus schools. By 1975 this had risen to two thirds. By 1982 all selection in the public sector had been ended: three quarters of all secondaries provided six-year courses, and the rest of the public sector (about one in eight of all schools) were non-selective four-year schools in rural areas, mainly in the north-west Highlands and the western and northern Islands. At the same time, the already very small amount of single-sex secondary schooling had almost all disappeared in the public sector: by the 1980s, there remained only one, girls-only, secondary, Notre Dame Catholic school in Glasgow.

As well as this restructuring of the schools, the SED also encouraged a gradual move away from the grouping of pupils by ability, a practice that had probably been the norm in all schools until 1965 (McPherson and Raab 1988: 374, 391). Mixed ability had come to be regarded as part of the process of a truly comprehensive school, in contrast to the notion of the omnibus school with its internal differentiation that had been dominant in the 1930s (Stocks 2002: 28–9). For example, in an early evaluation of reorganisation by Ayrshire Fabian Society, it was commented that: 'pupils are all individuals who have different gifts and skill and ability, different aspirations and expectations, different frustration levels, and they are entitled to educational provision which has been tailored to meet their individual needs. This requires mixed ability' (Millar and White 1972: 24).

The SED found in a 1972 survey that around two thirds of schools were using mixed-ability classes, and reported that the headteachers of most comprehensive schools believed that this improved the motivation of the least able, and had beneficial social consequences for the most able (SED 1972d: 5, 9, 14). Only fifteen per cent of all secondary headteachers believed that mixed-ability classes held back the most able.

In other respects, though, the reform process was not as smooth as these trends might indicate, essentially because the SED had done little to prepare teachers for dealing with the resulting new demands that were placed on them (Watt 1991). The whole of the period from the 1970s until the end of the century may be understood as the gradual working through in practice of the consequences of the ending of selection, attempting to realise the full idealism of the reformers, just as the last three decades of the nineteenth century sought to deal with the problems that had not been solved by the 1872 extension of elementary education. There was a need to develop new curricula that would cater for a much broader range of abilities, to train and to offer advice to teachers on how to provide academic courses for children who would previously have left school early, to develop new systems of guidance for pupils themselves, to deal with rising levels of indiscipline, and to find new styles of educational leadership (Watt 1991). There were also grave shortages of teachers, especially in west-central Scotland, which the SED did not fully sort out until the mid-1970s (Marker and Raab 1993: 4–5). As one interviewee put it to Watt in his investigation of the process of introducing comprehensive schools in west-central Scotland:

> the main obstacle was the conceptual poverty which existed at all levels in the Scottish educational system at the time ... There was a signal failure on all sides to grasp the essential practical consequences of giving equality of educational opportunity to all children.
>
> (Watt 1989: 254)

The goal of ending selection did quite quickly lead to a reduction in social class segregation (McPherson and Willms 1987: 513, 526). This worked best in communities which were not themselves very socially segregated, such as the small burghs, sites of the longest-established omnibus schools, and the new towns that had been built in the 1950s and 1960s to re-house families from nineteenth-century slums in the cities (McPherson and Willms 1987: 526; Thomson 1968). The reform was particularly beneficial in this sense to the Roman Catholic sector (four fifths of which was in the west-central area). Before 1965, only five per cent of schools offering senior secondary courses were Catholic, even though about nineteen per cent of secondary pupils were Catholic (McPherson and Willms 1986). Over the following two decades, one policy consequence of creating this system of common schooling was that the inspectors' attention then moved to measuring the 'effectiveness' of each school on a common basis, generating a plethora of performance indicators, targets and school development plans (McPherson 1989).

This fitted the policies of the Conservative government in the 1980s, who extended it by devolving greater budgetary autonomy to headteachers and by encouraging schools to compete with each other, but – slightly ironically given the ideological provenance of these ideas – this also served to reinforce the sense that all schools ought to be equal. Scottish parents never took to the further idea that schools should become 'self-governing' by parents' voting to remove them from the administrative control of the education authorities: by the time the Conservative government lost power in 1997, only two small schools had done so (an Episcopal primary in Dunblane and the secondary school in Dornoch), and one other (a primary in Fort William) had voted for this but was awaiting official approval. Parents had sometimes used the opportunity of a ballot to force a postponement of a proposal to close a school, but these moves were always vetoed by the Government since restricting public expenditure had higher priority for them than parental power. So the persisting public character of nearly all secondary schools reinforced the sense of a common system.

Nevertheless, social class segregation did not end. In fact, it rose again somewhat in the 1980s, partly because unemployment and poverty grew in some places but not in others (Paterson 1997a: 14–16), and partly because in 1980 the Conservative government gave legislative recognition to the right of parents to choose the school to which their children would go (Adler et al. 1989). That right was exercised on behalf of some one in ten pupils entering the first year of secondary school in the mid-1980s, and levelled off at about one in eight in the 1990s (SED 1989a: 6; SOEID 1997d: 7). The segregation rose at first because middle-class parents were initially more likely to make such a choice than working-class parents (Echols et al. 1990), but the School Leavers Surveys in the 1990s showed a slow fall again back to the level in 1980. Calculating segregation as the proportion at the school level of the total variance of an indicator of membership in the semi-skilled and unskilled classes IV and V, the segregation index was 0.14 in 1980, 0.25 in 1990 and 0.15 in 1995. Exercising a choice was higher in the cities, where real choice was available – around a quarter in most of them. However, there too, segregation was falling again by the 1990s, although it was still higher than in 1980: the index value was 0.17 in 1980, 0.31 in 1990 and 0.27 in 1995. It could well have been, therefore, that the main source of segregation among schools remained residential segregation, and that its effects may eventually have been somewhat mitigated by the parental choice policy, as working-class parents learned to use the system as the middle class had done from the beginning. In any case, working against the educationally invidious effects of segregation were the redistributive powers of the large regional education authorities which had responsibility for schooling between 1975 and 1996: the mostly Labour-dominated Regions were able to direct resources to schools serving socially deprived neighbourhoods, despite the apparent ideology of central government (see, for example, Strathclyde Regional Council 1984).

One reason for persisting social segregation was the continued existence of the small private sector. Some of the late-nineteenth-century endowed schools had been taken over by the education authorities in the first few decades of the twentieth century because their endowments were so meagre, the most famous being James Gillespie's in Edinburgh, the setting for Muriel Spark's *The Prime of Miss Jean Brodie*. However, a couple of dozen secondary endowed schools survived outwith education authority management, though receiving grant aid from them and from the SED (Highet 1969). After 1965, one in eight of all secondary schools remained outside the public sector – the fully independent schools and the grant-aided schools, all but two of which chose to become independent. The Labour government of 1974–9 proposed to end these schools' grants, which had amounted to fifty-four per cent of their income in 1964, having been as high as sixty-three per cent in 1955 (SED 1957: 109; 1966: 89). The grant had dropped to under ten per cent of their income by 1979, causing several schools to close (Walford 1988: 145). The Conservative government in 1979 slightly increased this again, but then replaced it with the Assisted Places Scheme, bursaries to encourage entry to the schools by children whose parents could not afford the fees; the total received from this each year was much the same as the grant aid had been in the early 1980s (Walford 1988: 143). It, too, was withdrawn in 1997, by the Labour government.

The proportion of secondary pupils in this private sector never rose much above one in twenty nationally, a level that was lower than in the combined total of independent and grant-aided schools in the 1930s. In 1934, the grant-aided schools had contained 6.6 per cent of secondary pupils (that is, not including the Advanced Divisions), and the proportion in the independent schools which did not receive grants was probably around a further two per cent, judging by post-war levels (SED 1936c: 76–83; 1952a: 92). By 1965, the grant-aided and independent schools contained about 7.6 per cent of all secondary pupils (SED 1966: 100; 1969: 6). It dropped to 5.6 per cent in the 1991 School Leavers Survey, and 5.4 per cent in the annual school census in 1998 (Scottish Executive 1999c: 2). The proportion in Edinburgh and Glasgow in the 1980s and 1990s appeared to be much greater than the national average: for example, in the 1995 School Leavers Survey, it was around twenty per cent in Edinburgh and in Glasgow, but these figures take no account of pupils who travelled into the cities from surrounding areas. Because the schools charged fees, middle-class children were much more likely to attend them than were working-class pupils, despite the Assisted Places Scheme which benefited some 2,600 pupils each year up to the late 1990s, or about thirteen per cent of all pupils in the secondary independent schools (Walford 1988; SED 1989e: 3). Thus, in 1987, the national proportions of secondary pupils in the independent sector were eighteen per cent in the professional class, ten per cent in the intermediate class, five per cent in the skilled non-manual class, and one per cent or fewer in each of the manual classes (Echols et al. 1990: 213). This class gradient may have been less steep, however, than it had been half a century earlier: among pupils entering secondary school in 1947, the proportion attending an independent or grant-aided school was thirty-four per cent of those with a father who worked in a professional occupation, but only 1.4 per cent of those whose father was in a skilled manual job (SCRE 1953: 189). In one other respect, too, the overall small proportion in the independent sector understates its significance for pupils who took

Highers. In that sample of 1947 entrants, one quarter of pupils who achieved three or more Higher Grade passes or equivalent were attending independent or grant-aided schools (Macpherson 1958: 58). The independent schools no longer had such a significant share of pupils at that level in the 1980s and 1990s, but it was still higher than their share of pupils overall: in the School Leavers Surveys, 11.7 per cent in 1981, 10.2 per cent in 1991 and 12.3 per cent in 1995.

MOTIVATION AND CERTIFICATION

Altogether, however, the reorganisation provided educational opportunities to a much broader social spectrum of pupils, even though it did not eliminate the relevance of social class. These new opportunities then encouraged people to want more. In 1970, only thirty-one per cent of the age group had stayed on voluntarily to enter fifth year of secondary school. By the mid-1970s, this figure had risen to thirty-eight per cent (SED 1982: 29), and in 1983 it was fifty-two per cent (Paterson 1997a: 12). Dealing with all these new pupils required that attention be given to some of the problems which Watt (1989) recorded for the immediate aftermath of the ending of selection.

The first point was the question of motivation, and in the 1970s several studies found quite high levels of indiscipline and truancy. For example, the School Leavers Survey in 1977 showed that fourteen per cent of pupils reported that, during fourth year, they had truanted at least several days at a time, and that a further fifty per cent truanted for a day or a lesson here and there (Raffe 1986: 14). An SED committee set up to look into the problem reported in 1977 that truancy was only the most visible manifestation of wider disaffection (SED 1977c). As in primary schools, use of corporal punishment turned out to be much more widespread than the official policy of gradual elimination would seem to be acknowledging: thus only a third of girls and a mere four per cent of boys reported in the Scottish School Leavers Survey of 1977 that they had never been belted in secondary school; forty-seven per cent of boys and fourteen per cent of girls were belted 'quite often' or 'often' (McNally 1982: 43). The relationship to motivation was evident in the sharp differences in these rates between pupils who were on certificate courses and those who were not: among boys, sixty-one per cent of people who were sitting no O grades or Highers reported having been belted, in contrast to only twenty-two per cent of those who had sat Highers; for girls, the proportions were twenty-five per cent and two per cent (Gray et al. 1983: 174). Nevertheless, most pupils saw nothing wrong with this situation: two thirds of both boys and girls accepted that teachers should be allowed to punish pupils by the use of the belt (Pollock et al. 1977: 34).

These problems of motivation were further confirmed by a widely read research report from the Centre for Educational Sociology at Edinburgh University, which quoted numerous instances of young people feeling that the new comprehensive system was not providing for their interests and abilities (Gow and McPherson 1980). Another investigation of the curricular choices made by pupils in the second year of secondary school found persisting widespread belief among pupils, parents and teachers that the courses leading to the O grade were too difficult for most pupils (Ryrie et al. 1979: 80–1). There was, in fact, a subject hierarchy, in which the greatest social status was accorded to the traditional academic core, and in which access to that core was more common among middle-class pupils than among working-class ones (Gray et al. 1983: 80; Weir 1975).

The main response was to replace the O grade (Brown and Munn 1985). Two inquiries were set up by the SED. One was into curriculum, chaired by James Munn, who was rector of Cathkin High School in Glasgow. It recommended that all pupils should follow a broad and common curriculum to age sixteen, and justified this on similar grounds to those which had led the Advisory Council to propose the same in 1947:

> schools exist in and for a given society, and one of the main functions
> of schooling is to equip young people with the skills, the knowledge,
> and the social and moral attitudes which will fit them for full
> membership of the adult community.
>
> (SED 1977a: 15)

The other committee was concerned with assessment; it was chaired by Joseph Dunning, principal of Napier College of Commerce and Technology in Edinburgh. It recommended a new examination that would assess all pupils' achievements, as the outcome of this common curriculum; selection into different syllabuses for pupils of different ability should be postponed as late as possible (SED 1977b: 73–80).

Both committees made proposals for offering appropriate stimuli to very able pupils as well as providing courses for those who would not have attempted any O grades (SED 1977a: 60; 1977b: 78), reflecting what the committee on the curriculum described as 'concern ... that the ablest pupils may be disadvantaged in the comprehensive school' (SED 1977a: 13). The SED had in fact already made some changes aimed at this group, when it introduced the Certificate of Sixth Year Studies in 1968; this was intended to be at a level beyond the Higher Grade, and to encourage students to study independently in preparation for university (McPherson and Neave 1976).

The new structure of curriculum and examinations was introduced very gradually in the 1980s, the new examination being called the Standard Grade.

It was available at three levels, the top being intended to be more difficult than the O grade, and the bottom being for those pupils who would not have sat the O grade. The evidence was then that it had achieved some of its goals. Social class and gender differences in access to the curriculum at these ages narrowed as the broad curriculum was enforced. For example, the proportion of girls studying science rose from fifty per cent in 1977 to over ninety per cent in 1991; the proportion of boys increased from seventy-four per cent to over ninety per cent (Croxford 1994: 381). Gamoran (1995) found that, in the same period, the proportion studying English rose more rapidly among socially disadvantaged pupils than among the advantaged; the same was true for mathematics. By the mid-1990s, there was then some sign from the School Leavers Surveys of a reduction in class differences in high levels of attainment at this stage. For example, in 1981 the proportion passing five or more O grades in fourth year of secondary school was fifty-three per cent in the Registrar General's professional and intermediate non-manual classes, but only nineteen per cent in the semi-skilled and unskilled classes. In 1994, the analogous proportions in Standard Grade were seventy-one per cent and forty-two per cent, and so inequality, though still wide, had fallen.

Some of this was probably helped by the new system of guidance, which had been made more extensive from the mid-1980s (McLaren 1999), based on the same kinds of principles that lay behind the child-centredness of primary schools. These ideas also helped to bring social workers into schools (Bruce 1981), often through the most radical of the community schools that had been set up in the 1960s (Nisbet et al. 1980). The most notable exponent of the idea that comprehensive education required to be student-centred was the head-teacher R. F. Mackenzie, whose outspokenness brought him into conflict with the education authorities for which he worked in the 1960s and 1970s; one particular point of conflict was over his refusal to use corporal punishment. For that reason he has tended to be seen as a late-twentieth-century inheritor of the legacy of A. S. Neill, with whom in fact he spent an early part of his career as a teacher (Gordon 1988; Murphy 1998).

GROWTH OF POST-COMPULSORY SCHOOLING

All these reforms to courses, examinations and guidance then encouraged the staying-on rate in school after age sixteen to rise even further: it reached seventy per cent in the mid-1990s (Paterson 1997a: 12). The rates were generally about five per cent higher than this for girls, and the rate of staying-on among children of professional parents was around ninety per cent by the early 1990s (Paterson and Raffe 1995: 8). By that date, too, the social-class differences in staying on had begun to narrow. In 1980, two thirds of pupils whose fathers were in a non-manual occupation stayed on voluntarily into fifth year, compared to just a quarter of pupils whose fathers were in a manual job. In 1994, the proportion for the non-manual class had risen to eighty-two per cent, but that for the manual class had risen relatively much more, to fifty-six per cent (from School Leavers Surveys). Although there was some evidence that staying on was encouraged by rising youth unemployment, it did not fall back again as unemployment fell (Paterson and Raffe 1995). There was no evidence to support the claim of critics of comprehensive schools that they had damaged the chances of able working-class children. We noted earlier that Nisbet et al. (1972) found that, in the old selective system, working-class children did not have to show any undue intelligence before they could stay on beyond age fifteen. The same was true in surveys in Fife in 1980 and 1984 as part of the School Leavers Survey (see also Willms 1986): the average score in a verbal-reasoning test at age twelve among those who left from fifth or sixth years was not higher among working-class children than among the middle class, indicating that opportunities to make progress were not being denied to able working-class pupils. There remained, as in the study by Nisbet et al., large class differences in the attainment in that age-twelve test (Bondi 1991).

Problems of motivation did remain, and low-level disaffection and indiscipline persisted. Truancy fell at best slowly: by 1981–2, the proportion of people truanting for at least several days at a time had fallen to seven per cent (half that of 1975–6), although the proportion truanting occasionally remained around fifty per cent (Raffe 1986: 14). The pattern in the School Leavers Survey of 1994 was much the same. Surveys in the mid-1990s found that – despite lurid newspaper headlines – really serious misbehaviour was very rare, but also found that the cumulative effect of a great deal of minor disruption was very wearing on teachers (Munn and Johnstone 1992). The problems may have been exacerbated by the policy of 'inclusion', by which it became very difficult for schools to exclude pupils for anything other than extremely serious offences (Munn et al. 2000). In a sense, this indicated something of the success of comprehensive schooling, insofar as, before the 1970s, persistently disobedient pupils were sent to completely separate, prison-like establishments – the reformatory schools between 1894 and 1932 and the approved schools thereafter (Lloyd 2000; Scotland 1969: 94–5, 216). The change in policy was part of the same climate as led to the abolition of corporal punishment (as noted in Chapter 7 above), and to the children's hearing system, dealing with child criminal offences as a matter of guidance and welfare rather than of punitive justice (Asquith 1992; Murphy 1992). It did, however, show the intractability of providing secondary courses that would suit everyone.

On the other hand, a majority of pupils now expressed satisfaction with what they had experienced in school. In the School Leavers Survey of 1994, for example, sixty-three per cent of leavers agreed with the statement that 'school has helped give me confidence to make decisions', and sixty-four per cent agreed that 'school has taught me things which would be useful for a job'. In contrast, only ten per cent agreed that 'school has been a waste of time' (Paterson 1997a: 13). Further, eighty-one per cent felt school work was worth doing, seventy-two per cent said teachers helped them to do their best, seventy-nine per cent said teachers often gave them homework, and sixty-three per cent felt there was a teacher they could talk to if they had a problem. Even among pupils who had not done well in school, satisfaction was quite high: for example, among school leavers with no formal passes in Standard Grade, fifty-five per cent said that school had taught them things that would be useful for a job, and no more than twenty-six per cent said school had been a waste of time. Wherever measures were available for comparison with earlier surveys, generally satisfaction had risen: for example, between the 1985 and 1996 School Leavers Surveys, the proportion of pupils who stayed on at school because they enjoyed it rose from thirty-four per cent to fifty-seven per cent, and between 1987 and 1996 the proportion saying that they had stayed on because they had found a particular course interesting rose from thirty-eight per cent to eighty-one per cent. There were also fairly high levels of satisfaction with the comprehensive system among the Scottish population generally. In the 1990s, the various Election Surveys and Social Attitudes Surveys found that, among the three quarters of people who had a view on the matter, around two thirds opposed a return to selection, a proportion that was over eighty per cent among people who were young enough to have experienced the comprehensive system as pupils or as parents of pupils; these views were similar in all social classes (Paterson 2000a: 24–5). In one survey in 1998, respect for teachers was high (see p. 26), and no more than twenty-seven per cent believed that standards were falling (see p. 51).

For the majority who were now staying on into post-compulsory schooling, attainment in the Highers was rising too: for example, in 1965 the proportion of school leavers who had passed three or more of them was twelve per cent; in 1981, it was twenty per cent; in 1996 it was thirty per cent (Paterson 1997a: 13). Detailed analysis of syllabuses and marking standards suggested that the quality of the examinations had not changed (Devine et al. 1996). Moreover, some aspects of social inequality in such attainment had been transformed. In attainment at Higher Grade, females overtook males in the late 1970s, as Table 8.1 illustrates, and by the late 1990s their relative performance was a reversal of the position four decades earlier. As in Standard Grade, moreover, female students gradually moved into traditionally male-dominated subjects at Higher Grade. For example, between 1962 and 1990, the female proportion among the students passing Higher Grade mathematics rose from thirty-three per cent to forty-five per cent (from the Scottish School Leavers Surveys). Likewise, the female proportion among those passing at least one science

Table 8.1 Percentage of School Leavers Passing Three or More Highers, 1951–97, by Gender

	1951–4*	1965	1975	1987	1997
Male	10	12	18	20	27
Female	6	11	18	23	34

*Criterion in 1951–4 is three or more Higher Grades or equivalent: see source.
Sources: Macpherson (1958: 63); SED (1988: 7); SOEID (1998b: 7).

Higher rose from thirty per cent to forty-nine per cent, and among those passing at least one social subject rose from forty-two per cent to forty-nine per cent. Female students retained their preponderance in biology and arts subjects: throughout the period from 1963 to 1990, female students made up around two thirds of passes in Higher biology, and the female proportion rose from forty-eight per cent to fifty-seven per cent of passes in English, and from fifty-three per cent to seventy-one per cent among those passing at least one modern language. By 1998, as a result, female students made up one half or more of Higher Grade passes in almost all the core areas of the academic school curriculum (SQA 1999: 89): around one half in mathematics, chemistry and geography; between about sixty and seventy per cent in English, biology, history and modern studies; and around three quarters in French and German. Among the core subjects, only in physics were they still in a minority of thirty-one per cent, but that figure too had risen from twenty-two per cent in 1970.

As in the primaries, however, these changes in the experience of female students probably owed little to official encouragement before the 1990s (Turner et al. 1995). The overall proportion of secondary teachers who were female was close to one half throughout the period – forty-two per cent in 1956, forty-four per cent in 1971 and fifty per cent in education authority schools in 1994 (SED 1957: 141; 1972c: 150; SOEID 1996c: 5). However, the powerful positions in schools were still mostly in the hands of men, although systematic data on this were available only in the 1990s: in 1994, only eighteen out of the 394 headteachers in education authority secondary schools were women, a number that nevertheless did rise sharply to forty-six out of 385 in 2000 (Scottish Executive 2001d: 13). Therefore, the changing experience of female students owed far more to popular pressure – to the transformation of gender relations that was taking place more generally – than to official action.

Catholic schools, now fully part of a common system, showed the same gains in the Higher Grade attainment of their pupils as non-denominational schools: between the School Leavers Surveys of 1981 and 1995, the proportion

Table 8.2 Percentage of School Leavers Passing Three or More Highers, 1960–94, by Social Class

Father's occupation	1960–3	1978	1986	1994
Non-manual	25	38	43	51
Manual	5	9	11	20

Sources: Gray et al. (1983: 204–5); Scottish School Leavers Survey.

of their pupils passing three or more Highers rose from twelve per cent to twenty-seven per cent, while that in the non-denominational schools rose from twenty per cent to thirty-one per cent (Paterson 2000c: 148; Payne and Ford 1977; Willms 1992). The Catholic schools seem to have been particularly effective for working-class pupils: the proportion of them passing three or more Highers rose from nine to twenty-one per cent in Catholic schools but from ten to nineteen per cent in the rest (Paterson 2000c: 150). There was less systematic evidence of any sort concerning pupils from minority ethnic groups, but, because their rate of entry to higher education was above that of white people (as we will see in Chapter 9), their school attainment must have been better too, despite suffering from persistent racism while at school (Hampton 1998). There was even some slow change in the most intractable dimension of social inequality in relation to Highers attainment, social class, as Table 8.2 shows: in the early 1960s, middle-class school school leavers were five times more likely than working-class school leavers to have reached the threshold of university entrance, whereas three decades later the ratio was less than three to one.

By the year 2000, all this expansion of opportunity in secondary schooling seemed to have produced levels of attainment in the senior years of secondary that were respectable by international standards. In contrast to the results of surveys in the early secondary and in primary (which we discussed in Chapter 7), the performance of pupils aged about fifteen in mathematics was fourth among twenty-nine countries in the Organisation for Economic Cooperation and Development; in science it was ninth (Scottish Executive 2002a). The inspectors' reiterated complaint from the 1970s to the 1990s that pupils' progress was too slow in the first two years of secondary may have missed the point (SED 1972; SOEID 1996: 7): perhaps the eventual outcome mattered more than the route by which it was reached. Nevertheless, the inspectors began to push schools back towards some elements of grouping by ability. In the early 1990s, over ninety-five per cent of all classes in the first two years of secondary school were being conducted as full mixed ability, up from the two thirds found in 1972 (SOEID 1997e: 8). The inspectors now perceived mixed ability as a cause of low achievement at age fourteen: in a controversial change of policy in 1996 they supported broad setting – the loose grouping of pupils into broad bands within each subject according to their prior attainment (SOEID 1996: 17–21). They continued to recommend strongly against streaming – that is, the practice of grouping pupils into the same classes for all subjects (see pp. 13–15).

REFORM OF THE HIGHERS

The rising levels of staying on then required further reform to the post-16 courses to which these new students were gaining access. Some of that had been forced also by the rise in youth unemployment during the 1980s and the fall in the availability of apprenticeships, discussed in Chapter 10 below (Fairley 1989: 40–1). Part of the Conservative Government's response was to try to introduce a stronger vocational element into the school curriculum, through the Technical and Vocational Education Initiative from 1984 until the early 1990s (Bell et al. 1989; Fairley and Paterson 1991). The inspectors and the schools resisted this innovation until the government had agreed that it would not displace the new Standard Grade courses, and that it would not be used to undermine the comprehensive system: there were fears that it could lead to a separate vocational track. The result was that the TVEI was 'domesticated', as Bell et al. (1989) put it, which meant in practice that it became complementary to the main academic curriculum, not a rival to it. One rather ironic outcome was that it became the basis for many local programmes to promote equal gender opportunities, taking advantage of the scheme's aim to encourage girls to study technological subjects, but extending that far beyond the government's intentions (Turner et al. 1995).

This combination of views then explains the path taken by the reform of courses beyond age sixteen. There were two specific sources of ideas for a radical overhaul of courses and assessment in the final two years of secondary school (McPherson 1992b). The first was the long-standing desire of the SED to do something about what the inspectorate considered to be the messy character of fifth and – especially – sixth year in secondary schools. Their earliest proposal in this respect had been made as far back as the late 1950s, when they suggested an advanced course that would resemble the A levels in the rest of the UK (Osborne 1966: 133). The sixth Advisory Council had also proposed such a course, to follow its leaving examination at age sixteen (SED 1947: 56–7). The eventual outcome was the Certificate of Sixth Year Studies (from 1968), but because universities were dissuaded from using it as their main entrance exam, it was never taken by more than about one in ten students. The problem had always been that if any new course took two years, replacing the Highers in fifth year, then it would threaten the viability and academic effectiveness of small schools, a matter of controversy in rural areas and in the socially deprived parts of the cities.

A catalogue of modular National Certificates was introduced after 1984, run by a new Scottish Vocational Education Council – largely as a reaction to the Conservatives' desire to strengthen the vocational aspects of schooling – and did help to postpone dealing with the problem of fifth and sixth year; this is discussed more fully in Chapter 10 below. The accusation was made, however, that this was a short-term expedient, not a coherent solution: the expansion of the National Certificate into areas traditionally reserved for the academic curriculum – such as languages and even philosophy – was regarded as unsatisfactory by those who distrusted the assessment techniques on which the modules were based and who were wary about what they saw as the Vocational Education Council's lack of expertise in devising curricula (Croxford et al. 1991; Fairley and Paterson 1991).

The second source of pressure for reform came from the universities. The Highers had never lost their initial purpose of performing the role of a university entrance exam. The cuts in university funding which the Conservative government had imposed in 1981 (see Chapter 9 below) had begun to reduce their leading influence over post-16 schooling in general. Their four-year honours degree was under threat as allegedly more wasteful than the normal three-year courses elsewhere in the UK. They were also facing competition from the central institutions. The universities chose to respond to these various pressures by restricting access: instead of allowing staff–student ratios to worsen, they made it more difficult for students to get in. The result, in Andrew McPherson's words, was that 'pupils whose fifth-year Highers would have been good enough to secure them entry to higher education from fifth year in the 1970s were obliged in the 1980s to return for a sixth year to upgrade their qualifications' (McPherson 1992b: 117).

In consequence, the sixth year became increasingly like a remedial year, not at all the opportunity for using the Certificate of Sixth Year Studies as an induction into mature, independent study.

The inspectorate, therefore, persuaded the government to establish a committee of inquiry, chaired by John Howie, who was professor of mathematics at St Andrews University (and had been a member of the Dunn committee). It produced a sweeping indictment of the existing system, on four main grounds (SOED 1992d). First, most students did not have coherent breadth in the Higher courses they followed in fifth and sixth year: for example, in 1990, twenty-seven per cent of fifth-year pupils attempted no more than one Higher, and forty-two per cent attempted no more than two (SOED 1992a: 18). The report claimed that was because the old academic style of the Highers was no longer suitable for the more diverse fifth and sixth year which comprehensive education had produced. Second, most students had extensive experience of failing courses in fifth and sixth year: for example, although eighty-four per cent of all fifth-year pupils attempted at least one Higher, only sixty-six per cent passed at least one, and – among people who failed at least one Higher in fifth year and who stayed on into sixth year – thirty-three per cent passed no further Highers in sixth year (see p. 26). Therefore, although the flexibility of Highers and National Certificate modules was undeniable, it was also wasteful. Moreover, third, 'the Scottish system offered few opportunities for searching scholarship' (SOED 1992d: 39), because of the relative unpopularity of the Certificate of Sixth Year Studies: this comment was partly a reaction to the growing proportion of students in the Scottish universities who had followed the more specialised A level courses in the rest of the UK, and the resulting belief in some of the universities that the Highers no longer provided an appropriate standard for university entry (a trend that will be discussed more fully in Chapter 9). And, fourth, although the Scottish system might have stood up well compared to that in the rest of the UK, in some respects it looked weak compared to other European countries. The report claimed that 'the key feature of most continental systems is that students cover a broad, quasi-mandatory programme, so ensuring substantial coverage of a whole range of subjects or curricular areas' (see p. 41). Such programmes also often allowed for deep study of a few areas. The report was full of rhetoric about Europeanism, in fact, but had little comment to make on the socially and academically exclusive character of Baccalaureate-style courses (Stronach 1992). As McPherson noted (1992b: 122–5), it saw Scottish students who passed only one or two Highers – thirteen per cent of all leavers – as failures of the system rather than as people who, in France as well as in England, would have achieved almost nothing meaningful at all at this level.

This critique was widely accepted, and made reform inevitable, but the committee's proposals were not, because they involved two pathways through fifth and sixth year – one academic and one vocational. Given the history of the previous seventy years, it was never likely that such ideas would be acceptable in Scotland: if fifth and sixth year had to be reformed because of the achievements of comprehensive education, then it was always bound to be in the direction of making academic education available more widely. The inspectorate's response in 1994 was to turn all the courses at that stage into a single system of modules – combining Highers, Sixth Year Studies and the National Certificate into a new programme entitled 'Higher Still' (SOED 1994). The examinations would be at five levels, thus taking forward the principles of Standard Grade which had three levels. The new system was to be run by a new body, the Scottish Qualifications Authority, formed by the merger of the Examination Board and the Vocational Education Council. The courses and examinations would be available in both schools and further education colleges.

This change may have seemed administratively neat, and it seemed to accept the view, which had attracted much support in the 1980s, that 'parity of esteem' between academic and vocational education required that they be organised in the same framework as academic education (for which debate, see Raffe et al. 2001). However, the reform did not still the controversy (Paterson 2000b: 82–98). The main point which the critics made was that the new courses interfered with worthwhile academic study, partly because they were divided into discrete modules, partly because students therefore had to be assessed in each subject at least three times during the year, but above all because – it was alleged – the values of vocationalism had swamped the principles of broad, academic study. Many of these concerns received much more publicity than they might otherwise have done when, during the first year of the new system's operation in 1999–2000, the Scottish Qualifications Authority failed to deliver accurate certificates on time to a substantial minority of candidates – at least one in nine, and perhaps as many as one in six (Paterson 2000b: 15–16, 21–2; Raffe et al. 2002). The resulting inquiry conducted by the Scottish Parliament's Education Committee found widespread support for the principle of extending courses and certification to all students in fifth and sixth year, just as had been successfully achieved in third and fourth year. Indeed, in a survey of teachers and students in late 2000, clear majorities were found in favour of this widening of access, and in particular for the new Intermediate courses that were set at a level just below that of the Higher (Scottish Executive 2001e; Raffe et al. 2002). The dissent stemmed from the modular assessment and excessive amounts of assessment, and from the apparent dilution of academic standards (Paterson 2000b: 132–56). There also seemed to be a widespread feeling that the reform had not paid adequate attention to questions of purpose. An editorial in the *Times Educational Supplement Scotland* on 21 July 1995 had warned that those designing the new courses must face up to the 'intellectually demanding task' of combining 'liberal education and vocational preparation'. To many critics of the SQA in 2000, that still seemed not to have happened: for example, the Association of Directors of Education in Scotland said in their submission to the parliamentary inquiry that:

> the decision to create a unified academic and vocational qualification
> system produced many fundamentally conflicting views and interests
> which could only have been reconciled through consultation on issues
> of philosophy, purpose and overall design. Consultation focused instead
> on mechanistic, instrumental issues relating to implementation.
>   (ADES 2000: 3.4; see also Paterson 2000b: 88)

Particularly prominent in this debate was an association representing English teachers, which attracted the signatures of around half of them to a petition re-asserting the subject's traditional role of forming the core of general education (Paterson 2000b: 90–4). One of the organisers of this, Tony McManus, who was an English teacher in Queensferry High School, argued in 1997 that the effect of the reforms would be to turn 'the teaching process into a mechanistic affair, training pupils towards the narrow needs of an overweening and inflexible assessment system'. The role of general education, he said, was to open 'the intellectual landscape to anyone who wishes to venture into it', which would provide the basis for 'a genuine social ethics as well as individual fulfilment' (McManus 1997: 35–6). As we have seen, these principles were common in thinking about English throughout the century, and they sum up rather neatly at the end of it the Scottish inclination to define educational democracy as access to an academic curriculum, not as an erosion of intellectual difficulty.

THE ROLE OF MYTH

We have seen, then, that the debates about secondary education at the end of the century were still about much the same things as had dominated it throughout: how to democratise access to broad, academic study. In effect, what had happened between 1945 and the 1970s was that the old omnibus schools had become the defining institutions of Scottish secondary schooling. In the fullest and most rigorous analysis of post-war secondary schooling that has been published, Andrew McPherson and his colleagues put this very well: 'the form of comprehensive education that sustains' the claims made by its advocates 'is not the one introduced by the post-1965 reorganisation, but one arising out of an older and traditional form of Scottish education' (Gray et al. 1983: 266).

However, the conclusions they drew from it – which have been influential on subsequent perceptions of Scottish education – are strangely contradictory. On the one hand, they argued that what they call the 'myth' of Scottish educational democracy was used to inspire reform, partly because many of the key people who made the policies had themselves come through these traditional omnibus schools, and so had a well-developed sense of what a common education would look like, and also had an appreciation that it could be achieved while maintaining high academic standards. That seems an accurate analysis of the Scottish reformers' understandings and motivation, and explains how the popular pressure for access to broad, general education could be translated into practice. On the other hand, the critique by Gray et al. of the myth was based only on its traditional form, not on the potentially democratic outcomes which this policy process may have created. Yet that critique of the traditional myth has now passed into educational folklore as if it were a critique of the myth's potential, so that many subsequent writers – as we noted in Chapter 1 – seem to have believed that Scotland was no nearer educational democracy than it had ever been.

A couple of examples may illustrate this. Gray et al. concluded in relation to the curriculum that 'inherited ideas of breadth ... have only been realised for a small minority of pupils' (see p. 303). However, the processes of pressure and politics from the 1970s onwards have gradually widened access to the main elements of a broad curriculum, as we have seen in this and the previous chapter. Indeed, they themselves document the first phases of that earlier in the book (on p. 78). Likewise, when they wrote that it is 'perhaps ironic that comprehensive education has extended the influence of the universities over secondary education' (see p. 135), they were positing a timeless image of the university tradition too. There is nothing at all ironic about such an outcome where the prevalent idea that has driven democratisation is that a broad, general education, defined ultimately by the university, ought to be available to everyone.

Maybe this contradiction is inevitable. It was precisely the stringency of the critique by McPherson and others which pushed reformers into trying to make the myth more real for a democratic age. Perhaps the critique of the inadequacies of Higher Still will push that reform back in the direction of greater academic rigour, while maintaining the democratising impulse which it inherited from Standard Grade and the ending of selection. Similarly, the persisting social inequalities at the end of the century encouraged new radicals to believe that the 1960s reforms were incomplete. Sociologists need to remember that the history of reform extends into the future, inspired often by sociology's own work in delineating the inequalities which have been inherited from the past: in Alasdair MacIntyre's words, 'an adequate sense of tradition manifests itself in a grasp of those future possibilities which the past has made available to the present' (MacIntyre 1981: 223).

CHAPTER 9

Higher Education

The universities were the one sector which the post-war Advisory Councils did not discuss, reflecting these institutions' growing absorption into a British realm of policy at that time. The Councils did not have much to say about the central institutions either, even in the seventh council's report on further education in 1952: it dealt with non-advanced courses. The teacher-training institutions were discussed, but they were never really at the heart of higher education. The result was that, in the 1940s and 1950s, there was no fundamental appraisal of Scottish higher education, and so the policies that were already in place simply drifted forward until the mid-1960s when the whole sector was transformed by the UK-wide effects of the 1963 report of the Robbins committee. There were two consequences of this. One was slow expansion. The other was an emerging dispute over what ought to be the true character of Scottish higher learning – an inherited, Scottish and putatively democratic one, or elite and British. These arguments were never very prominent in the 1950s, but they surfaced publicly in the 1970s and after, and in many respects were still unresolved at the end of the century, although by then officially almost completely ignored.

EXPANSION, 1950S–1970S

Each of the three main sectors providing under-graduate higher education grew slowly in the 1950s, as Table 9.1 illustrates. Assessing how many of the students were working at university level in 1950 in the central institutions remains difficult from official figures. The sixth Advisory Council had in fact recommended that most non-elementary work be removed from them (Cowper 1970: 79), but the seventh Council found that too much elementary work was still being done there (SED 1952b: 50). The SED's claim in 1953 that much of the elementary work had been transferred to education

Table 9.1 Numbers of Full-Time Under-Graduate Students, 1950–70

	1950	1960	1970
Students at university*	14,000	15,061	32,714
Non-graduate trainee teachers	3,130	4,625	10,765
Advanced students in central institutions	not available	3,762	8,836

*The four ancient universities in 1950 and 1960, and the eight universities in 1970: see text.
Sources: UGC (1952: 16; 1962: 22); SED (1951: 94; 1961a: 122–3, 133; 1972c: 73, 148);
DES (1973: 3).

authorities therefore seems implausible (SED 1953b: 5). From 1958 onwards the SED annual reports show the higher-education work separately, and from then until the early 1960s there were over 3,500 full-time students at that level (SED 1959: 103). In 1960, there were also a further 1,894 part-time students at higher-education level. For Table 9.1, an adjustment has to be made to avoid double-counting of the students in the Royal College in Glasgow, which was partly funded by the University Grants Committee but was administratively the responsibility of the SED. It is almost certain that the numbers reported by the SED in the central institutions included students at the Royal College, because, in the SED's 1964 report (although not in the earlier ones), there was an explicit note to that effect (SED 1965c: 114). Therefore, in Table 9.1, the figures for the universities in 1950 and 1960 refer only to the four old universities.

In short, the total number of people embarking on full-time study at first degree or diploma level in higher education rose from around 21,000 in 1950 to about 23,000 in 1960, or from four per thousand population to 4.5. The latter figure was two thirds more than the 2.7 per thousand in the late-1930s (Chapter 5 above). Nevertheless, despite this expansion, there were complaints that qualified applicants were not being admitted – 304 of them, it was claimed, in 1962 (Scotland 1969: 246). This was the Scottish instance of the pressure that led to the setting up of the Robbins committee, and its recommendations in 1963 that there should be a large increase in the number of higher-education students by the 1980s. Its recommendations for Scotland included establishing one wholly new university, the location of which was eventually settled on Stirling; it opened in 1967. In Glasgow, the Royal College merged with the Scottish College of Commerce to become Strathclyde University in 1964. Heriot Watt College in Edinburgh became Heriot Watt University in that same year, and the Dundee campus of St Andrews University regained its independence as Dundee University. Table 9.1 illustrates the subsequent growth in the 1960s: in 1970, the figure of around 52,000 students represented ten full-time students per thousand population, a doubling in a decade and more than a tripling since the 1930s.

All this expansion from the 1950s to the 1970s then occasioned a great deal of debate about the Scottish university tradition. There were three main topics – access, curriculum and cultural loyalty. The process of selecting students to the universities changed as new institutions were founded, and as some of them tried harder to recruit more widely throughout the UK. A UK-wide entrance system for the universities was started in 1961, although Aberdeen, Strathclyde and Glasgow universities did not fully join it until the 1980s. The attestation of fitness was dropped in 1968, and individual faculties started to impose their own entrance requirements (Scotland 1969: 248). The new universities no longer required that all entrants have Higher passes in both mathematics and a language, although all continued to insist on English and some breadth. These administrative changes themselves had significance for the social basis of the universities: they weakened the direct links with Scottish schools and began to disrupt the practice of a common educational ethos stretching from primary to university.

The introduction of state grants for all students in higher education in 1962 also modified the old patterns of recruitment (Cazaly 1986: 95–6; Scotland 1969: 251). The change was greatest for university students. In the 1950s – as a result of the 1946 Education (Scotland) Act which systematised earlier legislation stretching back to 1918 – Scottish students could receive bursaries from local authorities: for example, in 1960–1, 6,852 university students were holding local authority bursaries, about one half of all university students from Scotland, as were almost all higher-education students in teacher-training colleges and central institutions (SED 1961a: 138). The new grants after 1962 were available to everyone, and were intended to cover all costs, in contrast to the local authority bursaries which the SED had always recognised as being inadequate, and so students could afford to travel further afield (Cazaly 1986: 96, 101).

The expansion did lead to a slow rise in the participation of women in the universities, the proportion who were female being twenty-seven per cent in 1950 and thirty-three per cent in 1970. The proportion of students on non-graduate teacher-education courses – which were mainly for primary teaching – also grew, from eighty-one per cent in 1950 to eighty-four per cent in 1970. Information on the gender composition of students in the central institutions was not supplied routinely in the 1950s, but the SED annual reports showed the number of such students in receipt of education authority bursaries, and these indicated a fall in the proportion who were female, from forty-five per cent in 1950 to thirty-eight per cent in 1960 (SED 1952a: 106; 1962: 138); in 1970, when full information was published, thirty-seven per cent of full-time higher-education students in the central institutions were female. Because the universities contained many more higher education students than these colleges, however, this fall from the early 1950s was not enough to offset the growth in female participation.

Table 9.2 Percentage of School-Leaver Entrants to Full-Time Higher
Education who were Working Class, 1963–90

	1963	1972	1980	1990
Universities*	34	28	26	18
Colleges and central institutions	47	47	37	36

* The four ancient universities in 1963, and the eight universities thereafter.
Sources: Scottish School Leavers Survey.

In contrast, whether the growth led to any change in social-class differences
in opportunities to enter university is doubtful. The proportion of middle-
class school leavers who entered degree courses rose from twelve per cent in
the early 1950s through sixteen per cent in the early 1960s to twenty-three per
cent in the mid-1970s; the working class proportions kept pace, but probably
did not converge: they were two per cent, three per cent and four per cent
(Gray et al. 1983: 204–5). Because the overall size of the working class was
falling – from fifty-eight per cent in the census of 1951 to forty-nine per cent
in 1971 (McCrone 1992: 139) – this fairly constant differential meant that the
proportion of students who were working class was declining as well, as the
first two columns of Table 9.2 show. The level of self-recruitment by professions such as law and medicine remained as high as it had ever been (Kelly
1976: 185–7). The working class, then, probably benefited from the expansion
to the same extent as did the middle class, and so in that sense opportunity to
enter the universities was extended, but the relative disadvantage of the
working class did not change.

The other sectors of higher education remained much more open to
working-class entrants, as Table 9.2 also shows. Therefore, in 1963, the overall
proportion of school-leaver entrants to the non-university institutions who
were working class was thirteen points higher than in the universities; in 1972,
it was nineteen points higher. The working-class proportions were much the
same in the different parts of the non-university sector – mainly at this date
the central institutions and the colleges of education (Raffe 1977: 102). (We
return to the rest of Table 9.2 later.)

The universities were also becoming less local. There were two aspects to
this. One was a slow decline in the connections between the universities and the
regions of Scotland, exacerbated by the 1960s expansion. In 1952, the four
older universities were still almost as firmly rooted in their regions as they had
been before the war (Mackay 1969: 56). In Aberdeen, seventy-three per cent of
all students came from the north east and twelve per cent from the Highlands
and Islands. In Edinburgh, fifty-four per cent came from the east-central
region and six per cent from the Borders. In Glasgow, seventy-seven per cent
came from the west-central area. Only in St Andrews was the traditional region

in a minority: forty-six per cent were from the east-central region. This pattern had probably still not changed much by 1962, although directly comparable data have been published only for Aberdeen University, where the total from Aberdeenshire remained roughly constant at about one half between 1950 and 1960 (Hargreaves and Forbes 1989: 141). In 1962, across Scotland as a whole, two thirds of school-leaver entrants to university went to their local university (Paterson 1993: 239). However, by 1972, this had fallen to fifty-four per cent, and a decade later it was under one half. In Aberdeen, the proportion from Aberdeenshire fell from fifty-one per cent in 1960 to thirty-nine per cent in 1970 (Hargreaves and Forbes 1989: 141). Encouraging this process was the building of residences, which were used by twenty-three per cent of students in 1970, double the level of 1960 and 1950 (DES 1973: 16; UGC 1952: 10; 1962: 12). This went along with a fall in the proportion living in their parental home from fifty-seven per cent in 1950 to forty-one per cent in 1970. These proportions were much the same for men and women, although slightly higher proportions of women were in residences (for example, twenty-seven per cent in 1970). The proportion living at home was highest in Glasgow city: Glasgow university had three quarters of its students doing so in 1950 and 1960, and two thirds in 1970. The figures were similar for the Royal College in 1950 and 1960 and for Strathclyde University in 1970. In contrast to all this decline in university localism, throughout the two decades from 1962, around sixty per cent of entrants to the non-university sector of higher education entered an institution in their local region (Paterson 1993: 240).

The other aspect of the decline of localism was the beginnings of a slow fall in the proportion of university students who came from Scotland. The proportion of under-graduate students at the universities from Scotland was around eighty per cent in 1952 (Mackay 1969: 56), and around seventy-five per cent throughout the 1970s (SED 1972c: 116; 1989b: 9), but by the 1980s Dundee and Stirling had fewer than sixty per cent from Scotland, and St Andrews had under forty per cent (SED 1989b: 4). At the same time, the non-university sector remained much more Scottish in its recruitment: in 1980, ninety per cent of its entrants were from Scotland (SED 1989c: 11).

The universities, old and new, were therefore gradually becoming less local, less Scottish and – compared to the higher-education colleges – less working class. This provided the sociological background to controversies over the curriculum, the second topic of debate around expansion between the 1950s and 1970s. The earliest prominent contribution was George Davie's *The Democratic Intellect* in 1961. Although cast as a critique of the 1889 reforms (as we have seen in Chapter 5), it was also an intervention in a current debate: could the generalist tradition survive in an age when the price that was being paid for massive expansion was that higher education be more tightly related to policy makers' perceptions of the needs of the economy?

In the universities, the curricular specialisation which provoked this had started in the 1950s. In 1950, it was still the case that more than half (fifty-one per cent) of all degrees obtained in the universities were arts (UGC 1952: 24–5). In 1960, this had fallen to forty-three per cent (UGC 1962: 29). The proportion of science degrees had risen from thirty-two per cent to thirty-nine per cent. The curricular shifts towards vocationalism and away from the traditional arts curriculum accelerated. Neither the four new universities in the 1960s, nor the central institutions and colleges, even tried to replicate the old breadth of the Ordinary MA, and the older universities gradually abandoned the tight requirements, aided by the Universities (Scotland) Act of 1966 which removed the stipulation that all four universities had to agree on curricular changes (Scotland 1969: 247). The traditionalists tended to ignore the central institutions and the teacher-training colleges altogether in their contribution to the debate, but including them in the totals would have increased the proportion of science degrees even further, since most of the students in the growing central institutions were scientists or technologists, and since, throughout the period, they outnumbered the students training to be teachers. The trends in the universities were partly halted in the 1960s by the growth in social science, which emerged out of arts as a recognisable area of study in that decade: in 1970, the combined total of arts and social science was again at forty-nine per cent, and the science proportion was constant at forty per cent; the big fall proportionately was in medicine, from eighteen per cent in 1950 and 1960 to eleven per cent in 1970 (although, in absolute numbers, it too had grown).

After the 1970s, social science grew even further, mainly because of the popularity of business studies (SOED 1991: 6; Scottish Executive 2001b: table 16). This in turn was partly because the initial training of several of the large professions was shifting from apprenticeship to the universities. For example, before 1960, there were no full-time academic accountancy staff in the Scottish universities, although there had been part-time professors in Edinburgh since 1919 and in Glasgow since 1926. Then, in 1961, the Institute of Chartered Accountants of Scotland required that all its trainees spend one full-time year in an academic institution, and in 1973 it went even further and moved almost all the initial period of training into the universities or onto the new Higher National Diploma in accounting (ICAS 1974; Paisey and Paisey 2000: 35–6; Parker 1997). Thus, whereas in 1968 only seventy of the 269 new trainees were graduates, by 1980 all but seventeen of the 536 new trainees held a degree or the diploma (ICAS 1970, 1980).

Accompanying the growth of specialisation was the growth of post-graduate degrees. In 1950, there were 1,132 full-time or part-time post-graduate students in the Scottish universities, seventeen per cent of them women (UGC 1952: 16–17). In 1960, the number had grown to 2,094, fifteen per cent of whom were women (UGC 1962: 22–3), but by 1970 this had more than doubled, to 5,952, twenty per cent women (DES 1973: 3 and 37). The growth in higher degrees since 1950 had thus been more than fivefold, whereas first degrees had no more than doubled in number.

The specialisation was interpreted as an undermining of the Scottish tradition – even the growth of social science, since in the epistemology of that tradition the study of society was not considered to be distinguishable from the study of human thought, and since directly vocational study was not believed to be the role of first-level degrees. There was a similar reaction to the sense that many more students were driven by vocational motives. One analysis of school-leaver entrants to higher education in 1972 found that fifty-eight per cent of men and fifty-four per cent of women were motivated primarily by vocational considerations such as seeking training for a particular occupation; only twenty-four per cent of men and thirty per cent of women were influenced by educational factors, such as being interested in a particular subject; the remainder saw higher education as a means of postponing decisions about their future (Jones and McPherson 1973). The new social science courses were also, at this time, seen to be of low status compared to science, medicine or the traditional arts subjects, and the increasing competition for entry to arts, medicine and science was narrowing the school curriculum of able students. Among school-leaver entrants to university in 1970, the most able students had already specialised in their school curriculum in order to achieve entry to either science or arts, so that almost all university science entrants had concentrated on science at school and most university arts entrants had taken two foreign languages at school; the social scientists tended to have lower attainment at school overall (Hutchison and Littlejohn 1975: 6–7). A UK committee – chaired by Sir Frederick Dainton – examined the supply of science graduates, and praised the Scottish system because its breadth seemed to be able to avoid deterring able students from entering science (Council for Scientific Policy 1968). However, that had one drawback for encouraging broad university studies in that it tended to push most students who were qualified to enter science into science, even if they had also been qualified to enter social science or arts (Jones et al. 1974). Perhaps Scotland was then producing scientists who had some acquaintance with non-science study – especially through the liberal studies element of the English courses at school – but this did leave those professions which recruited from social science degrees with little advanced understanding of science and technology.

The curricular change that provoked the most hostility from advocates of the Scottish tradition was the declining popularity and status of the Ordinary Degree. This was still seen as the very embodiment of generalism, and of the unity of the whole education system: as the SED itself put it in 1972, 'the Scottish ordinary degree course represents a natural extension into university education of the secondary school curriculum', insofar as both provided a curriculum that is 'broadly based' (SED 1972b: 7). Scottish evidence to the Robbins committee also made this link, although the report of the committee had little to say on either the Ordinary Degree specifically or the Scottish curricular tradition generally (Committee on Higher Education 1963a: 96–7; McPherson 1972: 14). The proportion taking the Ordinary Degree was still high in the 1950s: sixty-nine per cent in 1950, sixty-seven per cent in 1960 (UGC 1952: 24; 1962: 29). Then, however, in a decade, the proportion fell to fifty-five per cent, the start of a process that saw the degree eventually collapse to thirty-two per cent of graduates in 1990 (DES 1973: 54; UFC 1992: 61). The proportion among women had in fact remained high: seventy-five per cent in 1950, seventy-two per cent in 1960 and sixty-eight per cent in 1970. Among men, however, the fall was much larger: from sixty-seven per cent in 1950 to forty-eight per cent in 1970. McPherson (1972: 18–19) also found that, in the mid-1960s, for both women and men, the average number of Highers passed at secondary school was lower among students who took the Ordinary Degree than among those who did Honours.

The Ordinary MA Degree, in fact, was becoming the normal route into secondary school teaching, while the specialist Honours science degree was acquiring the high status associated with the attempted modernisation of the British economy that had been inaugurated by the Labour government of 1964–70. In the mid-1960s, the proportions entering colleges of education upon graduation were around one half of all female graduates – Honours or Ordinary, arts or science (McPherson and Atherton 1970: 38). One third of male arts graduates did the same, again whether Honours or Ordinary, as did one third of male Ordinary science graduates. However, school teaching was shunned by male Honours science graduates: only thirteen per cent of them entered it. This was highly significant: male Honours science graduates were three quarters of all male science graduates, and fifty-five per cent of all science graduates. Another way of expressing these figures is to say that of all graduate entrants to school teaching, sixty-two per cent had graduated with an Ordinary Degree.

Changes in the colleges of education themselves in the 1960s tended to reinforce this perception of a diminished status for school teaching. The expansion of secondary schooling and the working-through of the large post-war birth-cohorts of school pupils required an expansion of teacher numbers, and so the SED expanded the colleges, building three new ones – in Ayr, Hamilton and Falkirk – and accepting Stirling University's innovation of training a small number of teachers in so-called concurrent degrees, in which students took university courses and the professional courses at the same time (Marker and Raab 1993). There continued to be the four large colleges in the four cities, two Catholic colleges, and one specialist college for teachers of physical education. Following Robbins, the four city colleges inaugurated BEd degrees, which, as Marker (1994: 48) comments, were in fact Ordinary Degrees providing prospective primary teachers with something like the concurrent courses that had been common at the beginning of the century, and that the Stirling courses also resembled. These, however, never flourished, partly because of tensions between the universities and the colleges over the role of academic work in a professional degree, and partly because the degree never proved very popular (Kirk 1996: 111). For example, in 1971, when it had been in existence for at least four years in all four colleges, it contained only seven per cent of all teacher-training students, or only eight per cent of students entering the colleges directly from school (SED 1972c: 148). It was alleged also that the introduction of the BEd had been designed by the management of the older universities as a means of further marginalising the Ordinary Degree, with its importance as the route into teaching: typical of this view was the comment by R. E. Bell, who was in the school of education at the Open University, that the BEd had 'paved the way for ending the universities' general commitment to the world of educational studies' (Bell 1987: 30).

Altogether, then, the status of school teaching was being threatened by three processes: by the separation of the universities from the cultural world of the colleges, by the tendency within the universities for those students who were destined to enter school teaching to be concentrated in the Ordinary, especially Ordinary Arts, degrees, and by the lack of any sustained thinking about the educational purpose of these degrees themselves. The setting up of a General Teaching Council in 1965 – in theory providing an element of self-regulation to the teaching profession through its power to regulate professional standards – did not really halt this sense of decline, and neither did the coming of a nominally all-graduate profession in the 1980s through a renaming of the primary diploma courses as degrees (using the same title of BEd to mean something much less academic than the joint degree of the 1970s). In the minds of the critics of this process, the backbone of the Scottish tradition – the route from school to university and then back again as teacher – was thus becoming a ghetto, and was allegedly dragging down the whole education system with it.

This sense was intensified by controversies over governance, the third topic of debate at this time. The universities were moving increasingly into a British funding realm, their planning associated with the policies of the University Grants Committee. In 1950, sixty-nine per cent of the income of the Scottish universities came from government grants, and ninety-three per cent of that came via the UGC (UGC 1952: 35–6). This was already nearly double the level in the 1930s (see Chapter 5 above). In 1960, the proportion had risen to seventy-seven per cent, now ninety-six per cent from the UGC (UGC 1962: 39). In 1970, it was back down slightly, to seventy-two per cent, but that was only because, as a share of total income, research grants and contracts had reached ten per cent, and most of that came from the new research councils that had been created in 1965 with UK-wide responsibilities (DES 1973: 86). Research income had been five per cent in 1960 and was too small to be listed separately in 1950. By contrast, the central institutions remained firmly within the Scottish political realm. In 1960, for example, they received sixty-two per cent of their income from the SED, up from fifty-eight per cent in 1950; in 1960, only one fifth came from the UGC and other UK-government sources (SED 1961a: 105). By 1970, once the Royal College, the Scottish College of Commerce and Heriot Watt College had been wholly transferred to UGC responsibility, the proportion of the remaining income belonging to the central institutions that came from the SED was ninety-two per cent (SED 1972c: 193). The teacher-training institutions were almost exclusively Scottish in their income: for example, in 1960, sixty-three per cent came from the SED, and twenty-one per cent from education authorities.

This absorption of the universities into a British realm of policy had come about partly because their relations with the SED had deteriorated even further between the 1930s and the 1950s than they had done before. For example, when it had become clear in the late 1930s that Scottish local authorities were less generous in providing grants to universities than those in England, it had been proposed that the SED make compensatory payments out of the Education (Scotland) Fund (Hutchison 1992: 58). The SED was very reluctant, partly because they did not want the Treasury to examine in any great detail its expenditure on non-university education in Scotland (see p. 61). After the war, the universities therefore looked upon the UGC as a much safer source. It was only when, in the 1980s, protection in Whitehall seemed to be at an end that there were the beginnings of a shift in the universities' position.

MASS HIGHER EDUCATION, 1980s–1990s

Two of these three controversies – over access and over accountability – then shaped the Scottish response to the emergence of a mass system of higher education in the 1980s and 1990s. The odd absence was the official silence on the curriculum and on higher education's cultural purpose.

Growth was both spectacular and accelerating, as Table 9.3 shows – by a quarter in the 1970s, by a third in the 1980s, and by two thirds in the 1990s. The rate of participation in full-time under-graduate courses by people aged under twenty-one grew from nine per cent in 1962 to eighteen per cent in 1975, twenty-six per cent in 1990 and fifty per cent in 2000 (Committee on Higher Education 1963b: 26; SED 1983b: 6; Scottish Executive 2002b: table 6). Part-time study also grew sixfold from the early 1960s, to 66,806 at the end of the

Table 9.3 Numbers of Full-Time Under-Graduate Students, 1970–2000

	1970	1980	1990	2000
Numbers	52,315	65,400	85,977	143,913
Percentage in the eight older universities	63	61	54	50

Sources: SED (1972c: 73, 118, 148; 1989c: 11); SOED (1992c: 6); Scottish Executive (2001b: table 17).

century (DES 1973: 36; SED 1972c: 71; Scottish Executive 2001b: table 5). Numbers of post-graduate students rose, at first mainly in the universities. There were 7,842 post-graduate students in the universities in 1980, about a third more than in 1970 (UGC 1982: 12–13). By 1990, this had grown to 12,759, and there were then also 4,952 in the central institutions and colleges (SOED 1992c: 6–7). In the next decade, the market for vocationally specific post-graduate diplomas and masters degrees had grown enormously, and there were 48,669 post-graduates in total in 2000 (Scottish Executive 2001b: table 5), although about a third of this apparent growth in the decade was due to the inclusion of continuing education students in the statistics for the first time.

From the 1980s, the growth was largest in the non-university sector, as is also shown in Table 9.3. This was partly because of restrictions on the expansion of the universities imposed by government (Love and McNicoll 1990: 481). One difference between the sectors was the proportion on multi-disciplinary courses, the legacy of the Ordinary Degree in the universities – in 1990, twenty per cent of full-time degree students in the universities, but under four per cent in the non-university sector (SOED 1992c: 6). The shift to the central institutions and colleges marked, therefore, a further step in the decline of that programme. The central institutions and colleges also tended to have greater proportions in applied subjects: in 1990, thirty per cent of their full-time under-graduates were studying business, compared to six per cent in the universities, and twenty-one per cent were studying technology compared to sixteen per cent in the universities. The universities, correspondingly, had more pure science (twenty-one per cent against ten per cent), and their medical courses were mainly to train doctors rather than nurses and other health professionals. This practical orientation suited the predilections of politicians in all the main parties. So, too, did the relative cheapness of educating students in the central institutions rather than the universities: in 1982, for example, the average annual costs per full-time student were £4,628 in the universities, £3,663 in the colleges of education and £3,074 in the central institutions (SED 1985: 153). These differentials also, however, provoked complaints that students outside the universities were receiving a poorer quality of education.

This process culminated in the ending of the distinction between universities and colleges altogether: in 1993, all the central institutions, colleges of education and colleges of agriculture were put on the same funding and planning basis as the universities, and indeed five of the central institutions were given the title of university. Several of the smaller colleges – including all the colleges of education – merged with neighbouring universities (Kirk 1999). By the end of the 1990s, despite these mergers, sixty-seven per cent of all under-graduate students (and fifty per cent of full-time under-graduates) were outside the eight older universities (Scottish Executive 2001b: tables 1, 17, 18).

Within the non-university sector, an increasing share was taken by the further education colleges; as we will see in Chapter 10, these were founded, mainly after 1950, to provide non-advanced technical training, but after the 1970s they also developed increasing amounts of advanced work. As a proportion of all entrants to full-time under-graduate courses, the colleges made up twenty-four per cent in 1980 and thirty-six per cent in 1999 (SOED 1991: 9; Scottish Executive 2001b: table 10). Their most important role, however, was in the expansion of part-time higher education: they attracted ninety-five per cent of entrants to part-time courses in 1980 and seventy-one per cent in 1999 (Schuller et al. 1999; SOED 1991: 10; Scottish Executive 2001b: table 10). As a result, in 1999, fifty-two per cent of entrants to any kind of under-graduate higher education course were entering a college. But most of their work was at the level of higher education diplomas, not degrees: by the 1990s, over ninety-five per cent of their students (whether full-time or part-time) were taking diplomas (SOED 1991: 6–7; Scottish Executive 2001c: table 1h).

The main explanation of all this growth was the successful outcomes of the secondary-education reforms of the 1960s and 1970s (Burnhill et al. 1988). Because of the expansion and rising attainment at that level, growing numbers of parents of school leavers had more than a minimal amount of secondary schooling: for example, the proportion of leavers with at least one parent who had at least four years of secondary schooling rose from twenty per cent in 1976 to thirty-three per cent in 1986, then reached fifty-eight per cent in 1994 (Burnhill et al. 1988: 72; Scottish Schools Leavers Survey of 1995). The proportion with a parent who had at least five years of secondary schooling was eleven per cent in 1976, fourteen per cent in 1986 and twenty-eight per cent in 1994. These better-educated parents passed on to their children a sense that higher education was a realistic goal, and thus inspired them to attempt and to pass the Highers that would gain them a place on a higher education course. Since the government funding of higher education was largely determined by statistical forecasts of student numbers that were themselves based on this rising trend of Higher Grade attainment, the expansion was in a real sense a response to popular pressure.

Whether this mass expansion was achieved without any deterioration of quality is difficult to say, although higher education was subject to much more formal quality assurance than ever before (Sharp et al. 1997). Class sizes rose, but small classes had never been a feature of the Scottish universities, as had been pointed out in a UGC report in 1964 (UGC 1964: 16). The proportion of students who failed to complete their courses, even in the late 1990s, was only twelve per cent, and so, with a rate of entry that was relatively high by European standards, Scotland probably had one of the largest proportions of young people graduating (SHEFC 2000). By contrast, allegations that quality was deteriorating tended to be rhetorical, lacking any basis in systematic research (see, for example, Walker 1994).

In a formal statistical sense, then, the expansion seemed to have come close to making much more of a reality of the putative tradition of open access to university. Moreover, the democracy lay not only in the sheer size of the system, but also in some large shifts in its social base, in three respects – gender, age and social class. The share taken by women continued to rise. As a proportion of all entrants to full-time higher education, women made up forty-three per cent in 1980 and fifty-five per cent in 1999 (SOED 1991: 9; Scottish Executive 2001b: table 10); in 1999, the female proportion in part-time higher education was fifty-seven per cent. By that last date, fifty-three per cent of women aged under twenty-one were entering full-time higher education, compared to forty-two per cent of men. A similar shift came about among post-graduate students: the proportion who were female rose from twenty-eight per cent in the university courses in 1980 to forty-eight per cent of the total in 1999. Although rising female entry to university courses was initially in part a response to rapid contraction in the colleges of education in the 1970s and 1980s, the sustaining of the trend thereafter showed that the main impetus – as in the schools – was not so much official policy as young women's changing aspirations: thus, during the 1970s, the intentions of female school leavers converged with those of male leavers (Burnhill and McPherson 1984). Following the changes in female students' participation in the Higher Grade curriculum at school, there also emerged large changes in the kinds of subjects which they took in higher education, as Table 9.4 shows: by the 1990s, only in technology did the female participation lag far behind (Paterson 1994).

Table 9.4 Percentage of Women among Full-Time Under-Graduate University Students, 1960 and 1990

	1960	1990
Arts and social science	43	54
Pure science	25	42
Medicine	25	50
Technology	3	15

Sources: UGC (1962: 27); UFC (1992: 14–15).

After the fall in the proportion of students who were aged over twenty-one in the earlier part of the century, there was now a slow rise again, the second way in which access was widening. In the 1970s and 1980s, only one in five entrants to full-time higher education courses were aged over twenty-one; by 1999, the proportion was one third, and in the further education colleges it was over one half (Gallacher 2002; SED 1972c: 71, 117; SOEID 1996b: 10; Scottish Executive 2001b: table 13). One aspect of the same phenomenon (not included in these figures) was the Open University which had been founded in 1969 to provide access by means of distance learning and broadcasting: numbers in it rose from 5,242 in 1980 to 8,982 in 1990 and 13,607 in 1999 (Paterson 1997b: 43; Scottish Executive 2001b: table 14).

Social class differences – the third aspect of changing patterns of access – were more intractable, but the expansion did start to erode them by the 1990s (Tinklin and Raffe 1999: 18). In 1980, the proportion entering full-time higher education was thirty-three per cent among school leavers whose father was in a non-manual job, but only eight per cent among those whose father was in a manual occupation, a ratio that was only slightly less than between the 1950s and 1970s. By 1993, the non-manual proportion had grown to fifty-one per cent, but the working-class proportion had proportionately grown more, to twenty-four per cent. One of the reasons was that the most rapidly growing sectors – the central institutions and the further education colleges – were better at attracting working-class entrants (Paterson 1995; Raab 1998: 39). The further education colleges, in particular, provided routes into higher education for people who did not gain enough certificates from school to enter directly; they could take Highers courses there, then move to a higher education diploma, and subsequently transfer to a degree course in a university (Gallacher et al. 1997; Robertson 1992).

Another reason for the slow narrowing of the class inequality may have been the various schemes that were set up in the 1980s specifically to encourage working-class entry – for example, by special summer schools, or by recognising routes into universities or colleges by means of non-advanced courses at further education colleges. In the early 1990s, there were around 2,000 students on such access courses, and the consensus of evaluations of them was that they were indeed attracting students who would not otherwise have entered (Gallacher 1994, 2002; Munn et al. 1993). Their biggest impact, however, was on the vocationally relevant courses in the central institutions (or their successors) and the further education colleges. These access courses, by their very nature, tended to appeal most to older students (Munn et al. 1993; Tett and Blair 1999). On the whole, with adequate support while at university or college, the access students seem to have performed as well as people who entered by traditional routes (McPake and Watt 1998; O'Dea and McPhee 1994).

The forty-seven further education colleges were also much more geo-graphically dispersed and therefore more local than the other sectors of higher education, and so had become the main repository of the Scottish tradition of local access, although the central institutions maintained this too. The older universities, by contrast, had became far less local by the 1990s than they had been only two decades earlier: in 1990, among school-leaver entrants, only forty per cent entered a university in their local region, not much more than would have been expected if students had randomly chosen a location (Paterson 1993: 239). Some of the universities had also, by the 1980s, started to recruit large proportions of their students from outside Scotland altogether. The overall proportion from outside remained at around the one in five that it had been throughout the century (Paterson 1997b: 39), but in St Andrews it was over one half. Particular controversy was raised when the trends in non-Scottish entry to Edinburgh University went in the same direction in the late 1980s – from seventy-one per cent of entrants being from Scotland in 1980 to forty-three per cent in 1993 (SED 1989b: 12; Paterson 1997b: 40). There were then accusations that the universities were designing their first-year classes to suit entrants with A levels, rather than people who had followed a broader but less specialised school curriculum from Scotland, since most of the non-Scots came from England: the proportion of all university under-graduate students from outside the UK remained at under one in ten until the end of the century, as it had been throughout (SED 1989c: 11; Scottish Executive 2001b: table 8). Scots themselves preferred to remain in their own country, despite the decline in choosing a local university: only around six to seven per cent of entrants to full-time under-graduate courses left Scotland, and – throughout the period from 1971 until the end of the century – seventy per cent or more of graduates who were originally from Scotland stayed in Scotland for their first job or for a post-graduate course (Paterson 1997b: 38; Scottish Executive 1999d: 16; SED 1979: 9). Whatever else they may have been, the higher education institutions remained the training ground of new generations of the Scottish middle class, and the old nineteenth-century role of supplying professional men for the Empire had died with it between the 1920s and the 1950s (Hargreaves 1994; Mackay 1969: 96).

The decline in localism is probably one reason why, consistently from the 1960s to the 1990s, the older universities tended to have relatively low and declining proportions of their students from working-class families (Paterson 1995: 89). Another reason may be that the sheer strength of the further education colleges siphoned off working-class entrants who might otherwise have gone into university (Osborne 1999: 45). In 1998, in the eight universities that dated from the 1960s or earlier, only one fifth of entrants aged under twenty-one to full-time under-graduate courses had fathers who were in manual occupations; in St Andrews University the proportion was only fifteen per cent, and in Edinburgh University it was thirteen per cent (SHEFC 2000: table 1b). By contrast, Paisley University, a former central institution, had as many as forty-one per cent, and in Abertay University the figure was thirty-nine per cent, not far short of the forty-four per cent which the Scottish Household Survey of 1999 found to be the working-class proportion among adults in the general population. The situation in this regard in the older universities may in fact have deteriorated in the 1980s and 1990s, although directly comparable information is not available: in 1984, for example, the working-class proportion was twenty-six per cent among all entrants with Scottish qualifications to under-graduate courses anywhere in the UK (over nine out of ten of whom went to Scottish universities) (UCCA 1986: 16–17). Although that fall from one quarter to one fifth between 1984 and 1998 was no more than the fall of about five percentage points in the size of the manual working class in Scotland as a whole, over a longer time-span the older universities probably did lose working-class students in numbers that were disproportionate to the demographic change. Thus in Glasgow University, the most socially open of the older institutions – and the one for which the most detailed data on social class had always been collected – the proportion of its students who were working class had remained at around one third from the 1930s to the 1960s, but – among entrants aged under twenty-one – had fallen to one fifth by 1998, a sharper decline than the fall of nine percentage points between 1961 and 1999 in the size of the manual working class in Scotland as a whole (McDonald 1967: 53; SHEFC 2000: table 1a; McCrone 1992: 139; Scottish Household Survey 1999). The pattern in these figures is confirmed for school-leaver entrants: see the final two columns of Table 9.2 above. In the 1970s and 1980s, the working-class proportion in the colleges and central institutions fell roughly in line with the shrinking size of that class, but dropped by around a third in the universities to a level that was not much more than half that of the early 1960s.

Edinburgh and St Andrews Universities also had around forty per cent of these young entrants from independent schools. Such schools supplied seventeen per cent of all entrants to the Scottish higher education institutions (and so the proportion would be lower if the courses in further education colleges were included), a proportion that had hardly changed since 1962, when the School Leavers Survey had found the independent-school proportion to be twenty per cent among entrants to the universities and sixteen per cent among entrants to higher education as a whole. The disproportionate representation of these schools was mainly because their leavers tended to gain better results in school examinations (Tinklin 2000: 377), but – in the case of these two universities – it was also because they recruited fairly large minorities of their students from England, where the independent sector was larger. Whether these better school results were actually a better preparation for university was not clear: some research suggested that cramming for examinations might gain entry, but might then be a less effective preparation for truly autonomous study than passing fewer Highers at a school where university entry was not the norm (Robertson 2000).

Students from the newer minority ethnic groups started to enter higher education in proportions that were around twice those of their size in the general population. The data were collected only from the early 1990s onwards: from 1990, around two to three per cent of entrants to full-time under-graduate courses in the older universities were from such groups, around twice their proportion in the population: for example, in Glasgow in the mid-1990s, thirty-three per cent of school leavers in minority ethnic groups entered higher education, but only fourteen per cent of white leavers did so (Paterson 1997a: 13). For under-graduate higher education as a whole, this pattern was also found by Raab for the year 1996–7 (Raab 1998: 42).

CULTURE AND PURPOSE

Three themes run through the Scottish debate about access, accountability and curriculum. On access, first, there was the persistent belief that higher education ought to be broadly available: there was almost no public sense at all in Scotland that a mass system was dubious. The most visible instance of this concerned the issue of student fees and grants. The real value of the student grant fell in the 1980s, and in 1991 the Conservative government started the process of replacing grants with loans. In 1997 the Labour government announced that it would abolish grants altogether, and would require students to pay fees. Both these moves were highly controversial in Scotland, on the grounds that they threatened the principle of democratic access. The issue of student finance and student hardship then became one of the most prominent topics during and after the first elections to the new Scottish Parliament in 1999 (Smith and Taylor 1999). The result was the ending of fees for Scottish students, their replacement by a form of graduate tax, and the partial restoration of grants for students with low incomes (Paterson 2003).

On accountability, there was a background debate throughout the period from the 1970s about whether higher education was and ought to be Scottish. The universities continued to receive around three quarters of their income from the University Grants Committee or the UK research councils (UGC 1982: 12–13). They managed to have themselves excluded from the powers of the proposed Scottish Assembly at that time, but when that was not established the issue of their Scottishness returned, encouraged partly by the new Conservative government's sharp cuts in funding (Paterson 1998). A committee of inquiry reported in 1985, recommending that responsibility for all Scottish higher education be transferred to the Scottish Office (SED 1985).

This eventually happened in 1993, when responsibility for funding all higher education institutions was passed to the new Scottish Higher Education Funding Council. The immediate occasion was the Conservative government's decision to end the distinction between polytechnics and universities throughout the UK, but they could, in theory, have done that by transferring the central institutions and the colleges to a new UK-wide funding body (Scott 1995). That they did not do so was for political reasons: to have removed such a significant part of Scottish education from Scottish administrative control would have meant risking even further undermining the Scottish credentials of a party that was already gaining no more than about one quarter of the vote. The structurally unified system was then readily transferrable to the Scottish Parliament after 1999, with almost none of the controversy that had arisen in the 1970s (Paterson 1998). Thereafter, the higher education institutions remained attached to a formal UK political realm only through the UK-wide research councils, which provided about a fifth of the income of the eight older universities, but under one twentieth of the income of the others (SHEFC 1995: 23). Nevertheless, voluntary links remained strong: the funding councils shared processes of quality inspection for both teaching and research, there remained a common UK-wide system for admitting under-graduates, and salary scales were still the same in all parts of the UK.

Higher education had therefore become the focus for political debate, and its expansion gave it a political significance analogous to that which secondary education had had in the first three quarters of the century. There are indeed more detailed parallels. The creation of a unified system after 1993 and the mergers between many of the former colleges and the universities thereafter might be taken to be analogous to the combination in 1923 of the Higher Grade, Higher Class and endowed schools into one secondary sector. The subsequent debate about the role of the further education colleges would then appear to be analogous to the discussions in the 1920s and 1930s about a secondary education that would be on the same basis for all: as in the 1930s with the inferior funding of the Advanced Divisions compared to the secondary schools, it has been pointed out frequently that, even for higher education courses, annual funding per student is lower in the colleges than on similar courses in the higher education institutions. The Scottish Executive estimated that in 2001, the average funding per full-time higher-education student was about £2,900 in the FE colleges but £3,900 in the higher education institutions (Gallacher 2002). Some opinion then suggested that a common but still differentiated system of lifelong learning be established: for example, a discussion paper from the Scottish parliamentary committee that was responsible for lifelong learning recommended in March 2002 that everyone be entitled to the equivalent of two years of post-school education, funded on the same basis and monitored by a single agency (Scottish Parliament 2002). Consistent with this was the tendency of groups of FE colleges to form consortia to provide specialist courses: the most well-developed by the end of the century was the network in the Highlands and Islands which, it was intended, would eventually become a university for that area (Leech 1999: 56; Robertson 1999: 252). If a common system of post-school education did come about, then the next stage of the debate would – as in secondary schooling between 1936 and 1965 – probably be about a system of lifelong learning that was truly comprehensive.

What was notable, however, as this massive expansion took place, was the absence of much official encouragement to debate about the social role of the curriculum, and hence about purpose – the third feature of the debate. Higher education had become more democratic in a formal sense, but this had not been accompanied by any official discussion of what university democracy might mean culturally – nothing to resemble the Advisory Council's thinking about mass secondary education, for example. Davie's book did shape the thinking of many on the vaguely nationalist left, such as Beveridge and Turnbull (1989), Kane (1992), Kelman (1991) and Walker (1994). The general intellectual climate in which Davie wrote his work influenced the report of the Robbins committee in 1963: their statement that one of the aims of higher education should be 'the transmission of a common culture and common standards of citizenship' would not have been out of place in the main Scottish tradition, although they did not acknowledge any Scottish precedents for this aspect of their recommendations (Committee on Higher Education 1963a: 7). Such thinking in Scotland was also part of an intellectual climate in which a proper sociological evaluation of the twentieth-century reality of the tradition could take place, notably in the work of the Centre for Educational Sociology at Edinburgh University, which, under the leadership of Andrew McPherson between 1972 and the mid-1990s, achieved for the analysis of comprehensive education and university expansion what the Scottish Council for Research in Education had done for the expansion of the secondary system between the 1930s and the 1960s. The Centre then became associated with the mainstream Scottish support for the principles of comprehensive, public schooling and an accessible system of higher education, principles that sometimes brought it into heated conflict with Conservative ministers such as Michael Forsyth. The nationalist and academic currents of thought came together in 1989 in a declaration of principles for Scottish education, issued by a committee that included Davie and McPherson, together with several others who were critical of the Conservative government's policies, such as Brian Boyd (whose writing on the primary curriculum was cited in Chapter 7 above) and Kenneth Alexander, whose report on community education in 1975 is discussed in Chapter 10 below. The declaration endorsed the potential of the tradition, arguing that 'we are seeking ... to use history as a means to understanding better how we got where we are, and to identify the elements of a positive tradition in Scottish education' (SCESR 1989: 8).

However, these intellectual currents vanished from officially sponsored debates about higher education, in the UK as a whole as well as in Scotland (Scott 1990). Thus they barely impinged on, for example, the Scottish report of the UK-wide Committee of Inquiry into Higher Education that the Conservatives set up before the 1997 election and which reported to the Labour government in July 1997 (NCIHE 1997), or on a book published earlier in the same year by the principals of the Scottish higher education institutions (Crawford 1997); both of these were dominated by arguments that were vocational and technocratic, and their brief mention of philosophical and cultural questions was decidedly shallow. There was also a lack of any thorough attention to culture and to purpose in the Scottish Executive's inquiry into student finance (ICISF 1999) and the Parliament's inquiry into lifelong learning (Scottish Parliament 2002). Even the important institutional developments went ahead largely without much airing of questions of philosophy. For example, the absorption of the colleges of education into the universities occasioned almost no public debate, in striking contrast to the controversies at the beginning of the twentieth century over the SED's refusal to allow the universities a significant role in teacher training. The growing role of further education colleges in providing higher education raised no official debate about whether there was any deep difference between vocational and academic further education – no sense, for example, that converting a network of colleges into a University of the Highlands and Islands might require more than a quantitative change in the kinds of courses which they provided. Moreover, anything beyond managerial considerations was wholly absent from the 1993 ending of the distinction between central institutions and universities, which was announced in a government document that related to the whole of the UK and had absolutely nothing to say about aims or curricular content (DES 1991); the different degree structures, curricular traditions and cultural role of the two sectors were legislated out of existence without official comment. Politicians' justifications tended to be based on the same kinds of rhetoric about 'parity of esteem' between academic and vocational education as was leading to the reform of the examinations in secondary school, and thus assumed that institutional unification could bring about deep cultural change without affecting the character or quality of the educational programmes that were on offer. It is as if the entire tradition of democratic intellectualism as articulated by George Davie in the 1960s or Herbert Grierson in the 1930s had been reduced to the matter of who got access, with the philosophical and cultural discussions forgotten. Likewise, it is as if Scottishness had become merely the question of political accountability.

In the absence of explicit debate about purpose at the end of the century, the new system was then being shaped by the same Scottish predilections for general education in formal institutions as had earlier forced the SED to pay attention to popular preferences in secondary education. Thus the central institutions adopted the title 'university' enthusiastically, the further education colleges interpreted educational democracy as moving away from their technical college origins into providing a significant share of higher education, and the principles of comprehensive access to formal education that had become and remained popular after the 1970s were being extended to education beyond age eighteen. In an era of student choice and modular curricula, imposing a unified interpretation of a cultural tradition would have been much more difficult in any case, especially when most students were being exposed at school to the sorts of broad intellectual preparation that the democratic intellect was originally intended to be about. However, in the longer term, that is unlikely to be enough. As Carnochan (1993: 126) concludes about the similar lack of 'adequate criteria of purpose' in debates about US higher education: 'the universities need not only to understand their own history better and how that history intersects with the larger history of the nation but also (once more) to understand what they have been trying individually and collectively to do'.

CHAPTER 10

Further and Community Education

T he history of non-university adult education in the second half of the century can seem sometimes like a recapitulation of the events of the first half. It started with the creation of a new sector, the technical colleges which were properly recognised by the SED in the 1950s; but, just as the central institutions drifted away from their original purpose and eventually became universities, so the colleges took on a life of their own, as the beginnings of a network of community colleges on north American lines. The Education (Scotland) Act of 1945 also defined for the first time a sector which it called 'informal adult education', but, as before, this struggled in the face of official indifference, lack of legislative entrenchment and the preference of most Scots for learning based inside institutions. Yet the irony is that it was in debate about adult education in the 1980s and 1990s that the notion of democratic intellectualism received its most critical scrutiny, linking back to the Scottish Labour Colleges in an effort to modernise the Scottish radical tradition.

TECHNICAL EDUCATION

The seventh Advisory Council reported on further education in 1952. Young comments on the Council's approach here that 'the source of the problem was the infancy of the whole sector', drawing on disparate origins in adult educa- tion, technical education, continuation classes and recreational classes (Young 1986: 390). Whereas technical education and continuation classes had looked to the state for support, adult education – as we saw in Chapter 6 – had not. Thus, unlike in its inquiries into primary and secondary education, the Council had much greater scope to define something new here.

It sought to impose a classically Scottish liberal interpretation: 'we regard primary, secondary and further education as stages in the education of the whole man and not as three different types of education', and it reiterated the purpose which the sixth Council had given to secondary education in 1947: 'to foster the full and harmonious development of the individual' (SED 1952b: 24–5). The goals of further education should be to extend literacy to the whole population, to provide opportunities to understand human culture, to strengthen the moral basis of society and to encourage worthwhile recreation and hobbies of a kind that are 'consonant with human dignity' (see pp. 25–30). It should also help people to gain employment and to contribute as citizens to the life of the community (see pp. 30–2). Part of that would be helping parents to build strong families (see p. 31). The central institutions would be able to divest themselves of elementary work if local technical colleges were set up (see p. 50). For younger trainee technicians, it proposed that the problem of 'leakage' from the continuation classes – students leaving before they had finished a course – be dealt with by bringing these classes into closer contact with the secondary schools, by learning from the schools that students' motiv- ation could be improved by increasing the choice which they had over their programmes of study, and by paying more attention to matching the courses to students' abilities (see pp. 46–50). It reiterated the recommendation of the sixth Council that the training of young workers should become the responsi- bility of junior colleges.

The SED never did develop these, but it did sanction the building of tech- nical colleges, and in 1949 created Regional Advisory Councils to oversee their growth as they took over from the continuation classes that had been developed before the war (Butt 2000; Scotland 1969: 237). Its discussion paper on tech- nical education in 1956 accepted that government had the responsibility of coordinating the colleges, and proposed spending £10 million on extending technical education. By 1961, the actual expenditure had been £17 million, at a time when, for example, the Scottish universities received about £1.6 million each year in non-recurrent grants for building work (UGC 1962: 43). This had created over fifty colleges (Scotland 1969: 238). The results were that in 1956 there were 4,363 students enrolled in full-time courses in the further education colleges (SED 1957: 127) and that by 1965 this had grown to 10,248 (SED 1966: 110). At that latter date there were also 299,768 part-time students. Almost all of these full-time or part-time students were in non-advanced courses, and so the colleges were then much more significant providers of these than the central institutions, which had only 2,685 full-time and 2,025 part- time students at this level (SED 1966: 111–13).

The development of technical education at this time was believed to be particularly significant for the Highlands and Islands, where it tended to be seen in the same light as the other public efforts to renovate the economy of the region, such as through the extension of access to the electricity network (Thompson 1972–4). One example of the sorts of rural development theories on which this thinking drew was in the work of Duncraig Castle in Wester Ross.

It had been owned by Sir Daniel Hamilton, who had impressed Mahatma Gandhi by his work in promoting technical education in Bengal. Hamilton believed that similar ideas could help the Highlands. This did not in fact flourish at first, but by the late 1940s Duncraig was operating successfully as a school for the domestic training of girls, under the management of Ross and Cromarty County Council. It was joined in 1947 by Balmacara House technical school for training boys in farming and forestry (that building having been left to the Council by Hamilton's widow). By the 1960s, much larger technical colleges had been established in Inverness and in Thurso (to serve the nuclear power station at Dounreay). The Golspie technical school that had been founded by the Duchess of Sutherland had developed into a further education centre, and a similar college was established at Lews Castle in Stornoway.

The Advisory Council had made only a few suggestions concerning the curriculum for technical education, and the first serious attempt to give a philosophy to it came in 1963 from a committee chaired by John Brunton, head of the schools inspectorate (SED 1963b). It sought to coordinate the work of the colleges with that of the secondary schools. Although it saw the main purpose of technical education as being to provide skilled workers to help the economy, it linked that to more humanistic aims (see p. 7): 'experience has shown that it is through courses of further education that the young worker can deepen his knowledge, widen his vision and learn to do his job with greater efficiency and understanding'. The courses ought then to be 'of the most general nature', and should take forward the students' general education, especially in English which (as in the tradition we have seen from secondary education) could convey the capacity to understand and communicate (see p. 32). The teaching methods that would be appropriate to this would be student-centred: 'young people should be taught by methods which take account of their natural interests and attitudes, and of differences in individual ability, aptitudes, attainment and temperament' (see p. 37). That would not have been out of place in the Primary Memorandum two years later. The report also, notably, insisted that girls as much as boys were entitled to a full vocational education: 'girls can give valuable service in a much wider variety of jobs than has so far been open to them', and in particular – contrary to the common view that women's training would be wasted because they would leave the labour force when they married – 'many married women return later to industry or commerce, and the training they have received before marriage is therefore by no means entirely lost' (see p. 14).

The report was generally judged later in the 1960s to have made less of an impact than it could have done (Scotland 1969: 239), although most education authorities carried out experiments in linking schools and the colleges. Part of their problem in the 1960s was the maintenance of the Scottish preference for seeing academic education as more respectable, and for defining educational democracy as providing access to it. The SED had little success in developing technical courses for the Higher Grade examinations: the universities preferred, for example, good passes in mathematics and physics even for entry to engineering (Osborne 1966: 186). This preference for academic education had the effect of allowing into university people who might otherwise have entered technical colleges. The Robbins report found that alongside the 7.4 per cent of boys and 6.1 per cent of girls who had passed three Highers and two Lowers at school, there was also 1.7 per cent of boys and 2.2 per cent of girls who fell just short of this, with two Highers and three Lowers (Osborne 1966: 186). However, in that latter group, as many as forty-five per cent of boys entered university and seventy-three per cent of girls entered teacher training (see p. 187). This siphoned off from technical education into academic courses some of its most able potential recruits.

The political interest in training skilled workers did not abate, and after 1964 technical education received more systematic attention from the new Industrial Training Boards, the remits of most of which covered the whole of Britain (Fairley 1989: 37–41). Although responsibility for training lay with firms, the Act which established them empowered the Boards to raise a levy to finance training, for example by offering grants to small firms (see p. 38). However, the political fashion for strong intervention lasted less than a decade. The Boards were first weakened and then replaced by the new Manpower Services Commission which was set up in 1973, also with British scope (see p. 39). That was faced in the 1970s and 1980s by a collapse in traditional apprenticeships and by a massive growth in youth unemployment. Between 1978 and 1982, unemployment among people aged under nineteen grew from 19,726 to 30,608, and, in addition to that, the number in the short-term and generally poor-quality Youth Opportunities Programme grew from 5,400 to 30,100 (Raffe 1984: 189, 204–7). By the mid-1980s, only a third of sixteen-year-olds had found a job within a year of leaving school (Brown 1989: 16). The technical education of young school leavers then acquired a wholly different purpose: at best, enabling them to find any job at all, at worst simply including them in temporary training schemes to keep them out of the unemployment queues (Fairley 1989: 42–59). The quality of these training schemes did improve during the 1980s, and the second version of the Youth Opportunities Programme's successor, the Youth Training Scheme in 1986, offered reasonable two-year programmes for sixteen-year-olds. By this date, a quarter of males and a fifth of females were entering the scheme within a year of their sixteenth birthday, and about a half of these had found a job two years later (Raffe and Courtney 1988: 16, 19). By their very nature, however, all the training schemes acquired a low educational status from their being mainly occupied by school leavers who had poor academic records at school (Hendry and Raymond 1986; Raffe and Courtney 1988: 20–4).

These schemes may have started as temporary expedients, and may never have been seen as proper education, but the context which created them stimulated some fundamental re-thinking about the role and character of technical education. The most visible was the SED's complete reorganisation of all non-advanced vocational education in the 1984 'Action Plan' (SED 1983a). This turned all these courses into short modules, under the general title of the National Certificate, which students could, in principle, combine in any way that suited them. The proposal reiterated the view that had been maintained by Brunton and by the Advisory Council that vocational education should not involve the 'abandonment of broadly-based education' (Raffe 1985: 27). David Raffe of the Centre for Educational Sociology summed up the resulting epistemological confusion, one that was to be long-lasting. Noting that the modular approach entailed the 'atomisation of knowledge' and the 'individual-isation of the learning experience', he warned that this might 'sustain ... a bureaucratic, credentialist view of education as modules-to-be-completed' (see p. 31). As we saw in Chapter 8, this was precisely how the modular approach had come to be seen a decade and a half later when this initially vocational reform was extended to all courses and examinations for ages sixteen to eighteen.

Nevertheless, at the time the Plan was enthusiastically welcomed, partly because it represented the SED asserting its educational control over training, keeping the Manpower Services Commission at arm's length: the scheme was overseen by a new Scottish Vocational Education Council (Fairley and Paterson 1991). By the end of the 1980s, almost all formally recognised vocational training in Scotland was organised through the National Certificate modules: in 1990–1, among all student registrations in further education, forty-eight per cent were taking National Certificates, nineteen per cent were studying for Standard Grades, O Grades or Highers, and twenty-seven per cent were not studying for any nationally recognised qualification (SOED 1993: 12).

The individualisation of learning in further education was also stimulated by similar developments to those which led to child-centred education in primary schools. Guidance was provided for the first time. It was argued that, whereas students in the 1950s or 1960s were motivated by gaining qualifications for their current or prospective job, from the 1970s 'new-type students had no present job, and were not directly preparing for a particular occupation' (Ryrie 1984: 3). Ryrie also noted that the Action Plan required guidance: 'students will need to be offered systematic help or guidance when choosing their modular course, and in some cases when reviewing and changing their choice' (see pp. 19–20). Guidance was also needed because the growth of unemployment had created a crisis of identity for young people, removing from young men especially what had been the normal route into adult life for over a century (Hendry and Raymond 1986).

All these changes had one further, institutional effect: they strengthened the experience and diversity of the further education colleges. The Conservative government removed nearly all of them from the control of the local authorities in 1992, citing the principle that market-like competition among them would be beneficial to choice and quality (Munn 1992). In practice, the colleges continued to work closely with the authorities and with schools, but now from a position of greater independence (Finlay 1995). Just before this change, the government had also transferred the Scottish responsibilities of the Manpower Services Commission to two new bodies, Scottish Enterprise and Highlands and Islands Enterprise, where these were combined with the responsibility for promoting industrial development (Fairley 1996).

FURTHER EDUCATION AND GENERAL EDUCATION

The growth of the further education colleges did not involve only technical education, however, and in providing courses of general education they were repeating a move which we have seen several times before – in the development of the Higher Grade schools and of the junior secondary schools as well as of the central institutions. The start of the process may be dated to 1962, when, for the first time, the colleges were allowed to provide courses leading to the new O Grade and to Highers (Osborne 1966: 133). There was then a rapid growth, so that by 1968 about a quarter of students in the colleges were following these courses (Ferguson 1971: 101). One study of the motivation of such students in a college in Glasgow found that non-vocational reasons were common – cited by a quarter of all candidates, and by forty-eight per cent of those aged over thirty (Ferguson 1971: 104). Thereafter, the proportion of college students engaging in general courses of these types remained at between one quarter and one fifth for the next three decades: for example, as we noted, it was nineteen per cent in 1990.

The other means by which the colleges became providers of general education was through their courses of higher education. We have noted the scale of this in Chapter 9, and the result was that students on higher education courses formed a significant minority of all the students in these colleges – in 1993, for example, one third of full-time students and one fifth of part-time ones (SOEID 1996b: 4; 1996e: 3). The consequences were that colleges formed many links with neighbouring universities, because the distinction between non-advanced and advanced education did not in fact correspond very well to students' needs for progression in steps that would not be discouraging. The colleges mainly did not become sub-contractors for university courses (as is common in England and the USA): the most common type of link was 'articulation', by which people who successfully completed a college course would be given entry to the second or later years of a degree course at a university

(Alexander et al. 1995: 29). This strengthened the sense that the colleges were independent providers, and many of them consolidated that by forming diverse links with many universities: in the mid-1990s, two thirds of colleges had articulation links with more than one university, and a fifth had links with more than five (see p. 31). The universities to which they linked tended to be the newer ones: fifty-eight per cent of links were to them, twelve per cent to other higher education institutions, and only twenty-nine per cent to the eight older universities, even though – as we saw in Chapter 9 (Table 9.3) – these contained around fifty per cent of all full-time students in higher education institutions (Alexander et al. 1995: 34).

INFORMAL ADULT EDUCATION

What the 1945 Act called 'informal adult education' grew as people had more leisure time in the 1950s and 1960s. This amorphous sector encompassed adult education that was not vocational and was not in the graduating courses at the universities, central institutions or teacher-training colleges. In 1952–3, there were 104,000 enrolments; by 1966 there were 185,000, and by 1972 there were 218,000 (SED 1975: 99). The number of students involved was about 95,000 in the mid-1950s, 145,000 in the mid-1960s and 167,000 in the early 1970s (Kelly 1992: fig. 10; SED 1975: 99). About seven out of ten of the students were female. The largest providers were the education authorities, through their evening classes: in the mid-1960s, ninety per cent of enrolments in adult education were in these evening classes, ten per cent were in university extra-mural classes, two per cent were in analogous classes provided by the central institutions, and only one per cent were in classes directly provided by the WEA (SED 1975: 99–101). The pattern was similar in the early 1970s.

These figures indicate the displacement of the Workers' Educational Association during the 1950s (Duncan 1999: 114). It was paralleled by the equally stark decline of the Labour Colleges which wound themselves up in 1962, by which date their numbers had fallen to 1,477 students; they were replaced by a more narrowly defined education service for trade unionists (Henderson 1978; Roberts 1970: appendix ii). There was almost no official encouragement to these voluntary movements, and W. H. Marwick noted in 1953 that the Scottish Labour Party 'seems increasingly thirled to the doctrine of public rather than voluntary provision, in the sphere of adult education as elsewhere' (Marwick 1953: 13). Nevertheless, unlike the Labour Colleges, the WEA did not die: in 1972, although still only providing a tiny share of all adult education courses, its number of enrolments had more than doubled since 1966, from 1,930 to 4,666 (SED 1975: 101).

Much the same could be said for University extra-mural courses at this time, holding a precarious place in their institutions but not disappearing, and indeed being supplemented by new departments in the new universities of the 1960s (Robertson 1974). The other segments of informal education that had been important until the 1930s were also in decline, notably – for children – the Sunday schools of the presbyterian churches, which collapsed in a very short space of time in the early 1960s, for reasons that are not fully understood by historians (Brown 1997: 160). The Socialist Sunday Schools vanished altogether at the same time (Reid 1966). Newbattle Abbey College managed to survive as an adult residential college with a few dozen students, despite indifference or hostility from the SED and the education authorities (Ducklin and Wallace 2000: 295–6). A few Labour politicians supported it, for example Margaret Herbison MP, who wrote in a memorandum in 1951 that 'I should hate to think that we couldn't afford one Adult College to provide more or less liberal education for any of our people who have been denied it' (see p. 297). However, most of her colleagues were hostile, as was the Conservative government in the 1950s. With the apparent achievement of secondary education for all, and with the system of higher education already expanding as never before, the attractions of the institutional route to education seemed to be vindicated.

Yet there remained a sense that adult education had a potential that was not being fulfilled, and could do more to underpin citizenship. That was the intention behind the setting up of a committee of inquiry in 1970, one of the last actions in Scotland of the Labour government before it was defeated in the June election of that year. Its chair was Kenneth Alexander, professor of economics at Strathclyde University, who had been an economics adviser to the Labour government. It reported in 1975 after the party had been returned to power (SED 1975).

It defined the aims of adult education in ways that were consistent with the general Scottish preference for liberal studies, and implicitly rejected the adjective 'informal' which had been attached to it since 1945: 'Learning is a basic characteristic of life ... Continuing education ... is thus a series of learning experiences organised, structured or deliberately created by the learner or by others' (SED 1975: 25).

This ought to be thought of as being for all adults, not as a 'marginal'. In a classic statement of the educational aims of social democracy, it set four purposes: the affirmation of individuality, education as a means to the effective use of the resources of society, the fostering of pluralism, and 'education for change itself' (see pp. 26–7). All this was above all to enable individuals to fulfil themselves through their social identity, through 'the mutual relationship between individual and social aims': 'society need not fear that by stressing individuality we are sowing the seeds of anarchy for it is only where people have developed their own unique individualities that social ideals of the highest order emerge' (SED 1975: 35).

It therefore recommended that adult education be recognised by legislation and overseen nationally by a Scottish Council for Community Education, and that local authorities should be required to make proper provision for it by combining adult education, community development and youth work. The leading role was therefore to lie in the public sector, not among voluntary organisations: the WEA, for example, was to concentrate on the educational needs of the socially, economically and educationally disadvantaged (see p. 64). Including people who had not done well in their school education ought to be the main aim of the whole of adult education, since the committee had found in a small survey of people who attended classes that most participants tended to be much more likely to be middle class than the population in general: they reported that eighty per cent of them were in non-manual occupations, whereas the 1971 population census had found only around fifty per cent of adults in these social classes (McCrone 1992: 139).

This statement of such aims, however, came at the very end of the period in which expansionist social democracy dominated British politics. Therefore Alexander's recommendations were never fully put in place, and his goal of extending participation was no more than partly realised. Absolute numbers did rise, although because the service remained non-statutory the education authority evening classes were cut in the late 1970s when central-government funding was cut. Thus the peak of enrolments in adult education was in fact in the mid-1970s, at around a quarter of a million (Horobin 1980: 6). Enrolments fell sharply in the late 1970s, and continued downwards to around 150,000 in the early 1980s (Horobin 1983: 8). Thereafter, participation rose steadily again, but not much beyond the 1970s peak: there were 240,000 adults taking part in the local authority sector in 1996 (SOEID 1998a: 3). Most of these classes were described as leisure rather than liberal studies: in 1980, forty-four per cent of enrolments in the education authority courses were in physical activities such as sport, twenty-seven per cent were in practical subjects such as needlework, four per cent were in basic literacy classes, and so only twenty-five per cent were academic (Horobin 1983: 6). Information on leisure classes is not available as a continuous series, although in the mid-1990s Tett (1994) also found that leisure classes dominated provision in Lothian region. Surveys asking about participation in adult education probably tended to pick up mainly the academic courses, since many people may not have defined leisure classes as education at all. One survey in 1999 found that the most popular academic classes were in computer studies, business studies, nursing and other health studies, foreign languages and engineering (Sargant 2000: 19). This was not dissimilar to adults' intentions for further learning reported two decades earlier by Munn and MacDonald (1988: 34).

Throughout this period, the dominant provider remained the education authorities, still with over three quarters of enrolments in 1980 (Horobin 1983: 9).

By the early 1980s, most education authorities had created unified community education services, but adult education remained a very small part of them. One survey in 1982 found only thirteen full-time staff for adult education in Fife, Tayside and Central Regions, which had an adult population of over half a million people (D. Alexander et al. 1984b: 44–5). Although, as the researchers acknowledged, part-time staff were bound to play an important role in adult education, the organisation of courses required full-time coordinators. Total numbers of staff in community education nationally were higher, at 785 in 1979, but the majority were dealing with young people. The total full-time community education staff increased to 1,391 in 1996, when there were also 716 part-time staff and 10,408 sessional workers. There was also probably a growth in the number of adults taking part in day-time classes in schools, although a consistent statistical series is not available: in 1990, there were 14,000 adults attending some classes (SOED 1992b: 2). By contrast, Newbattle College was eventually forced to close its residential courses by cuts in its funding in 1987, although these were restored when the Labour government was elected in 1997 (Ducklin and Wallace 2000: 299).

Local authorities were also the main providers of public libraries, which – following the universal coverage achieved by the end of World War II – continued to expand until the 1980s. There was some contraction during the 1990s, mainly occasioned by the reorganisation of local government in 1995–6, although not back to the levels of the 1970s or earlier. In 1952, they had six million books in stock (up from 1.6 million in 1913); by 1980, this had grown to ten million, in 1990 there were thirteen million and in 1998 fourteen million (Aitken 1971: 350; CIPFA 1982, 1992, 1999). Using 1952 as the base, expenditure per head in real terms grew by a factor of 4.6 by 1980, reached 6.1 in 1990, but then fell back to 5.2 in 1998. Book borrowing followed a similar trajectory: there were 29.5 million issues in 1952, 40.1 in 1980, 51.6 million in 1990 and 41.1 million in 1998. So, despite the contraction of the 1990s, libraries were still very important sources of public learning. In the 1990s, around twenty-nine per cent of adults were consulting a public library at least once per month (from the Scottish Household Survey of 1999 and from Carey et al. 1997: 48). By the end of the century, moreover, computers and the Internet were available as a new means of learning for a substantial minority of the population: in 1999, twenty-nine per cent of Scottish adults had a computer at home, and, of these, thirty-eight per cent were connected to the Internet (Sargant 2000: 79).

The various forms of adult education were not, however, compensating for social inequalities in access to initial education. That same 1982 survey found only slightly broader participation than the Alexander committee had reported from its small study. Men still made up only about a third of students (D. Alexander et al. 1984a: 115). People who were not in paid employment made up thirty per cent of participants (see p. 123), and among those who could be allocated to a social class the semi-skilled and unskilled working class was under-represented compared to its share in the general population. In Dundee, for example, people in such occupations made up twenty-four per cent of all people who were not retired in the 1981 population census, but only sixteen per cent of participants (see pp. 122–3). Nevertheless, like the survey of 1938 which we saw in Chapter 6, the skilled working class was not under-represented – in Dundee, for example, forming thirty-six per cent of the whole non-retired population but forty-one per cent of participants.

These results for social class were confirmed by a national survey in 1986, although (like the 1938 survey) it found roughly equal numbers of male and female participants (Munn and MacDonald 1988): twenty-three per cent of people in the semi-skilled or unskilled social classes had taken part in adult education, in contrast to seventy-four per cent of people in the professional and semi-professional classes (see p. 11). The patterns were similar in a survey in Fife by Rougvie in 1996: only fourteen per cent of people in semi-skilled or unskilled work had taken part in any education in the year preceding the survey, compared to forty-seven per cent of people in professional and semi-professional jobs (Rougvie 1997: 54). University extra-mural classes were probably even more socially selective: the annual reports of Glasgow University's department, which recorded social-class data until 1984, regularly found that only about five to eight per cent of students were in manual jobs (see, for example, University of Glasgow 1984: 28). There were also social-class differences in access to computers and to the Internet and in using public libraries. In the Scottish Household Survey, fifty-four per cent of non-manual workers had a computer at home, in contrast to a third of manual workers. As a result, twenty-eight per cent of non-manual workers had Internet access from home, but only thirteen per cent of manual workers. These figures would make the relative social-class difference in owning a computer or in Internet access about the same as in access to university among school leavers in the mid-1990s, where, as we saw in Chapter 9, the entry rates were fifty-one per cent and twenty-four per cent in these two broad social classes. The class difference in using public libraries, on the other hand, was somewhat lower than in any of these: in 1999, thirty-three per cent of people in non-manual occupations used a public library at least once a month, and twenty-two per cent of people in manual occupations did so (from Scottish Household Survey).

All of these surveys found that the more initial education which people had had, the more likely they were to take part in adult education. Nevertheless, nearly a half of Scots were still inclined to regard education as finishing with formal education: in 1999, only one third of them had recently taken part in any courses, and forty-three per cent had not taken part in any education since leaving full-time initial education (Sargant 2000: 8).

CONCLUSIONS

The patchy record in the 1980s and 1990s did, however, have the effect of encouraging a debate about the implications of the Alexander committee's proposals (D. Alexander 1994; D. Alexander and Martin 1995; Crowther et al. 1999; Martin 1996; Tett 1995). This debate was also provoked by the apparent triumph of vocational courses in adult education, and the concomitant growth in so-called 'competence-based assessment', the idea that learning could be reduced to discrete segments and that these were to be judged solely by students' acquisition of behavioural competence, rather than by, say, their knowledge or understanding. These were thus similar concerns to those which were expressed in the secondary schools about the Higher Still reforms in the late-1990s (Chapter 8 above). There was also a sense that the whole area of technical education was drifting, a feeling that allowing even this sector to be driven by the immediate apparent needs of the economy was not a very wise way of planning for the future (Fairley 1996).

Two principles emerged from the community education debate. One was to re-assert the value of 'purposeful learning' (D. Alexander et al. 1984b: 50). This was an assertion of intellectual seriousness against both vocational courses and undemanding leisure courses. The other principle was the claim that adult education ought to have a social purpose (Duncan 1999: 114–15). These two principles were sometimes expressed as a re-interpretation of the Scottish common-sense school of philosophy. For example, David Alexander and Ian Martin – lecturers in community education at Edinburgh University – wrote in 1995 that vocational and modularised courses for community workers create merely the 'illusion of autonomy', and provide no assessment of 'the ability to teach or to think' (D. Alexander and Martin 1995: 85–6). Drawing on George Davie's writing, they reiterated the Scottish philosophical tradition in which the purpose of education is to refine the common sense of the community, and linked that to Gramsci's idea that it should challenge the hegemonic culture (see pp. 88–9); that also linked back to John MacLean and the Labour Colleges (see p. 91). By creating the intellectual conditions for what Alasdair MacIntyre called 'common public debate', education could thus provide 'a type of humane and civic incorporation' (see p. 91).

One of the few sustained attempts to put such ideas into practice was in the Adult Learning Project in the Gorgie-Dalry district of Edinburgh, which was also inspired by the ideas of the Brazilian educator Paulo Freire; it managed to survive, with local authority funding, continuously from 1979 (Kirkwood and Kirkwood 1989). But the significance was wider, because this strand of thinking, and that project in particular, tended to be particularly prominent in the campaigning for a Scottish Parliament in the 1990s (Hearn 2000; Shaw and Martin 2000).

The very vibrancy of that community education debate highlighted the absence of similar questioning of cultural purpose in most of the official discussion of the other parts of education. In one sense, the dominance of the Scottish interpretation of educational democracy could hardly have been more complete: at no time during the century had adult education been its main repository, and the enormous increases in participation in the formal institutions of school, college and university seemed to have confirmed the belief that this type of democracy was possible and sufficient. But, in another sense, the sheer instrumentalism of it all had left any truly democratic debate behind. So, at the beginning of the new century, the debate about the Scottish tradition of radical education was strangely dislocated from most people's main experience of education. The most explicit links between education and democracy were being made by a radical minority within a marginalised sector that had never even been given proper statutory recognition.

CHAPTER II

Conclusions

There are two ways in which we can conclude. One is to follow the organisational principle of this account, and summarise the long view of what happened in each broad sector – primary, secondary, university, vocational, adult. The other is to return to the themes which were discussed in Chapter 2, indicating the ways in which they have pervaded the analysis. Neither is enough on its own. Themes of democratisation, of intellectualism, of the importance of socialising students into a common, democratic citizenship have appeared in connection with all the sectors, and so also has the counterpoint of growing individualism. But all these have appeared through their embodiment in particular institutions, with particular histories that are the practical forms taken by inherited but adapted ideals. Institutions cannot be ignored because without them we cannot explain in detail how the grand themes bear on reality. Take individualism, for example. It is true but somewhat trite to note that individualism has intensified. If the statement is left at that level of generality, moreover, there seems to be nothing distinctive about the Scottish system, or indeed about any other in the developed world. Much more revealing is then how a growing sense that students ought to be treated as creative individuals came to influence the practice of teachers, the expectations of students themselves, and through these the organisation of progression, assessment and opportunity. That needs an attention to institutions – to the character of the primary school, and what happens inside it, to the ways in which secondary education links backwards to young ages and forwards to the universities and the professions, and to the various institutional barriers that, to successive generations, have seemed to restrict the realisation of individual merit. The results of such inquiries then have taken us into highly distinctive features of the Scottish system, features that are invisible when too gross a level of generality is used in sociological classification. 'Child-centred methods' then may describe everything from the benign anarchy of A. S. Neill through the socialised individualism that characterised the 1965 Primary Memorandum to the common curriculum through which individual talent was meant to flower in a socially acceptable manner from the 1980s onwards. Where Scotland lay along this spectrum was as much a matter of a highly distinctive history as of sharing international developments.

INSTITUTIONS

Primary education, first, shows that merely measuring participation is not enough, necessary though such quantitative assessments are. Universal provision was achieved by the beginning of the century, and yet fundamental changes were yet to take place. The resulting revolution was ultimately as great as anything that happened in the more obviously changing secondary and university sectors. The most important shift is indeed best characterised as individualising. Teachers slowly learnt how to treat children as unique, primary schools gradually developed an ethos that was much more friendly and relaxed than they had mostly been at the turn of the century, and discipline eventually became – at least in aspiration – a matter of self-control rather than of physical harshness. None of this happened easily, or quickly, and probably few people other than those currently in charge at any moment have ever been anything other than ambivalent about one or other aspect of it. Children, it was always believed, had to be socialised, and their learning this had to be shaped by responsible adults. A common curriculum, therefore, far from being an alien imposition – as it was frequently felt to be in English education in the 1980s – was the very epitome of what was needed. Being common not only ensured that social needs were respected, but also underpinned a shared sense of individual entitlement. Of course this all may also be interpreted as confusion, or even as hypocrisy: the easy way to describe the caution about individual freedom is as a legacy of Calvinist authoritarianism. However, that is glib. Constraining unfettered freedom is bound to look conservative in any country, because it is bound to take the form of asserting inherited social values against radical challenge. But, unless Neill-type freedom is the route to be taken – and no education system has seriously attempted that – then acceptable freedom is bound to be compromised, and the compromise will be shaped by specific national beliefs about the nature of society.

These compromises also affected secondary education, but the main story here has been of structural change forced by struggle between official and popular views about the meaning of opportunity and about the extent of educability. The outcome by the 1970s was irreversibly that secondary education had to mean the same kind of full secondary education for all. Here too, though, the character of that outcome was the result of inherited ideas.

The democratisers and the conservative officials shared an interpretation of real learning as being academic, and ultimately that was what made the wide diffusion of secondary schooling acceptable. The specifically Scottish element here was in the belief that academic study was not only not necessarily for an elite only; it was also the best preparation for common living in a democracy. Of course, the resolution of the conflicts was never quite as simple as that, since there is no one meaning of academic, and it could be, after all, that democratic intellectualism is a much better description. The words matters less than the concept, though – the sense that a worthwhile education must be intellectually demanding, that there is a common core of culture that we all have to struggle with in order to realise our human potential, and that breadth of study of this sort not only stretches the intellect but also prepares us for life with others in society. These kinds of principles underpinned all the pressure for democratic reform until the 1980s. In the last decade of the century, though, the sense that academic study might be intrinsically undemocratic became more widespread, and so – for the first time in a very long time – Scottish secondary education found itself bereft of a guiding, inherited philosophy.

For the first half of the century, the standard of democratic intellectualism continued to be set by the universities. They still offered a broad education, their leading thinkers still believed that they ought to be the focus of national culture, and they still were rooted in local communities. That role, however, then dwindled, partly because the universities turned away from Scottish debates, and partly because of the parallel system of mainly vocational higher education which the Scottish Education Department had established in the central institutions and the teacher training establishments. These did, it is true, acquire an academic standing from the same sense that intellectual rigour was socially useful; but the separation left a vacuum in thinking for the long term. There was little that was distinctively Scottish about the official debates in the 1960s or 1970s over university expansion, and so the democratisation of the secondary schools was not followed by a coherent and relevant democratisation of universities and colleges. Instead, the enormous numerical widening of access to higher education in the 1980s and the 1990s took place with almost no public attention to questions of purpose, or of cultural role, or even of what might be distinctive about higher learning as opposed to other kinds. The cultural emptiness of the debates about secondary schooling at the end of the century was therefore no mere accidental accompaniment of the similar lack of thoughtful direction in higher education; the two were symptoms of the same causes, and fed each other – of an unshaken belief in democratic access, but of an official forgetting about the intellectual rationale that, in earlier decades, had provided the standard by which any worthwhile educational democracy would be judged.

There are two ways, then, of interpreting the Scottish approach to vocational education. The common one in the last couple of decades of the century was to claim that it was relatively undeveloped, and that this was partly the result of what has sometimes been called academic drift – the tendency of originally vocational colleges (such as the central institutions) to copy the universities on grounds solely of social prestige. Since this is indeed probably what happened in England, there is no doubt some truth in it for Scotland, precisely because, by the middle of the century, the universities had attached themselves to a British culture that still commanded high status. However, that is not the only explanation, because the alternative is that the central institutions were always intended to be academically respectable, that the teacher-training colleges became increasingly academic as they sought in the 1920s and 1930s to take over from the universities the proper education of teachers, and that the dominant Scottish view was therefore always that the best vocational preparation ought to be as intellectually rigorous as any university degree. The economic use of knowledge was, according to this view, not in principle different from its social use: the educational preparation for being an economic citizen was the same as for being a democratic one. To the extent that this view influenced reform, the development of the colleges was not academic drift at all but the realisation of their founding ideals.

The potential coincidence of vocational and civic interpretations of democratic intellectualism should also warn us against seeing it as inevitably radical. In the way that I have described it here, it was usually reformist, but for most of the century it was highly cautious, as respectful of the imperatives of existing institutions as of the voices outside them insisting that they live up to their claims to be accessible. Nevertheless, there has always been a more thoroughly radical interpretation, albeit intermittently, often in connection with adult education. Unlike in secondary and higher education, moreover, the most sustained of such critiques came towards the end of the century, inspired in part by the failure of liberal adult education to secure a firm place in official policy. Radical debates about adult education in Scotland were therefore nationally distinctive in their attention to questions of serious educational purpose, and in an insistence that a worthwhile democratic education had to be intellectually demanding. By the end of the century these ideas were also entwined with the most radical ideas about the kind of democracy which a Scottish parliament could stimulate, and so formed part of the intellectual foundation of Scotland's new system of government.

THEORIES

All of these sectoral changes also therefore had consequences for the kind of society that Scotland was becoming. Three general points about this may be made in conclusion.

The first is about the role of education in shaping the relationship between individual and community. Duncan MacGillivray's perception in 1919 that collective concerns were outweighing individualism does indeed seem to characterise the emerging view that came to dominate policy making in the middle of the century – the belief that the fairest and most efficient way to organise education was through the public provision of common institutions. This principle had already been well-established before the century started, in the school boards that had governed the public system after 1872, and they in turn inherited the presbyterian idea that education ought to be governed as a public good. The same belief underpinned the key Act of 1918, not only in its renovation of the 1872 structures, but also in its absorption of the Roman Catholic and Episcopal schools. That entrenched the very limited scope for institutional diversity which the Scottish system afforded: these churches could have some influence, but their schools were no longer their own, and their role was much more constrained than it would have been had they continued to manage a distinct voluntary sector. This principle of common provision then inspired the pressure for universal secondary education, and the common system of that schooling which emerged after the 1960s. All of this happened overwhelmingly under public control, the independent sector having already contracted to cater for fewer than ten per cent of pupils by the 1930s, and falling in size thereafter to fluctuate at around one in twenty from the 1980s until the century's end. The institutions of higher education continued to be regarded as public, and the universities never managed to escape their legacy from the nineteenth century and earlier: receiving over three quarters of their income from public sources by the second half of the century, this history ensured that any claim to be private would never have much resonance.

However, to leave this first point at that would be to miss an important motive for this public provision, and then would be to mis-represent what happened after the 1970s. The purpose of common provision was always to free individuals. We have seen numerous instances of this throughout – of the attempts to take account of individual preferences in order to promote individual learning and, thereby, individual citizenship. That was most evident in the slow growth of child-centred methods in primary teaching, and in the development of the guidance movement. The individualism was also, however, at the heart of Scottish faith in meritocracy: ultimately, common provision, and teaching in groups of mixed ability, were supported because they were seen as the fairest and most efficient way of promoting individual talent. Critics of the alleged uniformity of comprehensive secondary schooling frequently missed this point: in the eyes of most contemporaries from the 1940s to the 1960s, it was the selective system that categorised pupils too rigidly, and only common educational structures could underpin truly common individual rights.

That then also helps to explain Scottish reactions to the market-type individu-alism of the Conservative government in the 1980s and 1990s. For most Scots, it seemed perfectly possible to go along with the individualism without rejecting the common institutions, precisely because promoting individual freedom had been the goal all along. Parental choice of school, or student choice in post-school education, seemed to be a natural fulfilment of a century of cautious attempts at liberation, even though these then caused problems of equity and for the very meaning of a university education. As the comprehensive reforms seemed to be narrowing all sorts of invidious differences in educational progress – such as in relation to gender, religion, ethnicity and even class – there seemed no need at all to reject common schooling in order to achieve equal opportunities. Perhaps the very ambiguity of the Scottish tradition of educational democracy was, after all, peculiarly suited to this ideological adjust-ment. Because it was a democratic aspiration that had always been about promoting individual talent, it did not find an individualistic, even competitive, interpretation of collective reforms at all difficult.

This was helped, secondly, by the dominant belief in a broad, general education as the only kind of education that was seriously worthwhile. Real learning meant book learning, fostered first of all by the humanising study of literature. A common citizenship could be educated by a common curriculum, with literacy at its core, the twentieth-century legacy of the old common-sense philosophy in which learning forms the bonds of a common culture. If that sometimes looked like respect for academic education, most Scots would not have demurred, because general education was usually defined to be primarily academic. We see that in the very notion of democratic intellectualism: though the emphasis in the last couple of decades of the century tended to be more on the democratic aspects of this, taking for granted the quality of the intellect to which it would give access, the fuller interpretation would remember that the nature of education had to be recurrently debated too. It is fairly easy, as we have seen, to find support for this among professors, policy makers and mem-bers of official committees; but it was an attitude that was dispersed more widely, as the recurrent popular reaction to reforms shows. Teachers, parents and students simply refused to give the same respect to alternative types of education as they gave to the mainstream academic tradition – to courses leading to the Higher Grade of the Leaving Certificate, and to degree courses in university. This may offer a further clue as to why the comprehensive secondary school became and remained popular. Scots took the reform to their hearts because they interpreted it as being about widening access to academi-cally respectable education. For that same reason, they were sceptical of alle-gations that it lowered standards. Having high expectations and high standards for everyone required that all receive the opportunity to take part in the same kind of academic programmes.

If there was debate about standards, it did not come until the 1990s, well after the initial comprehensive reform, and it came at a time when the academic character of courses in secondary and higher education may well have seemed to be under threat from modularisation and from the encroachments of an allegedly philistine vocationalism. It is too soon to assess whether these developments really do threaten to undermine the academic tradition, and therefore even less possible to predict the reaction that might then ensue. One thing is clear, though, about these recent developments. Most of the old cultural leadership class has largely stopped debating matters of philosophy and purpose in public, as we saw for secondary schooling in Chapter 8, for higher education in Chapter 9 and for community education in Chapter 10. This is a very recent and very striking contrast to the first three quarters of the century. The SED officials, the inspectors, the university principals and most of the directors of education have concentrated on planning and responding to the minutiae of expansion, rather than questioning what it might be for in the way their predecessors frequently did. Contributions from academics have come only from those with a specialist interest in Scottish studies, rather than from across the disciplines as happened in the nineteenth century. The Advisory Council has not been convened since 1961. This lack of debate about purpose may simply be the Scottish instance of a much wider crisis of confidence among cultural elites that spreads across Europe and north America, or it may be a sign that the managerial elites who now run education systems are so confident in their own values that – unlike their more liberal predecessors – they see no need to debate these publicly. But the persistence of debate about these matters alongside the official silences suggests that the Scottish appetite for defining educational democracy as a cultural matter will not go away, especially since this unofficial debate has been closely linked to the political campaigning for national self-government.

If the main twentieth-century tradition was academic, it was also institutional, the third conclusion. Throughout the century, the nature of the general education to which democracy was meant to give access was defined by ideal interpretations of the institutions which had been inherited from the past. That started with the legacy of the parish school and the inexpensive, socially open university. As these were reformed, the legacy that mattered next was the public elementary school and the large civic institutions of higher education; re-establishing the link between these became the measure of any reconstructed system of post-elementary education. That explains the pressure that converted the Higher Grade schools into full secondaries, the Advanced Divisions into junior secondary courses offering general education, at least in principle, and then converted them and the senior secondary courses into a common system. So, when that secondary debate settled on the idea that secondary education for all had to mean a single kind of secondary school for

all, the institutional legacy of comprehensive schooling became the criterion
against which popular views judged the expansion of post-school education.
The further education colleges and the more astute universities appreciated
this, and sought to recover the older idea of open access. Some of the older
universities did not, and were finding the transition to mass higher education
distinctly awkward, fearing a tension between international academic lustre
and widening access, and thus failing to understand the academic motives that
had impelled Scottish educational democracy all along.

The point here is not whether any of these recurrently re-formed ideals
were accurate: they were always inaccurate to a certain extent, because they
always idealised the past, as ideals inevitably do. Thus the Higher Grade
schools were more democratic than the Higher Class schools, but the
Continuation Classes and the Advanced Divisions ensured that the reformers
would not stop there. The junior secondary courses were more democratic
than these, in their attempts to provide a general education for at least a
substantial minority of their students, but their relative failure ensured that
they, too, could not be the epitome of democracy, and were bound to be
succeeded by common schooling. These were all profound changes, but they
also all came from within a tradition that developed in response to popular
aspirations and struggle. The inherited ideals formed a utopian basis for
radical reconstruction, but did so without causing any revolutionary rupture
to the inherited institutions which were their main practical carriers. One
consequence was that most of the radicalism we have seen in this history has
come from professionals and parents, encouraged by the occasional visionary
official and supportive academic, and able to push the bureaucracy in a
reforming direction only by popular pressure. Politicians entered only to
sanction the key changes long after they had become more or less inevitable,
very rarely as their instigators. The obvious explanation of this is that it was
because there was no Scottish parliament, and that the public spaces in which
debate about change took place were thus in the networks of committees that
surrounded the Scottish Education Department. That is all true, but is as
much a sympton as a cause. The deeper reason is that the ideas for reform
emerged from the reinterpretation of inherited ideals, these ideals were
embodied in the inherited institutions, and so the main exponents of the
ideals were some of the professionals who inhabited them and some of the
students who passed through them. These people may have been influenced
by wider political ideals – especially from the Labour movement – but they
formed their educational aspirations first of all out of direct experience.
Scottish schools and universities were indeed, in this sense, far more public
spaces than the SED networks; they were the popular legislature of the
nation's educational destiny. However, because educational institutions
are never just that, and are always primarily concerned with socialisation,

learning and attainment, the scope for radical change was much slower than it might have been if political pressure had been more sustained, ideologically determined and centralised in a national legislature.

This Scottish experience was both particular and universal. It was universal because it participated in much broader trajectories. Scots shared enthusiastically in the shift from education by ascription to education as a right – education according to class of birth, or gender, or religion to education in the same terms for all. They shared in the growing belief that, with appropriate conditions, most people could learn far more than tradition had expected of them. Moreover, they developed the resulting sense that education could liberate people, even if that meant – to the disquiet of many on the political left – that people exercised their freedom by losing contact with some of the collective social experiences that had frustrated the educational opportunities of their parents and grandparents. The clearest example was the demise of the attempt at a working-class education that would be autonomous of the state and of the dominant culture, a collapse that was made inevitable by the individualising results of the meritocratic, academic learning which people acquired within institutions that were slowly becoming more accessible.

All this was common to many countries, but the Scottish way of doing these things was also peculiar because, as do all countries, it acquired its values from the country's institutional legacy – the schools, colleges and universities that were the embodiment of inherited ideas about education. Scots were open to the extension of opportunity because they had an inherited sense that this was right. The problem with the notion of the lad o pairts, as repeated generations of reformers have seen it, was not the principle of promoting individual talent, but that the inherited interpretation of it was felt to be too narrow. The Scots were open to taking public, collective action because they acquired from their religious histories such a strong attachment to social liberalism and then social democracy that even voluntary provision was suspect. In addition, they found no difficulty in accepting the liberatory potential of collective reform because of their inherited belief in competitive individualism.

The result is now a paradox and a dilemma. Scottish education at the beginning of the twenty-first century has been created by a belief that access to a coherent academic tradition, based in recurrently modernised forms of the inherited institutions, is the only worthwhile standard of educational democracy. However, the educational individualism which has resulted from this democratisation is now so extensive as apparently to bring into question the very notion of a relevant tradition. When that is combined with a questioning of the value of academic knowledge, and by a leadership class that seems to have forgotten about tradition altogether, the institutions and practices that have been built up since 1872 may seem anachronistic, even oppressive. Yet they are the only context in which thinking about the nation's educational future can happen. We started this account with the words of the sixth Advisory Council in 1947, advocating radical reform, but interpreting that within an evolving tradition. The historical inescapability of that delicate balance between legacy and change has rarely been put so well, or analysed so trenchantly, as by Scotland's most distinguished philosopher of the late-twentieth century, Alasdair MacIntyre, who concludes (1981: 221):

> what I am ... is in key part what I inherit, a specific past that is present to some degree in my present. I find myself part of a history ... whether I like it or not, whether I recognise it or not, one of the bearers of a tradition.

Bibliography

NOTE ON SOURCES

Two bibliographies are essential in any study of Scottish education in the twentieth century – the second of the two volumes by Craigie (Craigie 1974), which deals with publications in the period from 1872 to 1972, and the continuation of that to 1990 by Harrison (1994). The best general histories of Scottish education in this period are by Anderson (1983a, 1985, 1995), McPherson (1992a), Osborne (1966) and Scotland (1969), and there are useful papers in the collections edited by Bryce and Humes (1999) and Holmes (2000), and in the *Scottish Educational Review* (1978–present) and its predecessor *Scottish Educational Studies* (1967–77). Sources of specific information are indicated in the usual way throughout the book, and are listed below: this is a list of references, not of all the works consulted. There are three broad omissions from the listing. Wherever data on the general population is used, it is taken from the most recent Scottish population census, and no specific references are given to that: these took place in 1901, and then every decade apart from 1941. Second, wherever financial data are presented in terms adjusted for inflation, the calculations have been carried out using the Economic History web site, which applies to British data the methods set out by McCusker (2001). The other set of exceptions concerns data sets covering the period after the early 1960s. In Chapters 8 and 9 especially, extensive use is made of the surveys of school leavers that were mostly carried out by the Centre for Educational Sociology at Edinburgh University. These went under a variety of names, but are referred to here as the Scottish School Leavers Survey; see also Burnhill et al. (1987), Lynn (1994) and Tomes (1988). Although many of the research papers and books cited in these chapters made use of these surveys, new analysis is also reported here. Occasional use is also made of the Scottish Household Survey of 1999, full information on which is available at the survey's web site, and the Scottish Election Surveys and the British and Scottish Social Attitudes Surveys from 1983 onwards, information on which is in, for example, Paterson et al. (2001: Appendix).

REFERENCES

Adams, C. (1989), 'Women in teaching between the wars', *Scottish Educational Review*, 21, pp. 117–22.
Adams, F. (1997), 'Does Scotland have a national curriculum?', *Scottish Educational Review*, 29, pp. 66–75.

Adams, F. (1999), '5–14: origins, development and implementation', in Bryce, T. G. K. and W. M. Humes (eds), *Scottish Education*, Edinburgh: Edinburgh University Press, pp. 349–59.

Addison, P. (1975), *The Road to 1945*, London: Quartet.

ADES (2000), *Response of the Association of Directors of Education in Scotland*, submission to exams inquiry of the Scottish Parliament Education, Culture and Sport Committee, 27 September, http://www.scottish.parliament.uk/official_report/cttee/archive/educ-oo.htm#pap.

Adler, M., A. Petch and J. Tweedie (1989), *Parental Choice and Educational Policy*, Edinburgh: Edinburgh University Press.

Aitken, W. R. (1971), *A History of the Public Library Movement in Scotland to 1955*, Glasgow: Scottish Library Association.

Alexander, D. (1994), 'The education of adults in Scotland: democracy and curriculum', *Studies in the Education of Adults*, 26, pp. 31–49.

Alexander, D., T. Leach and T. Steward (1984a), *A Study of Policy, Organisation and Provision in Community Education and Leisure and Recreation in Three Scottish Regions*, Nottingham: Department of Adult Education, Nottingham University.

Alexander, D., T. Leach and T. Steward (1984b), 'Adult education in the context of community education: progress and regress in the Tayside, Central and Fife Regions of Scotland in the nine years since the Alexander Report', *Studies in the Education of Adults*, 16, pp. 39–57.

Alexander, D. and I. Martin (1995), 'Competence, curriculum and democracy', in Mayo, M. and J. Thompson (eds), *Adult Learning, Critical Intelligence and Social Change*, Leicester: National Institute for Adult and Continuing Education, pp. 82–96.

Alexander, H., J. Gallacher, J. Leahy and B. Yule (1995), 'Changing patterns of higher education in Scotland: a study of links between further education colleges and higher education institutions', *Scottish Journal of Adult and Continuing Education*, 2, pp. 25–44.

An Comunn Gaidhealach (1907), *The Teaching of Gaelic in Highland Schools*, Liverpool: Henry Young and Sons.

An Comunn Gaidhealach (1936), *Report of Special Committee on the Teaching of Gaelic in Schools and Colleges*, Glasgow: An Comunn Gaidhealach.

Anderson, R. D. (1983a), *Education and Opportunity in Victorian Scotland*, Edinburgh: Edinburgh University Press.

Anderson, R. D. (1983b), 'Education and the state in nineteenth-century Scotland', *Economic History Review*, 2nd series, 36, pp. 518–34.

Anderson, R. D. (1985), 'Education and society in modern Scotland: a comparative perspective', *History of Education Quarterly*, 25.

Anderson, R. D. (1987), 'Scottish university professors, 1800–1939: profile of an elite', *Scottish Economic and Social History*, 7, pp. 27–54.

Anderson, R. D. (1988), *The Student Community at Aberdeen, 1860–1939*, Aberdeen: Aberdeen University Press.

Anderson, R. D. (1995), *Education and the Scottish People, 1750–1918*, Oxford: Clarendon.

Archer, M. S. (1979), *Social Origins of Educational Systems*, London: Sage.

Asquith, S. (1992), 'Coming of age: 21 years of the children's hearings system', in Paterson, L. and D. McCrone (eds), *Scottish Government Yearbook 1992*, Edinburgh: Unit for the Study of Government in Scotland, pp. 157–72.

Bain, A. (1998), *Towards Democracy in Scottish Education: The Social Composition of Popularly Elected School Boards in Fife (1873–1918)*, Auchderran: Fife Council Education Service.

Bain, W. (1995), '"A picture of variable light and shade": the SED annual reports and primary education', *Scottish Educational Review*, 27, pp. 146–53.

Barker, R. (1972), *Education and Politics, 1900–1951: A Study of the Labour Party*, Oxford: Clarendon.

Beaton, E. (1991), 'The Sutherland technical school: pioneer education for crofters' sons', *Review of Scottish Culture*, no. 7, pp. 35–51.

Beck, U. (1992), *Risk Society*, London: Sage.

Begg, T. (1994), *The Excellent Women: the Origins and History of Queen Margaret College*, Edinburgh: John Donald.

Bell, C., C. Howieson, K. King and D. Raffe (1989), 'The Scottish dimension of TVEI', in Brown, A. and D. McCrone (eds), *Scottish Government Yearbook 1989*, Edinburgh: Unit for the Study of Government in Scotland, Edinburgh University, pp. 92–103.

Bell, R. E. (1975), *Godfrey Thomson and Scottish Education*, unpublished manuscript.

Bell, R. E. (1983), 'The education departments in the Scottish universities', in Humes, W. and H. M. Paterson (eds), *Scottish Culture and Scottish Education*, Edinburgh: John Donald, pp. 151–74.

Bell, R. E. (1987), 'The institutional structure', in Mitchell, A. and G. Thomson (eds), *Higher Education in Scotland*, Edinburgh: Unit for the Study of Government in Scotland, pp. 25–38.

Bell, R. E. and M. Tight (1993), *Open Universities: a British Tradition?*, Buckingham: Open University Press.

Benavot, A. and P. Riddle (1988), 'The expansion of primary education, 1870–1940: trends and issues', *Sociology of Education*, 61, pp. 191–210.

Bernstein, B. (1971), *Class, Codes and Control*, London: Routledge and Kegan Paul.

Beveridge, C. and R. Turnbull (1989), *The Eclipse of Scottish Culture*, Edinburgh: Polygon.

Bloomer, K. (2001), *Learning to Change: Scottish Education in the Early 21st Century*, Edinburgh: Scottish Council Foundation.

Boli, J., F. O. Ramirez and J. W. Meyer (1985), 'Explaining the origins and expansion of mass education', *Comparative Education Review*, 29, pp. 145–70.

Bondi, L. (1991), 'Attainment in primary schools: an analysis of variation between schools', *British Educational Research Journal*, 17, pp. 203–17.

Bone, T. R. (1968), *School Inspection in Scotland, 1840–1966*, London: University of London Press.

Bone, T. R. and T. D. Morrow (1975a), 'Primary education in Scotland ten years later', *Times Educational Supplement Scotland*, 14 February, p. 1.

Bone, T. R. and T. D. Morrow (1975b), 'Emergence of child-oriented education', *Times Educational Supplement Scotland*, 21 February, p. 4.

Bone, T. R. and T. D. Morrow (1975c), 'Training teachers for a new-style primary education', *Times Educational Supplement Scotland*, 28 February, p. 18.

Boucher, L. (1982), *Tradition and Change in Swedish Education*, Oxford: Pergamon.

Bourdieu, P. (1971), 'Systems of education and systems of thought', in Young, M. F. D. (ed.), *Knowledge and Control*, London: Collier-Macmillan, pp. 189–207.

Bourdieu, P. (1986), 'Forms of capital', in Richardson, J. E. (ed.), *Handbook of Theory of Research for the Sociology of Education*, Westport: Greenwood Press, pp. 241–58, reprinted in Halsey, A. H., H. Lauder, P. Brown and A. S. Wells (eds) (1997), *Education: Culture, Economy, Society*, Oxford: Oxford University Press, pp. 46–58.

Bowles, S. and H. Gintis (1976), *Schooling in Capitalist America*, London: Routledge.

Boyd, B. (1994), 'The management of curriculum development: the 5–14 programme', in Humes, W. M. and M. L. Mackenzie (eds), *The Management of Educational Policy*, Harlow: Longman, pp. 17–30.

Boyd, W. (1944), *Evacuation in Scotland*, London: University of London Press.

Boyd, W. and W. Rawson (1965), *The Story of the New Education*, London: Heinemann.

Brown, A. (1989), 'The context of change: the Scottish economy and public policy', in Brown, A. and J. Fairley (eds), *The Manpower Services Commission in Scotland*, Edinburgh: Edinburgh University Press, pp. 3–33.

Brown, C. G. (1997), *Religion and Society in Scotland since 1707*, Edinburgh: Edinburgh University Press.

Brown, S. (1990), 'The national curriculum and testing: enlightened or imported?', *Scottish Educational Review*, 22, pp. 68–77.

Brown, S. and P. Munn (eds) (1985), *The Changing Face of Education 14 to 16*, Windsor: NFER-Nelson.

Bruce, N. (1981), 'Social work support for Scottish schools', *Scottish Educational Review*, 13, pp. 130–40.

Bryant, I. (1984), *Radicals and Respectables: The Adult Education Experience in Scotland*, Edinburgh: Scottish Institute of Adult Education.

Bryce, T. G. K. and W. M. Humes (eds) (1999), *Scottish Education*, Edinburgh: Edinburgh University Press.

Burnhill, P., C. Garner and A. McPherson (1988), 'Social change, school attainment and entry to higher education 1976–1986', in Raffe, D. (ed.), *Education and the Youth Labour Market*, Lewes: Falmer, pp. 66–99.

Burnhill, P. and A. McPherson (1984), 'Careers and gender: the expectations of able Scottish school-leavers in 1971 and 1981', in Acker, S. and D. W. Piper (eds), *Is Higher Education Fair to Women?*, Guildford: Society for Research in Higher Education, pp. 83–113.

Burnhill, P., A. McPherson, D. Raffe and N. Tomes (1987), 'Constructing a public account of an education system', in Walford, G. (ed.), *Doing Sociology of Education*, Lewes: Falmer, pp. 207–29.

Butt, J. (2000), 'Further education institutions', in Holmes, H. (ed.), *Scottish Life and Society: Education*, East Linton: Tuckwell, pp. 175–97.

Callen, K. M. (1952), *History of the Scottish Cooperative Women's Guild*, Glasgow: Scottish Cooperative Wholesale Society.

Carey, S., S. Low and J. Hansbro (1997), *Adult Literacy in Britain*, London: Stationery Office.

Carnegie Trust (1926), *Twenty-fourth Annual Report*, Edinburgh: Carnegie Trust.

Carnegie Trust (1936), *Thirty-fourth Annual Report*, Edinburgh: Carnegie Trust.

Carnochan, W. B. (1993), *The Battleground of the Curriculum: Liberal Education and the American Experience*, Stanford: Stanford University Press.

Cazaly, C. P. R. (1986), *The Bursary in Scottish Education, 1860–1960*, MEd thesis, Edinburgh University.

Chartered Institute of Public Finance and Accountancy (1982), *Public Library Statistics 1980–81: Actuals*, London: CIPFA.

Chartered Institute of Public Finance and Accountancy (1992), *Public Library Statistics 1990–91: Actuals*, London: CIPFA.

Chartered Institute of Public Finance and Accountancy (1999), *Public Library Statistics 1998–99: Actuals*, London: CIPFA.

Closs, A. (2000), 'Special education', in Holmes, H. (ed.), *Scottish Life and Society: Education*, East Linton: Tuckwell, pp. 198–217.

Cochrane, C. and D. M. Stewart (1944), *Survey of Adult Education in Scotland 1938–1939*, Edinburgh: British Institute of Adult Education (Scottish Branch).

Collier, A. (1938), 'Social origins of a sample of entrants to Glasgow University', *Sociological Review*, 30, pp. 161–85 and pp. 262–77.

Collins, R. (1979), *The Credential Society*, New York: Academic Press.

Committee on Higher Education (1963a), *Higher Education: Report of the Committee Appointed by the Prime Minister under the Chairmanship of Lord Robbins*, London: HMSO.

Committee on Higher Education (1963b), *Higher Education: Report of the Committee Appointed by the Prime Minister under the Chairmanship of Lord Robbins: Appendix 1, The Demand for Places in Higher Education*, London: HMSO.

Consultative Committee on the Curriculum (1983), *Primary Education in the Eighties*, Dundee: Consultative Committee on the Curriculum.

Consultative Committee on the Curriculum (1986a), *'More than Feelings of Concern': Guidance and Scottish Secondary Schools*, Dundee: Consultative Committee on the Curriculum.

Consultative Committee on the Curriculum (1986b), *Education 10–14 in Scotland*, Dundee: Consultative Committee on the Curriculum.

Cormack, W. S. (1972), 'A century of further education', *Scottish Educational Journal*, 55, 19 May, pp. 416–18.

Corr, H. (1983), 'The sexual division of labour in the Scottish teaching profession, 1872–1914', in Humes, W. M. and H. M. Paterson (eds), *Scottish Culture and Scottish Education*, Edinburgh: John Donald, pp. 137–50.

Corr, H. (1990a), 'An exploration into Scottish education', in Fraser, W. H. and R. J. Morris (eds), *People and Society in Scotland Vol. II, 1830–1914*, Edinburgh: John Donald, pp. 290–309.

Corr, H. (1990b), '"Home Rule" in Scotland: the teaching of housework in Scottish schools 1872–1914', in Paterson, F. M. S. and J. Fewell (eds), *Girls in their Prime*, Edinburgh: Scottish Academic Press, pp. 38–53.

Council for Scientific Policy (1968), *Enquiry into the Flow of Candidates in Science and Technology into Higher Education*, London: HMSO.

Cowper, H. E. (1970), *The Scottish Central Institutions*, MEd thesis, Edinburgh University.

Craigie, J. (1972), *The Scottish Council for Research in Education 1928–1972*, Edinburgh: Scottish Council for Research in Education.

Craigie, J. (1974), *A Bibliography of Scottish Education 1872–1972*, London: University of London Press.

Craik, H. (1884), *The State in its Relation to Education*, London: Macmillan.

Crawford, J. (1987), 'The library policies of James Coates in early twentieth-century Scotland', *Journal of Urban History*, 22, pp. 117–41.

Crawford, R. (1997), *A Future for Scottish Higher Education*, Glasgow: Committee of Scottish Higher Education Principals.

Creighton, M. A. (1984), *An Evaluation of the Development and Role of the Workers Educational Association in Scotland*, MSc thesis, Edinburgh University.

Crowther, J., I. Martin and M. Shaw (1999), *Popular Education and Social Movements in Scotland Today*, Leicester: National Institute of Adult and Continuing Education.

Croxford, L. (1994), 'Equal opportunities in the secondary school curriculum in Scotland', *British Educational Research Journal*, 20, pp. 371–91.

Croxford, L., C. Howieson and D. Raffe (1991), 'National certificate modules in the S5 curriculum', *Scottish Educational Review*, 23, pp. 78–92.

Cruikshank, M. (1970), *History of the Training of Teachers in Scotland*, London: University of London Press.

Darling, J. (1994), *Child-Centred Education and its Critics*, London: Paul Chapman.

Darling, J. (1999), 'Scottish primary education: philosophy and practice', in Bryce, T. G. K. and W. M. Humes (eds), *Scottish Education*, Edinburgh: Edinburgh University Press, pp. 27–36.

Darroch, A. (1914), *Education and the New Utilitarianism*, London: Longmans, Green.

Davie, G. E. (1961), *The Democratic Intellect*, Edinburgh: Edinburgh University Press.

Davie, G. E. (1986), *The Crisis of the Democratic Intellect*, Edinburgh: Polygon.

Dell, G. A. (1969), 'Thirty years of child guidance: the development of the Glasgow child guidance service', *Scottish Educational Studies*, 1, pp. 32–40.

Department for Education and Employment (1998), *Education and Training Statistics for the UK*, London: Stationery Office.

Department of Education and Science (1973), *Statistics of Education 1970: Volume 6 Universities*, London: HMSO.

Department of Education and Science (1991), *Higher Education: a New Framework*, London: HMSO.

Devine, M., J. Hall, J. Mapp and K. Musselbrook (1996), *Maintaining Standards: Performance at Higher Grade in Biology, English, Geography and Mathematics*, Edinburgh: SCRE.

Donaldson, W. (1986), *Popular Literature in Victorian Scotland*, Aberdeen: Aberdeen University Press.

Douglas, J. W. B., J. M. Ross, S. M. M. Maxwell and D. A. Walker (1966), 'Differences in test score and in the gaining of selective places for Scottish children and those in England and Wales', *British Journal of Educational Psychology*, 36, pp. 150–7.

Ducklin, A. and S. Wallace (2000), '"Ivory tower" or wasted asset? Why did residential adult education fail to take root in Scotland?', in Cooke, A. and A. MacSween (eds), *The Rise and Fall of Adult Education Institutions and Social Movements*, Frankfurt: Peter Lang, pp. 291–301.

Duffield, J. (1995), 'Advice and educational policy-making: Scotland and New South Wales 1942–1961', *Scottish Educational Review*, 27, pp. 37–47.

Duncan, R. (1992), 'Independent working class education and the formation of the Labour College movement in Glasgow and west of Scotland, 1915–1922', in Duncan, R. and A. McIvor (eds), *Labour and Class Conflict on the Clyde, 1900–1950: Essays in Honour of Harry McShane*, Edinburgh: John Donald, pp. 106–28.

Duncan, R. (1999), 'A critical history of the Workers' Educational Association in Scotland, 1905–1993', in Crowther, J., I. Martin and M. Shaw (eds), *Popular Education and Social Movements in Scotland Today*, Leicester: National Institute for Adult and Continuing Education, pp. 106–20.

Durkheim, E. (1956), *Education and Sociology*, New York: Free Press.

Earle, F. (1944), *Reconstruction in the Secondary School*, Bickley: University of London Press.

Echols, F., A. McPherson and J. D. Willms (1990), 'Parental choice in Scotland', *Journal of Education Policy*, 5, pp. 207–222.

Economic History Web Site, www.eh.net.

Educational Institute of Scotland (1939), *Report on the Primary School*, Edinburgh: EIS.

Educational Institute of Scotland (1943), *Educational Reconstruction*, Edinburgh: EIS.

Elliot, W. (1932), 'The Scottish heritage in politics', in Atholl et al., *A Scotsman's Heritage*, London: Alexander Maclehose and Co., pp. 53–65.

Elliott, B. J. (1979), '"Buroo" schools 1919–1941: the Scottish experience of an early government response to juvenile unemployment', *Scottish Educational Review*, 11, pp. 11–21.

Entwistle, H. (1979), *Antonio Gramsci: Conservative Schooling for Radical Politics*, London: Routledge and Kegan Paul.

Fairley, J. (1989), 'An overview of the development and growth of the MSC in Scotland', in Brown, A. and J. Fairley (eds), *The Manpower Services Commission in Scotland*, Edinburgh: Edinburgh University Press, pp. 34–70.

Fairley, J. (1996), 'Vocational education and training in Scotland: towards a strategic approach?', *Scottish Educational Review*, 28, pp. 50–60.

Fairley, J. and L. Paterson (1991), 'The reform of vocational education and training in Scotland', *Scottish Educational Review*, 23, pp. 68–77.

Farquharson, E. A. (1985), 'The making of the primary memorandum', *Scottish Educational Review*, 17, pp. 23–32.

Farquharson, E. A. (1990), 'History, culture, and the pedagogy of the primary memorandum', *Scottish Educational Review*, 22, pp. 30–7.

Feinberg, W. (1998), *Common Schools, Uncommon Identities*, New Haven: Yale University Press.

Ferguson, C. (1971), 'Vocational or adult? The significance of the growth of SCE courses in further education', *Scottish Educational Studies*, 3, pp. 101–8.

Finlay, I. (1995), *Bridges or Battlements?*, Glasgow: Scottish School of Further Education, Strathclyde University.

Fisher, D. (1999), '"A band of little comrades": socialist Sunday schools in Scotland', in Crowther, J., I. Martin and M. Shaw (eds), *Popular Education and Social Movements in Scotland Today*, Leicester: National Institute for Adult and Continuing Education, pp. 136–42.

Fitzpatrick, T. A. (1986), *Catholic Secondary Education in South-West Scotland Before 1972*, Aberdeen: Aberdeen University Press.

Forsyth, D. and G. Mercer (1970), 'Socio-economic origins and attainment at university: a case study', *Sociology of Education*, 43, pp. 451–8.

Fraser, H., A. MacDougall, A. Pirrie and L. Croxford (2001), *National Evaluation of the Early Intervention Programme: Final Report*, Edinburgh: Faculty of Education, Edinburgh University.

Fuller, B. and R. Rubinson (1992), 'Does the state expand schooling? Review of the evidence', in Fuller, B. and R. Rubinson (eds), *The Political Construction of Education*, New York: Praeger, pp. 1–28.

Gallacher, J. (1994), 'Widening access to higher education in Scotland: a discussion of the contribution of the Scottish Wider Access programme', *Scottish Journal of Adult and Continuing Education*, 1, pp. 6–16.

Gallacher, J. (2002), 'Parallel lines? Higher education in Scotland's colleges and higher education institutions', *Scottish Affairs*, no. 40, pp. 123–40.

Gallacher, J., J. Leahy and K. MacFarlane (1997), *The FE/HE Route: New Pathways into Higher Education*, Glasgow: Department of Learning and Educational Development, Caledonian University.

Gamoran, A. (1995), 'Curriculum standardisation and equality of opportunity in Scottish secondary education, 1984–1990', *Sociology of Education*, 69, pp. 1–21.

Gatherer, W. A. (1990), 'The primary curriculum and the politicians', in Roger, A. and D. Hartley (eds), *Curriculum and Assessment in Scotland: A Policy for the 90s*, Edinburgh: Scottish Academic Press, pp. 62–77.

Gordon, D. (1988), 'The legacy of R. F. Mackenzie', *Scottish Educational Review*, 20, pp. 32–41.

Gordon, E. (1991), *Women and the Labour Movement in Scotland 1850–1914*, Oxford: Clarendon.

Gow, L. and A. McPherson (1980), *Tell Them From Me*, Aberdeen: Aberdeen University Press.

Gray, J., A. McPherson and D. Raffe (1983), *Reconstructions of Secondary Education: Theory, Myth and Practice since the War*, London: Routledge and Kegan Paul.

Green, A. (1990), *Education and State Formation: the Rise of Education Systems in England, France and the USA*, Basingstoke: Macmillan.

Grierson, H. (1937), *The University and a Liberal Education*, Edinburgh: Oliver and Boyd.

Grieve, C. M. (1926), 'A. S. Neill and our educational system', *Scottish Educational Journal*, 5 March, pp. 241–3.

Hampton, K. (1998), *Youth and Racism: Perceptions and Experiences of Young People in Glasgow*, Glasgow: Scottish Ethnic Minorities Research Unit.

Hargreaves, J. D. (1994), *Academe and Empire: Some Overseas Connections of Aberdeen University 1860–1970*, Aberdeen: Aberdeen University Press.

Hargreaves, J. D. and A. Forbes (1989), *Aberdeen University 1945–1981: Regional Roles and National Needs*, Aberdeen: Aberdeen University Press.

Harrison, M. (1994), *Scottish Education Bibliography, 1970–1990*, Glasgow: Jordanhill Library, Strathclyde University.

Hartley, D. (1987), 'The convergence of learner-centred pedagogy in primary and further education in Scotland: 1965–1985', *British Journal of Educational Studies*, 35, pp. 115–28.

Hearn, J. (2000), *Claiming Scotland*, Edinburgh: Polygon.

Henderson, S. (1978), 'Trade union education in Scotland: problems and potential', *Scottish Journal of Adult Education*, 3, pp. 29–35.

Hendrie, W. F. (1997), *The Dominie: a Profile of the Scottish Headmaster*, Edinburgh: John Donald.

Hendry, L. and M. Raymond (1986), 'YTS and young people growing up: the adolescents' perspective', *Scottish Educational Review*, 18, pp. 100–9.

Highet, J. (1969), *A School of One's Choice*, London: Blackie.

Holmes, H. (ed.) (2000), *Scottish Life and Society: Education*, East Linton: Tuckwell.

Hope, K. (1978), 'The Scottish Mental Survey: its history and achievements', in *The Scottish Council for Research in Education: 50th Anniversary 1928–1978*, Edinburgh: Scottish Council for Research in Education, pp. 23–4.

Horobin, J. (1980), 'Adult education in Scotland from 1968 to 1978', *Scottish Journal of Adult Education*, 4, Spring, pp. 5–15.

Horobin, J. (1983), 'Adult education in Scotland from 1976 to 1981', *Scottish Journal of Adult Education*, 6, Spring, pp. 5–10.

Humes, W. (1986), *The Leadership Class in Scottish Education*, Edinburgh: John Donald.

Humes, W. and H. M. Paterson (eds) (1983), *Scottish Culture and Scottish Education*, Edinburgh: John Donald.

Hutchison, D. and G. M. Littlejohn (1975), 'The impact of social science on flows from school to university', *Research in Education*, 13, pp. 1–26.

Hutchison, H. (1973), *Scottish Public Educational Documents*, Edinburgh: Scottish Council for Research in Education.

Hutchison, I. G. C. (1992), 'The Scottish Office and the Scottish universities, c. 1930–c. 1960', in Carter, J. and D. Withrington (eds), *Scottish Universities: Distinctiveness and Diversity*, Edinburgh: John Donald, pp. 56–66.

Hutchison, I. G. C. (1993), *The University and the State: the Case of Aberdeen 1860–1963*, Aberdeen: Aberdeen University Press.

Illich, I. (1973), *Deschooling Society*, Harmondsworth: Penguin.

Independent Committee of Inquiry into Student Finance (1999), *Student Finance: Fairness for the Future*, Edinburgh: Independent Committee of Inquiry into Student Finance.

Institute of Chartered Accountants of Scotland (1970), *Report of the Council*, Edinburgh: ICAS.

Institute of Chartered Accountants of Scotland (1974), *Report of the Council*, Edinburgh: ICAS.

Institute of Chartered Accountants of Scotland (1980), *Report of the Council*, Edinburgh: ICAS.

Jamieson, L. (1990), '"We all left at 14": girls' and boys' schooling 1900–1930', in Paterson, F. M. S. and J. Fewell (eds), *Girls in their Prime*, Edinburgh: Scottish Academic Press, pp. 16–37.

Jamieson, L. and C. Toynbee (1992), *Country Bairns Growing Up 1900–1930*, Edinburgh: Edinburgh University Press.

Jarausch, K. H. (ed.) (1983), *The Transformation of Higher Learning, 1860–1930*, Chicago: University of Chicago Press.

Jardine, T. (1955), *The Challenge of the Primary School*, Glasgow: Corporation of Glasgow Education Department and Educational Institute of Scotland Glasgow Local Association.

Jones, C. L., G. M. Littlejohn and A. McPherson (1974), 'Predicting science-based study at university', *Journal of the Royal Statistical Society*, series A, pp. 48–59.

Jones, C. L. and A. McPherson (1973), *Varieties of Consumer Demand for Scottish Tertiary Education*, unpublished paper, Edinburgh: Centre for Educational Sociology, Edinburgh University.

Kane, P. (1992), *Tinsel Show*, Edinburgh: Polygon.

Kelly, A. (1976), 'Family background, subject specialisation and occupational recruitment of Scottish university students: some patterns and trends', *Higher Education*, 5, pp. 177–88.

Kelly, T. (1992), *A History of Adult Education in Great Britain*, Liverpool: Liverpool University Press, 3rd edition.

Kelman, J. (1991), 'Foreword', in Davie, G. E., *The Scottish Enlightenment and Other Essays*, Edinburgh: Polygon.

Kenneth, Rev. Brother (1968), 'The Education (Scotland) Act, 1918, in the making', *Innes Review*, 19, pp. 91–128.

Kirk, G. (1996), 'The training of secondary teachers', in Harrison, M. M. and W. B. Marker (eds), *Teaching the Teachers: The History of Jordanhill College of Education 1828–1993*, Edinburgh: John Donald, pp. 106–21.

Kirk, G. (1999), 'The passing of monotechnic teacher education in Scotland', *Scottish Educational Review*, 31, pp. 100–11.

Kirk, G. and R. Glaister (1994), *5–14: Scotland's National Curriculum*, Edinburgh: Scottish Academic Press.

Kirkwood, G. and C. Kirkwood (1989), *Living Adult Education: Freire in Scotland*, Milton Keynes: Open University Press.

Knox, W. (1984a), 'Introduction' in Knox, W. (ed.), *Scottish Labour Leaders, 1918–1939*, Edinburgh: Mainstream, pp. 15–57.

Knox, W. (1984b), 'Joseph Forbes Duncan', in Knox, W. (ed.), *Scottish Labour Leaders, 1918–1939*, Edinburgh: Mainstream, pp. 100–7.

Kogan, M. (1975), *Educational Policy Making*, London: Allen and Unwin.

Laurie, S. S. (1901), *The Training of Teachers and Methods of Instruction*, Cambridge.

Leech, M. (1999), 'Further education in Scotland post-incorporation', in Bryce, T. G. K. and W. M. Humes (eds), *Scottish Education*, Edinburgh: Edinburgh University Press, pp. 49–62.

Lenman, B. and J. Stocks (1972), 'The beginnings of state education in Scotland, 1872–1885', *Scottish Educational Studies*, 4, pp. 93–106.

Levitt, I. (1988), *Poverty and Welfare in Scotland 1890–1948*, Edinburgh: Edinburgh University Press.

Lindsay, I. (1992), 'Migration and motivation: a twentieth century perspective', in Devine, T. M. (ed.), *Scottish Emigration and Scottish Society*, Edinburgh: John Donald, pp. 154–74.

Lloyd, G. (2000), 'From ragged to residential schools: schooling away from home for troubled and troublesome children', in Holmes, H. (ed.), *Scottish Life and Society: Education*, East Linton: Tuckwell, pp. 254–69.

Lloyd, J. M. (1979), *The Scottish School System and the Second World War: a Study in Central Policy and Administration*, PhD thesis, Stirling University.

Lloyd, J. M. (1984), 'Tom Johnston's parliament on education: the birth of the sixth Advisory Council on Education in Scotland, 1942–43', *Scottish Educational Review*, 16, pp. 104–15.

Lynn, P. (1994), *The 1994 Leavers*, Edinburgh: Scottish Office.

Macbeath, J. (1988), *Personal and Social Education*, Edinburgh: Scottish Academic Press.

MacDougall, I. (ed.) (1981), *Militant Miners*, Edinburgh: Polygon.

MacGillivray, D. (1919), 'Fifty years of Scottish education', in Clarke, J. (ed.), *Problems of National Education*, London: Macmillan, pp. 1–41.

MacIntyre, A. (1981), *After Virtue*, London: Duckworth.

Macintyre, A. (1984), 'Patterns of uptake and use in schools', in Duncan, J. (ed.), *Broadcasting and School Education in Scotland*, Edinburgh: HMSO, pp. 67–71.

Mackay, D. I. (1969), *Geographical Mobility and the Brain Drain*, London: Allen and Unwin.

MacKenzie, M. (1967), 'The road to the circulars: a study of the evolution of Labour Party policy with regard to the comprehensive school', *Scottish Educational Studies*, 1, pp. 25–33.

Mackinnon, K. M. (1972), 'Education and social control: the case of Gaelic Scotland', *Scottish Educational Studies*, 4, pp. 125–37.

Mackinnon, K. M. (1995–6), 'Gaelic and the "other languages of Scotland" in the 1991 population census', *Scottish Language*, no. 14/15, pp. 104–17.

Maclellan, E. (1999), 'Mathematics', in Bryce, T. G. K. and W. M. Humes (eds), *Scottish Education*, Edinburgh: Edinburgh University Press, pp. 374–7.

Macmeeken, A. M. (1939), *The Intelligence of a Representative Group of Scottish Children*, London: University of London Press.

Macpherson, J. S. (1958), *Eleven-Year-Olds Grow Up*, London: University of London Press.

Malzahn, M. (1987), 'The industrial novel', in Craig, C. (ed.), *The History of Scottish Literature, Volume 4, Twentieth Century*, Aberdeen: Aberdeen University Press, pp. 229–42.

Marker, W. (1994), 'The Robbins Report and teacher education in Scotland', *Scottish Educational Review*, 26, pp. 41–50.

Marker, W. and C. D. Raab (1993), 'Advise and construct: the expansion of the Scottish colleges of education in the 1960s', *Scottish Educational Review*, 25, pp. 3–16.

Marshall, T. H. (1950), *Citizenship and Social Class and Other Essays*, Cambridge: Cambridge University Press.

Martin, I. (1996), 'Community education: the dialectics of development', in Fieldhouse, R. (ed.), *A History of Modern British Adult Education*, Leicester: National Institute for Adult and Continuing Education, pp. 109–41.

Marwick, W. H. (1937), 'The university extension movement in Scotland', *University of Edinburgh Journal*, 8, pp. 227–34.

Marwick, W. H. (1953), 'The Workers' Educational Association in Scotland', *Scottish Adult Education*, no. 8, August, pp. 10–13.

Marwick, W. H. (1974), 'Workers' education in early twentieth century Scotland', *Scottish Labour History Society Journal*, no. 8, pp. 34–8.

Maxwell, J. (1969), *Sixteen Years On: A Follow-Up of the 1947 Scottish Survey*, London: University of London Press.

McClelland, W. (1936), 'Social aspects of the teacher's preparation', *New Era in Home and School*, 17, April, pp. 92–4.

McClelland, W. (1942), *Selection for Secondary Education*, London: University of London Press.

McCrone, D. (1992), *Understanding Scotland*, London: Routledge, first edition.

McCrone, D. (2001), *Understanding Scotland*, London: Routledge, second edition.

McCrone, D., F. Bechhofer and S. Kendrick (1982), 'Egalitarianism and social inequality in Scotland', in Robbins, D. (ed.), *Rethinking Social Inequality*, Farnborough: Gower, pp. 127–48.

McCusker, J. (2001), *How Much Is That in Real Money? A Historical Price Index for Use as a Deflator of Money Values in the Economy of the United States*, Worcester, MA: American Antiquarian Society.

McDonald, I. (1967), 'Untapped reservoirs of talent?', *Scottish Educational Studies*, 1, pp. 52–8.

McEnroe, F. J. (1983), 'Freudianism, bureaucracy and Scottish primary education', in Humes, W. and H. M. Paterson (eds), *Scottish Culture and Scottish Education*, Edinburgh: John Donald, pp. 244–66.

McIntosh, D. M. (1963), 'The wishes of parents', *Scottish Educational Journal*, 46, 22 February, pp. 145–7.

McIntosh, D. M. and D. A. Walker (1970), 'The O-grade of the Scottish Certificate of Education', *British Journal of Educational Psychology*, 40, pp. 179–99.

McKechnie, W. W. (1944), 'The development of post-primary education in Scotland – the multilateral school', *Scottish Educational Journal*, 27, 22 September (pp. 492–3), 29 September (pp. 503–4), 6 October (pp. 525–6), 13 October (pp. 538–9).

McLaren, D. (1999), 'Guidance and personal and social education in the secondary school', in Bryce, T. G. K. and W. M. Humes (eds), *Scottish Education*, Edinburgh: Edinburgh University Press, pp. 415–24.

McManus, T. (1997), 'Education in the philistine society', *Cencrastus*, no. 59, pp. 33–6.

McNally, D. (1982), *The Theory and Practice of Corporal and Other Forms of Punishment in Scottish Secondary Schools*, MEd thesis, Edinburgh University.

McPake, J. and S. Watt (1998), 'Scottish special entry summer schools: a secret success story?', *Scottish Educational Review*, 30, pp. 29–40.

McPherson, A. (1972), *The Generally Educated Scot: An Old Ideal in a Changing University Structure*, Milton Keynes: Open University.

McPherson, A. (1973), 'Selections and survivals: a sociology of the ancient Scottish universities', in Brown, R. (ed.), *Knowledge, Education and Cultural Change*, London: Tavistock, pp. 163–201.

McPherson, A. (1983), 'An angle on the geist: persistence and change in the Scottish educational tradition', in Humes, W. and H. M. Paterson (eds), *Scottish Culture and Scottish Education*, Edinburgh: John Donald, pp. 216–43.

McPherson, A. (1989), 'Social and political aspects of the devolved management of Scottish secondary schools', *Scottish Educational Review*, 21, pp. 87–100.

McPherson, A. (1992a), 'Schooling', in Dickson, A. and J. H. Treble (eds), *People and Society in Scotland, Vol III, 1914–1990*, Edinburgh: John Donald, pp. 80–107.

McPherson, A. (1992b), 'The Howie Committee on post-compulsory schooling', in Paterson, L. and D. McCrone (eds), *Scottish Government Yearbook 1992*, Edinburgh: Unit for the Study of Government in Scotland, Edinburgh University, pp. 114–30.

McPherson, A. and G. Atherton (1970), 'Graduate teachers in Scotland – a sociological analysis of recruitment to teaching among recent graduates of the four ancient Scottish universities', *Scottish Educational Studies*, 2, pp. 35–55.

McPherson, A. and Neave, G. (1976), *The Scottish Sixth: a Sociological Evaluation of Sixth Year Studies and the Changing Relationship between School and University in Scotland*, Slough: National Foundation for Educational Research.

McPherson, A. and C. D. Raab (1988), *Governing Education*, Edinburgh: Edinburgh University Press.

McPherson, A. and J. D. Willms (1986), 'Certification, class conflict, religion, and community: a socio-historical explanation of the effectiveness of contemporary schools', in Kerckhoff, A. C. (ed.), *Research in Sociology of Education and Socialization*, Greenwich, CT: JAI Press, vol. 6, pp. 227–302.

McPherson, A. and J. D. Willms (1987), 'Equalisation and improvement: some effects of comprehensive reorganisation in Scotland', *Sociology*, 21, pp. 509–39.

Mercer, G. and D. Forsyth (1975), 'Some aspects of recruitment to school teaching among university graduates in Scotland, 1860–1955', *British Journal of Educational Studies*, 23, pp. 58–77.

Meyer, J. W. (1992), 'The social construction of motives for educational expansion', in Fuller, B. and R. Rubinson (eds), *The Political Construction of Education*, New York: Praeger, pp. 225–38.

Meyer, J. W., F. O. Ramirez, R. Rubinson and J. Boli-Bennett (1977), 'The world education revolution, 1950–1970', *Sociology of Education*, 50, pp. 242–58.

Meyer, J. W., F. O. Ramirez and Y. N. Soysal (1992), 'World expansion of mass education, 1870–1980', *Sociology of Education*, 65, pp. 128–49.

Mill, J. S. (1867), *Inaugural Address Delivered to the University of St Andrews*, London: Longmans, Green, Reader and Dyer.

Millar, H. and D. White (1972), *Comprehensive Education – Has it Changed Anything?*, Ayr: Ayrshire Fabian Society.

Moore, L. (1992), 'Educating for the "women's sphere": domestic training versus intellectual discipline', in Breitenbach, E. and E. Gordon (eds), *Out of Bounds: Women in Scottish Society 1800–1945*, Edinburgh: Edinburgh University Press, pp. 10–41.

Morris, I. (1990), 'The Primary Memorandum: twenty five years on', *Scottish Educational Review*, 22, pp. 23–9.

Morris, J. G. [I.] (1994), *Scottish Council for Research in Education, 1928–1993/4*, PhD thesis, Edinburgh University.

Morris, R. J. (1983), 'Skilled workers and the politics of the "Red" Clyde: a discussion paper', *Scottish Labour History Society Journal*, 18, pp. 6–17.

Moss, M., F. Munro and R. H. Trainor (2000), *University, City and State: the University of Glasgow since 1870*, Edinburgh: Edinburgh University Press.

Muir, A. B. (1934), 'Survey of nursery schools in Scotland', *Scottish Educational Journal*, 17, 20 April, pp. 478–9.

Munn, P. (1992), 'Devolved management of schools and FE colleges: a victory for the producer over the consumer?', in Paterson, L. and D. McCrone (eds), *Scottish Government Yearbook 1992*, Edinburgh: Unit for the Study of Government in Scotland, Edinburgh University, pp. 142–56.

Munn, P. (1993), 'Parents as school board members: school managers and friends?', in Munn, P. (ed.), *Parents and Schools*, London: Routledge, pp. 87–100.

Munn, P. and M. Johnstone (1992), *Discipline in Scottish Secondary Schools*, Edinburgh: Scottish Council for Research in Education.

Munn, P., M. Johnstone and K. Lowden (1993), *Students' Perceptions of Access Courses*, Edinburgh: Scottish Council for Research in Education.

Munn, P., G. Lloyd and M. A. Cullen (2000), *Alternatives to Exclusion from School*, London: Paul Chapman.

Munn, P. and C. MacDonald (1988), *Adult Participation in Education and Training*, Edinburgh: Scottish Council for Research in Education.

Murphy, J. (1992), *British Social Services: the Scottish Dimension*, Edinburgh: Scottish Academic Press.

Murphy, P. A. (1998), *The Life of R. F. Mackenzie*, Edinburgh: John Donald.

Myers, J. D. (1972), 'Scottish nationalism and the antecedents of the 1872 Education Act', *Scottish Educational Studies*, 4, pp. 73–92.

National Committee of Enquiry into Higher Education (1997), *Report of the Scottish Committee*, London: HMSO.

Neave, G. (1976), 'The development of Scottish education, 1958–1972', *Comparative Education*, 12, pp. 129–44.

Neave, G. and H. Cowper (1979), 'Higher education in Scotland', *European Journal of Education*, 14, pp. 7–24.

Neill, A. S. (1916), *A Dominie's Log*, London: Herbert Jenkins.

Nisbet, J. (1957), 'From eleven-plus to graduation', *Scottish Educational Journal*, 40, pp. 261–2.

Nisbet, J. (1978), 'The SCRE's contribution to research in education', in *The Scottish Council for Research in Education: 50th Anniversary 1928–1978*, Edinburgh: Scottish Council for Research in Education, pp. 7–9.

Nisbet, J., L. Hendry, C. Stewart and J. Watt (1980), *Towards Community Education*, Aberdeen: Aberdeen University Press.

Nisbet, J., J. Welsh and N. Entwistle (1972), 'Age of transfer to secondary education: a postscript', *British Journal of Educational Psychology*, 42, pp. 233–9.

Northcroft, D. (1992), '"Secondary Education" and the rhetoric of change', *Scottish Educational Review*, 24, pp. 76–92.

O'Dea, M. and A. McPhee (1994), 'The Scottish Wider Access Programme and the attainment of students in a college of education', *Scottish Educational Review*, 26, pp. 34–40.

OECD (1997), *Education at a Glance*, Paris: OECD.

Osborne, G. S. (1966), *Scottish and English Schools: A Comparative Survey of the Past Fifty Years*, Pittsburgh: University of Pittsburgh Press.

Osborne, R. D. (1999), 'Wider access in Scotland?', *Scottish Affairs*, no. 26, pp. 36–46.

Paisey, C. and N. J. Paisey (2000), *A Comparative Study of Undergraduate and Professional Education in the Professions of Accountancy, Medicine, Law and Architecture*, Edinburgh: Institute of Chartered Accountants of Scotland.

Parker, R. H. (1997), 'Flickering at the margin of existence: the Association of University Teachers of Accounting, 1960–1971', *British Accounting Review*, 29 (special issue), pp. 41–61.

Parliamentary Debates (1947), fifth series, vol. 440, 22 July, col. 1067.

Parliamentary Debates (1954), fifth series, vol. 523, 1–19 February, cols 1896–8.

Parliamentary Papers (1901), *Report of the Committee of Council on Education in Scotland*, PP XXII.

Parliamentary Papers (1908), *List of Day Schools Aided from Parliamentary Grant*, PP XXVIII.

Paterson, H. M. (1975), *Godfrey Thomson and the Development of Psychometrics in Scotland*, unpublished manuscript.

Paterson, H. M. (1983), 'Incubus and ideology: the development of secondary schooling in Scotland, 1900–1939', in Humes, W. and H. M. Paterson (eds), *Scottish Culture and Scottish Education*, Edinburgh: John Donald, pp. 14–21.

Paterson, L. (1993), 'Regionalism among entrants to higher education from Scottish schools', *Oxford Review of Education*, 19, pp. 231–55.

Paterson, L. (1994), 'Participation in science and engineering courses by entrants to higher education from Scottish schools, 1963–1990', *Scottish Educational Review*, 26, pp. 3–17.

Paterson, L. (1995), 'Social origins of under-achievement among school-leavers', in Dawtrey, L., J. Holland, M. Hammer, and S. Sheldon (eds), *Equality and Inequality in Education Policy*, Milton Keynes: Open University Press, pp. 77–92.

Paterson, L. (1997a), 'Student achievement and educational change in Scotland, 1980–1995', *Scottish Educational Review*, 29, pp. 10–19.

Paterson, L. (1997b), 'Trends in higher education participation in Scotland', *Higher Education Quarterly*, 51, pp. 29–48.

Paterson, L. (1998), 'Scottish higher education and the Scottish parliament: the consequences of mistaken national identity', *European Review*, 6, pp. 459–74.

Paterson, L. (2000a), *Education and the Scottish Parliament*, Edinburgh: Dunedin Academic Press.

Paterson, L. (2000b), *Crisis in the Classroom: the Exam Debacle and the Way Ahead for Scottish Education*, Edinburgh: Mainstream.

Paterson, L. (2000c), 'Salvation through education? The changing social status of Scottish Catholics', in Devine, T. M. (ed.), *Scotland's Shame? Bigotry, Sectarianism and Catholicism in Modern Scotland*, Edinburgh: Mainstream, pp. 145–57.

Paterson, L. (2003), 'The three educational ideologies of the British Labour Party', *Oxford Review of Education*, 29, to appear.

Paterson, L., A. Brown, J. Curtice, K. Hinds, D. McCrone, A. Park, K. Sproston and P. Surridge (2001), *New Scotland, New Politics?*, Edinburgh: Edinburgh University Press.

Paterson, L. and D. Raffe (1995), '"Staying-on" in full-time education in Scotland, 1985–1991', *Oxford Review of Education*, 21, pp. 3–23.

Paulston, R. G. (1968), *Educational Change in Sweden: Planning and Accepting the Comprehensive School Reforms*, New York: Teachers College Press.

Payne, G. and G. Ford (1977), 'Religion, class and education policy', *Scottish Educational Studies*, 9, pp. 83–99.

Penn, H. (1992), *Under Fives: The View from Strathclyde*, Edinburgh: Scottish Academic Press.

Perkin, H. (1989), *The Rise of Professional Society: England Since 1880*, London: Routledge.

Petrie, D. S. (1978), 'The development of special education in Scotland since 1950', in Dockrell, W. B., W. R. Dunn and A. Milne (eds), *Special Education in Scotland*, Edinburgh: Scottish Council for Research in Education, pp. 1–15.

Philip, H. (1992), *The Higher Tradition*, Dalkeith: Scottish Examination Board.

Pollock, G. J., W. G. Thorpe and S. Freshwater (1977), *Pupils' Attitude to School Rules and Punishments*, Edinburgh: Scottish Council for Research in Education.

Raab, G. (1998), *Participation in Higher Education in Scotland 1996–97*, Edinburgh: Scottish Higher Education Funding Council.

Raffe, D. (1977), 'Social class and entry to further education', *Scottish Educational Review*, 9, pp. 100–11.

Raffe, D. (1984), 'Youth unemployment and the MSC: 1977–1983', in McCrone, D. (ed.), *Scottish Government Yearbook 1984*, Edinburgh: Unit for the Study of Government in Scotland, pp. 188–222.

Raffe, D. (1985), 'The extendable ladder: Scotland's 16+ Action Plan', *Youth and Policy*, no. 12, spring, pp. 27–33.

Raffe, D. (1986), 'Unemployment and school motivation: the case of truancy', *Educational Review*, 38, pp. 11–19.

Raffe, D., K. Brannen, J. Fairgrieve and C. Martin (2001), 'Participation, inclusiveness, academic drift and parity of esteem: a comparison of post-compulsory education and training in England, Wales, Scotland and Northern Ireland', *Oxford Review of Education*, 27, pp. 173–203.

Raffe, D. and G. Courtney (1988), '16–18 on both sides of the border', in Raffe, D. (ed.), *Education and the Youth Labour Market*, Lewes: Falmer, pp. 12–39.

Raffe, D., C. Howieson and T. Tinklin (2002), 'The Scottish educational crisis of 2000: an analysis of the policy process of unification', *Journal of Educational Policy*, 17, pp. 167–86.

Ramirez, F. O. and J. Boli (1987), 'The political construction of mass schooling: European origins and worldwide institutionalisation', *Sociology of Education*, 60, pp. 2–17.

Reid, F. (1966), 'Socialist Sunday schools in Britain, 1892–1939', *International Review of Social History*, 11, pp. 18–47.

Ringer, F. (1979), *Education and Society in Modern Europe*, Bloomington: Indiana University Press.

Ringer, F. (1987), 'Introduction', in Müller, D. K., F. Ringer and B. Simon (eds), *The Rise of the Modern Educational System: Structural Change and Social Reproduction, 1870–1920*, Cambridge: Cambridge University Press, pp. 1–12.

Roberts, A. (1972), 'Scotland and infant education in the nineteenth century', *Scottish Educational Studies*, 4, pp. 39–45.

Roberts, J. H. (1970), *The National Council of Labour Colleges*, MSc thesis, Edinburgh University.

Robertson, A. (1974), 'Extra-mural education in Dundee and district', *Scottish Journal of Adult Education*, 1, pp. 41–8.

Robertson, B. (1999), 'Gaelic education', in Bryce, T. G. K. and W. M. Humes (eds), *Scottish Education*, Edinburgh: Edinburgh University Press, pp. 244–55.

Robertson, C. (1992), 'Routes to higher education in Scotland', *Scottish Educational Review*, 24, pp. 3–16.

Robertson, C. (2000), 'Schools' effects on attainment in university', unpublished paper, Glasgow: Department of Statistics and Modelling Science, Strathclyde University.

Robertson, D. (1990), '*Curriculum and Assessment in Scotland – a Policy for the 90s:* humanism or philistinism?', in Roger, A. and D. Hartley (eds), *Curriculum and Assessment in Scotland: A Policy for the 90s*, Edinburgh: Scottish Academic Press, pp. 78–94.

Robertson, J. J. (1957), 'Ten years after', *Scottish Educational Journal*, 40, 12 April, pp. 213–15.

Robertson, P. (1984), 'Scottish universities and industry, 1860–1914', *Scottish Economic and Social History*, 4, pp. 39–54.

Rose, J. (1906), 'The place and function of Higher Grade schools in Scotland', *Educational News*, 24 February (pp. 146–7) and 3 March (pp. 167–8).

Rosie, M. J. (2001), *Religion and Sectarianism in Modern Scotland*, PhD thesis, Edinburgh University.

Rougvie, A. (1997), 'Participation in part-time adult education and training in Fife', *Scottish Journal of Adult and Continuing Education*, 4, pp. 45–68.

Russell, J. A. (1957), 'Survey of the Junior Secondary school', *Scottish Educational Journal*, 40, 6 December, pp. 724–5.

Rust, V. D. (1989), *The Democratic Tradition and the Evolution of Schooling in Norway*, New York: Greenwood Press.

Ryrie, A. C. (1984), *Changing Student Needs in Further Education Colleges*, Edinburgh: Scottish Council for Research in Education.

Ryrie, A. C., A. Furst and M. Lauder (1979), *Choices and Chances: A Study of Pupils' Subject Choices and Future Career Intentions*, Edinburgh: Scottish Council for Research in Education.

Sanderson, M. (1972), *The Universities and British Industry, 1850–1970*, London: Routledge and Kegan Paul.

Sargant, N. (2000), *The Learning Divide Revisited*, Leicester: National Institute of Adult and Continuing Education.

Savage, M. (2000), *Class Analysis and Social Transformation*, Buckingham: Open University Press.

Schuller, T., D. Raffe, B. Morgan-Klein and I. Clark (1999), *Part-Time Higher Education*, London: Jessica Kingsley.

Scotland, J. (1969), *The History of Scottish Education. Volume Two: From 1872 to the Present Day*, London: University of London Press.

Scotland, J. (1975), 'Battles long ago – Aberdeen University and the training of teachers 1907–8, *Scottish Educational Review*, 7, pp. 85–95.

Scott, J. W. R. (1925), *The Story of the Women's Institute Movement in England, Wales and Scotland*, Idbury: Village Press.

Scott, P. (1990), *Knowledge and Nation*, Edinburgh: Edinburgh University Press.

Scott, P. (1994), 'Scottish higher education regained: accident or design?', *Scottish Affairs*, no. 7, pp. 68–85.

Scottish Centre for Economic and Social Research (1989), *Scottish Education: a Declaration of Principles*, Edinburgh: Scottish Centre for Economic and Social Research.

Scottish Consultative Council on the Curriculum (1994), *Languages for Life*, Dundee: SCCC.

Scottish Consultative Council on the Curriculum (1995), *The Heart of the Matter: Education for Personal and Social Development*, Dundee: SCCC.

Scottish Consultative Council on the Curriculum (1996), *Teaching for Effective Learning*, Dundee: SCCC.

Scottish Consultative Council on the Curriculum (1999), *A Curriculum Framework for Children 3 to 5*, Dundee: SCCC.

Scottish Council for Research in Education (1931), *Curriculum for Pupils of Twelve to Fifteen Years*, London: University of London Press.

Scottish Council for Research in Education (1939), *Scottish Primary School Organisation*, London: University of London Press.

Scottish Council for Research in Education (1953), *Social Implications of the 1947 Scottish Mental Survey*, London: University of London Press.

Scottish Council for Research in Education (1958), *Educational and Other Implications of the 1947 Scottish Mental Survey*, London: University of London Press.

Scottish Council for Research in Education (1961), *Gaelic-Speaking Children in Highland Schools*, London: University of London Press.

Scottish Council for Research in Education (1968), *Rising Standards in Scottish Primary Schools: 1953–63*, London: University of London Press.

Scottish Council for Research in Education (1970), *A Study of Fifteen-Year-Olds*, London: University of London Press.

Scottish Education Department (1913), *Report of the Committee of Council on Education in Scotland 1912–1913*, London: HMSO.

Scottish Education Department (1919a), 'Report of the Committee of the Privy Council on Education in Scotland for the year 1915–16', in SED, *Education (Scotland) Reports, &c. issued in 1916–1919*, Edinburgh: HMSO.

Scottish Education Department (1919b), 'Report of the Committee of the Privy Council on Education in Scotland for the year 1918–19', in SED, *Education (Scotland) Reports, &c. issued in 1916–1919*, Edinburgh: HMSO.

Scottish Education Department (1921), 'Circular no. 44', in SED, *Education (Scotland) Reports, &c. issued in 1920–1*, Edinburgh: HMSO.

Scottish Education Department (1928), *Report of the Committee of Council on Education in Scotland for the Year 1927–1928*, Edinburgh: HMSO.

Scottish Education Department (1936a), *Report of the Committee of Council on Education in Scotland for the Year 1934–35*, Edinburgh: HMSO.

Scottish Education Department (1936b), *Sixty-third Annual Report of the Accountant to the Scottish Education Department*, Edinburgh: HMSO.

Scottish Education Department (1936c), *Statistical Lists of Grant-earning Day Schools and Institutions and of Continuation Classes and Central Institutions for the Year 1934–35*, Edinburgh: HMSO.

Scottish Education Department (1936d), *Circular 30: Leaving Certificate Examination and Day School Certificate (Higher) Examination, 1937*, Edinburgh: HMSO.

Scottish Education Department (1937), *General Reports for the Years 1933–36*, Edinburgh: HMSO.

Scottish Education Department (1939a), *Report of the Committee of Council on Education in Scotland for the Year 1938*, Edinburgh: HMSO.

Scottish Education Department (1939b), *Memorandum Explanatory of the Day School (Scotland) Code, 1939*, Edinburgh: HMSO.

Scottish Education Department (1945), *Summary Report on Education in Scotland for the Year 1944*, Edinburgh: HMSO.

Scottish Education Department (1946), *Primary Education: a Report of the Advisory Council on Education in Scotland*, Edinburgh: HMSO.

Scottish Education Department (1947), *Secondary Education: a Report of the Advisory Council on Education in Scotland*, Edinburgh: HMSO.

Scottish Education Department (1950), *The Primary School in Scotland*, Edinburgh: HMSO.

Scottish Education Department (1951), *Education in Scotland in 1950*, Edinburgh: HMSO.

Scottish Education Department (1952a), *Education in Scotland in 1951*, Edinburgh: HMSO.

Scottish Education Department (1952b), *Further Education: a Report of the Advisory Council on Education in Scotland*, Edinburgh: HMSO.

Scottish Education Department (1953a), *Education in Scotland in 1952*, Edinburgh: HMSO.

Scottish Education Department (1953b), *Technical Education in Scotland*, London: HMSO.

Scottish Education Department (1955a), *Education in Scotland in 1954*, Edinburgh: HMSO.

Scottish Education Department (1955b), *Junior Secondary Education*, Edinburgh: HMSO.

Scottish Education Department (1956), *Education in Scotland in 1955*, Edinburgh: HMSO.

Scottish Education Department (1957), *Education in Scotland in 1956*, Edinburgh: HMSO.

Scottish Education Department (1959), *Education in Scotland in 1958*, Edinburgh: HMSO.

Scottish Education Department (1960), *Education in Scotland in 1959*, Edinburgh: HMSO.

Scottish Education Department (1961a), *Education in Scotland in 1960*, Edinburgh: HMSO.

Scottish Education Department (1961b), *Transfer from Primary to Secondary Education*, Edinburgh: HMSO.

Scottish Education Department (1962), *Education in Scotland in 1961*, Edinburgh: HMSO.

Scottish Education Department (1963a), *Education in Scotland in 1962*, Edinburgh: HMSO.

Scottish Education Department (1963b), *From School to Further Education*, Edinburgh: HMSO.

Scottish Education Department (1964), *Education in Scotland in 1963*, Edinburgh: HMSO.

Scottish Education Department (1965a), *Primary Education in Scotland*, Edinburgh: HMSO.

Scottish Education Department (1965b), *Circular No. 600: Reorganisation of Secondary Education on Comprehensive Lines*, Edinburgh: HMSO.

Scottish Education Department (1965c), *Education in Scotland in 1964*, Edinburgh: HMSO.

Scottish Education Department (1966), *Education in Scotland in 1965*, Edinburgh: HMSO.

Scottish Education Department (1969), *Education in Scotland in 1968*, Edinburgh: HMSO.

Scottish Education Department (1971a), *Education in Scotland in 1970*, Edinburgh: HMSO.

Scottish Education Department (1971b), *Scottish Educational Statistics 1970*, Edinburgh: HMSO.

Scottish Education Department (1972a), *Education in Scotland in 1971*, Edinburgh: HMSO.

Scottish Education Department (1972b), *Education in Scotland: A Statement of Policy*, Edinburgh: HMSO.

Scottish Education Department (1972c), *Scottish Educational Statistics 1971*, Edinburgh: HMSO.

Scottish Education Department (1972d), *The First Two Years of Secondary Education*, Edinburgh: HMSO.

Scottish Education Department (1975), *Adult Education: The Challenge of Change*, Edinburgh: HMSO.

Scottish Education Department (1977a), *The Structure of the Curriculum in the Third and Fourth Years of the Scottish Secondary School*, Edinburgh: HMSO.

Scottish Education Department (1977b), *Assessment for All: Report of the Committee to Review Assessment in the Third and Fourth Years of Secondary Education in Scotland*, Edinburgh: HMSO.

Scottish Education Department (1977c), *Truancy and Indiscipline in Schools in Scotland*, Edinburgh: HMSO.

Scottish Education Department (1979), *First Destinations of University Graduates*, Statistical Bulletin no. 8/H2/1979, Edinburgh: SED.

Scottish Education Department (1980), *Learning and Teaching in Primary 4 and Primary 7*, Edinburgh: SED.

Scottish Education Department (1982), *Full-Time Education After S4: a Statistical Study*, Dalkeith: Scottish Examination Board.

Scottish Education Department (1983a), *16–18s in Scotland: an Action Plan*, Edinburgh: HMSO.

Scottish Education Department (1983b), *Higher Education Projections*, Statistical Bulletin no. 7/J1/1983, Edinburgh: SED.

Scottish Education Department (1985), *Future Strategy for Higher Education in Scotland*, Edinburgh: HMSO.

Scottish Education Department (1987), *Curriculum and Assessment in Scotland: a Policy for the 1990s*, Edinburgh: SED.

Scottish Education Department (1988), *School Leavers' Qualifications*, Statistical Bulletin no. 11/E2/1988, Edinburgh: SED.

Scottish Education Department (1989a), *Placing Requests in Education Authority Schools*, Statistical Bulletin no. 1/B6/1989, Edinburgh: SED.

Scottish Education Department (1989b), *University Students*, Statistical Bulletin no. 3/H1/1989, Edinburgh: SED.

Scottish Education Department (1989c), *Scottish Higher Education Statistics*, Statistical Bulletin no. 9/J2/1989, Edinburgh: SED.

Scottish Education Department (1989d), *Student Enrolments in Non-Advanced Further Education Scotland 1980/81–1987/88*, Statistical Bulletin no. 10/F7/1989, Edinburgh: SED.

Scottish Education Department (1989e), *The Assisted Places Scheme*, Statistical Bulletin no. 6/C5/1989, Edinburgh: SED.

Scottish Education Department (1990), *School Leavers' Higher Grade Qualifications*, Statistical Bulletin no. 11/E4/1990, Edinburgh: SED.

Scottish Education Reform Committee (1917), *Reform in Scottish Education*, Edinburgh: Scottish Education Reform Committee.

Scottish Educational Journal (1944), 'What are people thinking about education?', 27, 12 May (pp. 254–5), 19 May (p. 274), 26 May (pp. 286–7), 2 June (p. 300), 9 June (p. 316), 16 June (pp. 324–5), 23 June (pp. 336–7).

Scottish Executive (1999a), *Students in Higher Education in Scotland: 1997–98*, Edinburgh: Scottish Executive.

Scottish Executive (1999b), *Early Intervention 1997–98*, Edinburgh: Scottish Executive.

Scottish Executive (1999c), *Summary Results of the September 1998 School Census*, Statistical Bulletin Edn/B1/1999/3, Edinburgh: Scottish Executive.

Scottish Executive (1999d), *Higher Education Graduates and Diplomates and their First Destinations 1986–87 to 1996–97*, Statistical Bulletin Edn/F6/1999/5, Edinburgh: Scottish Executive.

Scottish Executive (2000), *Detailed Results of the October 1999 School Survey of Information and Communication Technology*, Statistical Bulletin Edn/B9/2000/2, Edinburgh: Scottish Executive.

Scottish Executive (2001a), *Pre-School Education for Three Year Olds Increasing*, Press Release SE1699/2001, Edinburgh: Scottish Executive.

Scottish Executive (2001b), *Students in Higher Education in Scotland: 1999–00*, Edinburgh: Scottish Executive.

Scottish Executive (2001c), *Standard Tables on Higher Education and Further Education in Scotland*, Edinburgh: Scottish Executive.

Scottish Executive (2001d), *Summary Results of the September 2000 School Census*, Statistical Bulletin Edn/B1/2001/2, Edinburgh: Scottish Executive.

Scottish Executive (2001e), *National Investigation into the Experience of Higher Still Assessment in Schools and Colleges*, Edinburgh: Scottish Executive.

Scottish Executive (2002a), *Programme for International Student Assessment: Scottish Report*, Edinburgh: Scottish Executive.

Scottish Executive (2002b), *Students in Higher Education in Scotland: 2000–01*, Statistical Bulletin, Edinburgh: Scottish Executive.

Scottish Higher Education Funding Council (1995), *Higher Education Institutions: Financial Statistics 1993–94*, Edinburgh: SHEFC.

Scottish Higher Education Funding Council (2000), *Scots Universities Ahead of UK on Access*, press release PRHE 11/00, Edinburgh: SHEFC.

Scottish Household Survey web site, www.scotland.gov.uk/shs/.

Scottish Office (1996), *Government Expenditure and Revenue in Scotland 1994–1995*, Edinburgh: Scottish Office.

Scottish Office Education and Industry Department (1995a), *Provision for Pre-School Children*, Statistical Bulletin Edn/A2/1995/16, Edinburgh: Scottish Office.

Scottish Office Education and Industry Department (1995b), *Summary Results of the 1994 School Census*, Statistical Bulletin Edn/B1/1995/17, Edinburgh: Scottish Office.

Scottish Office Education and Industry Department (1996a), *Standards and Quality in Scottish Schools 1992–95*, Edinburgh: Scottish Office.

Scottish Office Education and Industry Department (1996b), *Scottish Higher Education Statistics*, Statistical Bulletin Edn/J2/1996/12, Edinburgh: Scottish Office.

Scottish Office Education and Industry Department (1996c), *Teachers in Scotland: September 1994*, Statistical Bulletin Edn/G5/1996/2, Edinburgh: Scottish Office.

Scottish Office Education and Industry Department (1996d), *Achievement for All*, Edinburgh: Scottish Office.

Scottish Office Education and Industry Department (1996e), *Students Registered in Vocational Further Education in Scotland 1993–94*, Statistical Bulletin Edn/F7/1996/1, Edinburgh: Scottish Office.

Scottish Office Education and Industry Department (1997a), *Summary Results of the 1996 School Census*, Statistical Bulletin Edn/B1/1997/3, Edinburgh: Scottish Office.

Scottish Office Education and Industry Department (1997b), *Improving Mathematics Education 5–14: a Report by HM Inspectors of Schools*, Edinburgh: Scottish Office.

Scottish Office Education and Industry Department (1997c), *Achievements of Primary 4 and Primary 5 Pupils in Mathematics and Science*, Edinburgh: Scottish Office.

Scottish Office Education and Industry Department (1997d), *Placing Requests in Education Authority Schools in Scotland: 1985–86 to 1995–96*, Statistical Bulletin Edn/B6/1997/2, Edinburgh: Scottish Office.

Scottish Office Education and Industry Department (1997e), *The Curriculum in Publicly Funded Secondary Schools in Scotland 1991–1995*, Statistical Bulletin Edn/C7/1997/5, Edinburgh: Scottish Office.

Scottish Office Education and Industry Department (1998a), *Community Education Statistics, 1996–97*, Statistical Bulletin Edn/H1/1998/2, Edinburgh: Scottish Office.

Scottish Office Education and Industry Department (1998b), *Scottish School Leavers and their Qualifications*, Statistical Bulletin Edn/E2/1998/6, Edinburgh: Scottish Office.

Scottish Office Education Department (1991), *Scottish Higher Education Statistics*, Statistical Bulletin Edn/J2/1991/12, Edinburgh: Scottish Office.

Scottish Office Education Department (1992a), *School Leavers and Related Statistics Presented to the Howie Committee*, Statistical Bulletin Edn/E7/1992/6, Edinburgh: Scottish Office.

Scottish Office Education Department (1992b), *Adults in Schools and Colleges*, Statistical Bulletin Edn/K1/1992/2, Edinburgh: Scottish Office.

Scottish Office Education Department (1992c), *Scottish Higher Education Statistics*, Statistical Bulletin Edn/J2/1992/18, Edinburgh: Scottish Office.

Scottish Office Education Department (1992d), *Upper Secondary Education in Scotland*, Edinburgh: Scottish Office.

Scottish Office Education Department (1993), *Students Registered in Vocational Further Education in Scotland 1990–91*, Statistical Bulletin Edn/F7/1993/9, Edinburgh: Scottish Office.

Scottish Office Education Department (1994), *Higher Still: Opportunity for All*, Edinburgh: Scottish Office.

Scottish Parliament (2002), *Interim Report on the Lifelong Learning Inquiry*, SP Paper 550, Edinburgh: Scottish Parliament.

Scottish Qualifications Authority (1999), *Annual Statistical Report*, Dalkeith: SQA.

Sharp, S., P. Munn and L. Paterson (1997), 'Quality assessment in higher education: the Scottish experience', *Higher Education Quarterly*, 51, pp. 286–307.

Shattock, M. (1994), *The UGC and the Management of British Universities*, Guildford: Society for Research into Higher Education.

Shaw, M. and I. Martin (2000), 'Community work, citizenship and democracy: re-making the connections', *Community Development Journal*, 35, pp. 401–13.

Simon, B. (1965), *Education and the Labour Movement, 1870–1920*, London: Lawrence and Wishart.

Simon, B. (1974), *The Politics of Educational Reform, 1920–1940*, London: Lawrence and Wishart.

Simon, B. (1991), *Education and the Social Order, 1940–1990*, London: Lawrence and Wishart.

Simon, S. (1948), *Three Schools or One? Secondary Education in England, Scotland and the USA*, London: Frederick Muller.

Smith, J. A. (1978–80), 'The 1872 Education (Scotland) Act and Gaelic education', *Transactions of the Gaelic Society of Inverness*, 51, pp. 1–67.

Smith, N. and P. Taylor (1999), '"Not for lipstick and lager": students and part time work', *Scottish Affairs*, no. 28, summer, pp. 147–63.

Smout, T. C. (1986), *A Century of the Scottish People, 1830–1950*, London: Collins.

Stark, R., T. Bryce and D. Gray (1997), 'Four surveys and an epitaph: AAP science 1985–1997', *Scottish Educational Review*, 29, pp. 114–20.

Steedman, H. (1987), 'Defining institutions: the endowed grammar schools and the systematisation of English secondary schooling', in Müller, D. K., F. Ringer and B. Simon (eds), *The Rise of the Modern Educational System: Structural Change and Social Reproduction, 1870–1920*, Cambridge: Cambridge University Press, pp. 111–34.

Stewart, J. (1999), '"This injurious measure": Scotland and the 1906 Education (Provision of Meals) Act', *Scottish Historical Review*, 78, pp. 76–94.

Stocks, J. (1970), 'Scotland's ad hoc education authorities, 1919–1930', in History of Education Society, *Studies in the Government and Control of Education since 1860*, London: Methuen, pp. 69–90.

Stocks, J. (1986), 'Broken links in Scottish teacher-training', *Scottish Educational Review*, 18, pp. 110–20.

Stocks, J. (1995), 'The people versus the department: the case of circular 44', *Scottish Educational Review*, 27, pp. 48–60.

Stocks, J. (2002), 'Social class and the secondary school in 1930s Scotland', *Scottish Educational Review*, 34, pp. 26–39.

Strathclyde Regional Council (1984), *Social Strategy for the Eighties*, Glasgow: Strathclyde Regional Council.

Stronach, I. (1992), 'The "Howie Report": a glossary and a commentary', *Scottish Educational Review*, 24, pp. 93–104.

Swann, J. and S. Brown (1997), 'The implementation of a national curriculum and teachers' classroom thinking', *Research Papers in Education*, 12, pp. 91–114.

Tamir, Y. (1993), *Liberal Nationalism*, Princeton: Princeton University Press.

Tawney, R. H. (1964), *The Radical Tradition*, Harmondsworth: Penguin.

Tett, L. (1994), 'Where have all the men gone? Adult participation in community education', *Scottish Journal of Adult Education*, 1, pp. 41–8.

Tett, L. and A. Blair (1999), 'Access for adults to higher education: some providers' views', *Scottish Journal of Adult and Continuing Education*, 5, pp. 49–60.

Thompson, F. G. (1972–4), 'Technical education in the Highlands and Islands', *Transactions of the Gaelic Society of Inverness*, 48, pp. 244–338.

Thomson, G. H. (1929), *A Modern Philosophy of Education*, London: Allen and Unwin.

Thomson, G. O. B. (1983), 'Legislation and provision for the mentally handicapped child in Scotland since 1906', *Oxford Review of Education*, 9, pp. 233–40.

Thomson, I. (1978), 'The origins of physical education in state schools', *Scottish Educational Review*, 10, pp. 15–24.

Thomson, I. (1986), 'Militarism and Scottish schools in the Boer War era', *Physical Education Review*, 8, pp. 110–19.

Thomson, W. P. (1968), 'After Newsom: a survey of secondary school pupils in a New Town', *Scottish Educational Studies*, 1, pp. 49–54.

Tilton, T. (1990), *The Political Theory of Swedish Social Democracy*, Oxford: Clarendon.

Tinklin, T. (2000), 'The influence of social background on application and entry to higher education in Scotland: a multi-level analysis', *Higher Education Quarterly*, 54, pp. 367–85.

Tinklin, T. and D. Raffe (1999), *Entrants to Higher Education*, Edinburgh: Centre for Educational Sociology.

Tomes, N. (1988), 'Scottish surveys since 1977', in Raffe, D. (ed.), *Education and the Youth Labour Market*, Lewes: Falmer, pp. 266–73.

Treble, J. H. (1978), 'The development of Roman Catholic education in Scotland 1878–1978', *Innes Review*, 29, pp. 111–39.

Treble, J. H. (1980), 'The working of the 1918 Education Act in Glasgow archdiocese', *Innes Review*, 31, pp. 27–44.

Turner, E., S. Riddell and S. Brown (1995), *Gender Equality in Scottish Schools*, Glasgow: Equal Opportunities Commission.

Universities Central Council on Admissions (1986), *Statistical Supplement to Twenty-Third Report, 1984–5*, Cheltenham: UCCA.

Universities Funding Council (1992), *University Statistics, 1990–91: Vol. I, Students and Staff*, Cheltenham: Universities' Statistical Office.

University Grants Committee (1921), *Returns from Universities and University Colleges in Receipt of Treasury Grant, 1919–1920*, London: HMSO.

University Grants Committee (1936), *Report for the Period 1929–30 to 1934–35*, London: HMSO.

University Grants Committee (1952), *Returns from Universities and University Colleges in Receipt of Treasury Grant, Academic Year 1950–51*, London: HMSO.

University Grants Committee (1962), *Returns from Universities and University Colleges in Receipt of Treasury Grant, Academic Year 1960–61*, London: HMSO.

University Grants Committee (1964), *University Teaching Methods*, London: HMSO.

University Grants Committee (1982), *University Statistics, 1980–81: Vol. I, Students and Staff*, Cheltenham: Universities' Statistical Office.

University of Glasgow Committee on Adult and Continuing Education (1984), *Annual Report 1982–3*, Glasgow: University of Glasgow.

Wade, N. A. (1939), *Post-Primary Education in the Primary Schools of Scotland, 1872–1936*, London: University of London Press.

Wake, R. (1988), 'Research as the hallmark of the professional: Scottish teachers and research in the early 1920s', *Scottish Educational Review*, 20, pp. 42–51.

Walford, G. (1988), 'The Scottish Assisted Places Scheme: a comparative study of the origins, nature and practice of the ASPs in Scotland, England and Wales', *Journal of Educational Policy*, 3, pp. 137–53.

Walker, A. L. (1994), *The Revival of the Democratic Intellect*, Edinburgh: Polygon.

Watt, J. (1989), *The Introduction and Development of the Comprehensive School in the West of Scotland 1965–80*, PhD thesis, Glasgow University.

Watt, J. (1991), 'Going comprehensive in the west of Scotland: natural progression or culture shock?', *Scottish Educational Review*, 23, pp. 32–42.

Weber, E. (1977), *Peasants into Frenchmen: The Modernisation of Rural France, 1870–1914*, London: Chatto and Windus.

Weir, A. D. (1975), 'The Scottish Certificate of Education: factors affecting pupil performance', *Scottish Educational Review*, 7, pp. 5–14.

Western European Education (1985), 'United Kingdom – Scotland: corporal punishment and the European Court of Human Rights', 17, pp. 69–71.

Williams, R. (1963), *Culture and Society, 1780–1950*, Harmondsworth: Penguin.

Williams, R. (1977), *Marxism and Literature*, Oxford: Oxford University Press.

Willis, P. (1977), *Learning to Labour*, Farnborough: Saxon House.

Willms, J. D. (1986), 'Social class segregation and its relationship to pupils' examination results in Scotland', *American Sociological Review*, 51, pp. 224–41.

Willms, J. D. (1992), 'Pride or prejudice? Opportunity structure and the effects of Catholic schools in Scotland', *International Perspectives on Education and Society*, 2, pp. 189–213.

Wiltshire, H., J. Taylor and B. Jennings (1980), *The 1919 Report: The Final and Interim Reports of the Adult Education Committee of the Ministry of Reconstruction, 1918–1919, Reprinted with Introductory Essays*, Nottingham: Department of Adult Education, Nottingham University.

Withrington, D. J. (1972), 'Towards a national system, 1867–72: the last years in the struggle for a Scottish Education Act', *Scottish Educational Studies*, 4, pp. 107–24.

Withrington, D. J. (1983), 'Scotland a half educated nation' in 1834? Reliable critique or persuasive polemic?, in Humes, W. M. and H. M. Paterson (eds), *Scottish Culture and Scottish Education, 1800–1980*, Edinburgh: John Donald, pp. 55–74.

Young, J. (1986), *The Advisory Council on Education in Scotland: 1920–1961*, PhD thesis, Edinburgh University.

Young, M. (1958), *The Rise of the Meritocracy, 1870–2033*, London: Thames and Hudson.

Index